# The
# Wisdom
# of Teams

# The Wisdom of Teams

## Creating the High-Performance Organization

Jon R. Katzenbach
Douglas K. Smith

THE McGRAW-HILL COMPANIES

London · New York · St Louis · San Francisco · Auckland
Bogotá · Caracas · Lisbon · Madrid · Mexico · Milan
Montreal · New Delhi · Panama · Paris · San Juan
São Paulo · Singapore · Sydney · Tokyo · Toronto

Published by
**McGraw-Hill Publishing Company**
Shoppenhangers Road, Maidenhead, Berkshire, SL6 2QL England
Telephone 01628 502500
Fax: 01628 770224

---

Further information on this and other McGraw-Hill titles is to be found at
http://www.mcgraw-hill.co.uk

British Library Cataloguing in Publication Data

A catalogue record for this book is available from the British Library

ISBN 0 07 711168 0

4  5  6   BB   3  2  1

Printed by Bell & Bain Ltd, Glasgow

To Michael Katzenbach and Alena and Eben Smith,
for borrowed time.

# Contents

# Acknowledgments

We approached the idea of a book on teams cautiously. After all, we thought, teams are a well-known subject and there must be a thousand books on the subject already. Still, we suspected that most of these books focused on persuading readers that "teams are important" or providing how-to advice on building teams as an objective in itself. We were interested, by contrast, in understanding what lessons actual teams and nonteams had for others who choose to struggle with change and performance. By going down this path, we hoped to discover something to say that was (in our minds at least) different from most books on the subject.

## THE CORE TEAM

Probably Carol Franco, our editor at the Harvard Business School Press, was the first to suggest that "we might all become a team." Our first bona fide team recruit was Nancy Taubenslag, a natural for us because of her role in the Rapid Response Team (Chapter 5). Nancy brought us the invaluable skills of disciplined project management, organized thinking, and skeptical but constructive criticism. We are also forever indebted to Nancy for constantly reminding us that teams have feelings too.

We next discovered Mark Voorhees, a professional freelance journalist who turned out to be the team's irritant member and secret weapon. Without Mark's relentless pursuit of the real story, we wouldn't have half the insights that we developed. Mark refuses to take anything on faith, has the natural instincts of a detective, and writes better color than the rest of us put together. We never quite converted him to consultantese (thank goodness), but we did move him a little toward the center.

Gigi Harned-Annonio and Tricia Hennessy had to type–retype, file–refile, find–refind, and keep track of all kinds of things we never used as well as what finally made the cut. We don't know how many late nights the two logged because of the book. But without their dedication and patience there would be no book. More important, they had to calm the frantic authors on more than one occasion when computer malfunctions, lost files, or misplaced materials caused panic. In fact, Katz managed to lose the entire Microsoft Windows software package, files and all, one weekend on Long Island, or so he thought. After a desperate midnight ride back into New York, his son Ray (a computer manager in Seattle) talked him through the basic recovery steps by long-distance telephone. We obviously owe Ray a special mention for that miracle.

Katz started the actual writing during his summer vacation in East Hampton, much to the dismay of his family. But there was method in his madness. He knew his wife Linda was a born editor and an outstanding reader, and he secretly hoped to get her involved. Linda, of course, was much too smart to fall for his first insidious efforts to lure her into the effort, but she finally agreed to do it if she could keep track of her hours so he would know just how much time she devoted to the book; it turned out to be literally hundreds of hours, and we will not tell you how much that will cost Katz. Linda was invaluable because she stayed with us through thick and thin (the kind of phrase she hates, by the way) and was a constant source of wisdom as well as detail.

The final member to join the team was Alan Kantrow, whose insightful editing brought the book to another level. Alan came at this book even more cautiously than we had—it took him a long while to believe there even *was* a book. But, eventually, he got hooked. And the time, dedication, and contributions that he made were clearly at core team levels. To the extent any real wisdom of ours is to be found in the book, Alan deserves much of the credit for drawing it out of us.

## OTHER KEY CONTRIBUTORS

A few people made the extra effort that deserves special mention. Dick Cavanagh, Don Gogel, and Roger Kline were kind enough to read an entire early manuscript and provide encouragement as well as constructive criticism. Cavanagh in particular went out of his way to offer special insights and introduce us to several teams. Fred Gluck, Ted Hall, and Bill Matassoni read our final draft and gave us badly needed encouragement regarding McKinsey relevance and support. We would also like to thank the anonymous "peer group" readers whom the Harvard Business School Press selected. Each took a great deal of time and effort to give us frank and detailed feedback on an early draft—and it was very helpful (even the comments of the person who absolutely hated it). Ken Kurtzman and Chris Gagnon did early work on the subject, which gave us our initial framework for thinking about teams as well as some excellent examples.

Robert Waterman and Tom Peters kindly spent several hours with Katz before we ever put pencil to paper, reacting to our initial ideas and helping us understand how to avoid some of the possible pitfalls of co-authorship. Many of their ideas have been instrumental in our thinking.

Frank Ostroff deserves special mention for his unique efforts in gaining us access to critical nonclient companies. Bob Kaplan, Mike Nevens, Dave Noble, and Bruce Roberson went out of their way to help us arrange discussions at and case examples from important companies. Gene Zelazny, McKinsey's gifted visual-aids consultant for nearly thirty years, created the visual charts and conceptual framework illustrations.

Bob Irvin strengthened our performance curve and our thinking about working groups at the top. Diane Grady and Ashley Stevenson furthered our understanding of how teams are critical to broad-based, frontline change. Steve Dichter shared his insights on teams and transformational change. Tsun-Yan Hsieh was extremely helpful in adding to our perspective on leadership and change teams. Mike

Murray deserves to be singled out for being the first to focus our attention on the performance ethic of a company.

In addition to Carol Franco, people at the Harvard Business School Press who helped were Gayle Treadwell, David Givens, Nat Greenberg, Sarah McConville, Billie Wyeth, and Leslie Zheutlin.

Others who guided our thinking with both insight and patience included: Dick Ashley, Susan Barnett, Charlie Baum, Molly Bayley, Marvin Bower, Esther Brimmer, Lowell Bryan, John Cecil, Steve Coley, Alison Davis, Dolf DiBiasio, Chuck Farr, Bob Felton, Peter Flaherty, Dick Foster, Peter Foy, Larry Kanarek, Jeff Lane, Gil Marmol, Scott Maxwell, Mike Pritula, Jim Rosenthal, Bror Saxberg, Charlie Schetter, Jane Smith, Andy Steinhubl, Warren Strickland, Robert Taylor, Denis Tinsley, Judy Wade, Peter Walker, and Don Waite.

Last, but not least, we acknowledge the dozens of actual teams and nonteams that shared their experiences and insights with us, nearly all of which are listed in the Appendix. They deserve most of the credit for whatever is useful and real in this book. Each gave of their time as well as their knowledge. But even more important, like all real teams, they took the risk of exposing themselves openly and honestly to relative strangers. We can never thank them enough, not only for enabling us to write this book, but especially for what we learned from them.

# A Note About What to Expect

TEAM is a word and concept well known to everyone. Accordingly, we first intended this book to explore teams in a broader organizational context. We also believed that our past experiences, plus the existing body of research knowledge, would provide us with most of the information we needed. We were wrong.

As we started our search for examples to confirm what we thought we knew, we quickly discovered how much we had overlooked and how rich the subject of teams actually is. As a result, we have spoken with hundreds of people in dozens of organizations, focusing on groups who were or might have been teams. (See Appendix.) We discovered no bad examples; we learned from all of them. We also came to recognize how much there is to be learned from such experiences.

What this book has to say is both obvious and subtle. Many people recognize the obvious about teams. For example, the elements of our definition are obvious. But the discipline they imply is not. Moreover, each element has an obvious meaning. But each also has more subtle implications. And finally, it is obvious that teams outperform individuals. We have researched and written this book, however, because it is not obvious how top management can best exploit that advantage.

For that reason, we have made actual team stories the focal point of this book. We rely on them for our insights, use them to make our points, and base our evidence on them. The stories we relate present a wide variety of performance challenges, types of people, and organizational environments. Probably none will perfectly match the specific team opportunities that you have experienced or faced. Nor will you find all the stories equally compelling. We hope, however, that they will be as rich a learning opportunity for you as they were for us.

We should emphasize that we are relating stories of teams, not whole organizations. We have purposely sought out teams in organizations with a wide range of performance records to better understand team dynamics in different settings. The team accomplishments, often extraordinary, are nonetheless only those of a team and, more or less, only coincide with the life of the team. Nonetheless, we have gained both knowledge and conviction by observing how consistently the conditions for team performance emerge across such a wide variety of business conditions and organizational settings.

As expected, we did find a lot of common sense in what makes teams perform. We also kept running into *uncommon* sense that made a difference in team performance. The purpose of this Prologue is to highlight for the prospective reader the most important findings in both these categories and indicate what we will be exploring and drawing lessons from in various team stories throughout the book.

## COMMONSENSE FINDINGS

If there is new insight to be derived from the solid base of common sense about teams, it is the strange paradox of application. Many people simply do not apply what they already know about teams in any disciplined way, and thereby miss the team performance potential before them. Common sense, for example, suggests that teams cannot succeed without a shared purpose; yet more teams than not in most organizations remain unclear *as a team* about what they want to accomplish and why. Throughout the book we will explore why it is so difficult to apply common sense about teams:

**1. A demanding performance challenge tends to create a team.** The hunger for performance is far more important to team success than team-building exercises, special incentives, or team leaders with ideal profiles. In fact, teams often form around such challenges without any help or support from management. Conversely, potential teams without such challenges usually fail to become teams.

**2. The disciplined application of "team basics" is often overlooked.** Team basics include size, purpose, goals, skills, approach, and accountability. Paying rigorous attention to these is what creates the conditions necessary for team performance. A deficiency in any of these basics will derail the team, yet most potential teams inadvertently ignore one or more of them.

**3. Team performance opportunities exist in all parts of the organization.** Team basics apply to many different groups, including teams that recommend things (e.g., task forces), teams that make or do things (e.g., worker teams, sales teams), and teams that run things (e.g., management teams at various levels). Each of these types of teams, of course, face unique challenges. But the commonalities are more important than the differences when striving for team performance. Unfortunately, most organizations recognize team opportunities in only one or two of these categories, leaving a lot of team performance potential untapped.

**4. Teams at the top are the most difficult.** The complexities of long-term challenges, heavy demands on executive time, and ingrained individualism of senior people conspire against teams at the top. In addition, how executives are expected to act often conflicts with effective team performance. As a result, there are fewer teams at the top of large organizations, and those that do exist tend to have fewer people. Importantly, however, we believe this is caused by a number of misplaced assumptions about teams and behaviors at the top.

**5. Most organizations intrinsically prefer individual over group (team) accountability.** Job descriptions, compensation schemes, career paths, and performance evaluations focus on individuals. Teams are often an afterthought in the "nice to have" category. Our culture emphasizes individual accomplishments and makes us uncomfortable trusting our career aspirations to outcomes dependent on the performance of others. "If you want to get something done right, do it yourself" is a common belief. Even the thought of shifting emphasis from individual accountability to team accountability makes us uneasy.

## UNCOMMONSENSE FINDINGS

We also have found a lot of uncommon sense that made a significant difference in team performance. Many of the highest-performing teams, for example, never actually thought of themselves as a team until we introduced the topic. Moreover, in high-performance teams, the role of the team leader is less important and more difficult to identify because all members lead the team at different times. From these teams and others, we found that—counterintuitively—teams and teamwork are *not* the same thing; team leaders are best distinguished by their attitude and what they do *not* do; and focusing primarily on the goal of "becoming a team" seldom works.

The most important uncommonsense findings that we will develop further throughout the book include:

1. **Companies with strong performance standards seem to spawn more "real teams" than companies that promote teams per se.** Teams do not become teams just because we call them teams or send them to team-building workshops. In fact, many frustrations with broad-gauged movements toward team-based organizations spring from just such imbalances. Real teams form best when management makes clear performance demands.

2. **High-performance teams are extremely rare.** Despite the attention teams have been receiving, the true high-performance team— that is, one that outperforms all other like teams, and outperforms expectations given its composition—is very rare. This is largely because a high degree of personal commitment to one another differ-

entiates people on high-performance teams from people on other teams. This kind of commitment cannot be managed, although it can be exploited and emulated to the great advantage of other teams and the broader organization.

**3. Hierarchy and teams go together almost as well as teams and performance.** Teams integrate and enhance formal structures and processes. Hierarchical structures and basic processes are essential to large organizations and need not be threatened by teams. Teams, in fact, are the best way to integrate across structural boundaries and to both design and energize core processes. Those who see teams as a replacement for hierarchy are missing the true potential of teams.

**4. Teams naturally integrate performance and learning.** We have yet to meet anyone who disagrees with the aspiration implied in the "learning organization." Yet, many people also express concerns over how to balance short-term performance emphasis with longer-term institution building. Teams, we discovered, do just that. By translating longer-term purposes into definable performance goals and then developing the skills needed to meet those goals, learning not only occurs in teams but endures.

**5. Teams are the primary unit of performance for increasing numbers of organizations.** Managers cannot master the opportunities and challenges now confronting them without emphasizing teams far more than ever before. The performance challenges that face large companies in every industry—for example, customer service, technological change, competitive threats, and environmental constraints—demand the kind of responsiveness, speed, on-line customization, and quality that is beyond the reach of individual performance. Teams can bridge this gap.

Much of the wisdom of teams lies in the disciplined pursuit of performance. We explore this throughout the three parts of the book. Part I, *Understanding Teams*, examines why teams increasingly matter to the performance of large organizations, why rigorous attention to the basic elements of our team definition leads to achieving team performance, and why truly high-performance teams are so rare. Part II, *Becoming a Team,* describes how and why the performance of groups varies, including both teams and non-teams. It also covers what it takes to become a team from the team's perspective, including what successful team leaders do, and why the basic team discipline becomes even more essential when teams get stuck. Part III, *Exploiting the Potential,* concentrates on top management's role in getting the most out of the performance potential of teams across an organization, including its own group at the top. Part III also explores how and why teams are so critical to managing the major changes in skills, values, and behaviors essential to most companies that aspire to become high-performing organizations.

We certainly do not know all there is to know about teams. There is more to be learned, for example, about teams at the top, inter-locking teams, the role of teams in high-performing organizations, and the impact of real teams on those around them. Moreover, we have not subjected either the stories we relate or the lessons gleaned to the standards of statistical or scientific proof. Indeed, we have included more stories and in greater detail than might otherwise be needed because we sincerely hope readers will derive their own con-clusions by comparing what is offered here with their own team experiences. We also believe the wisdom of teams is far more ac-cessible in stories than in distilled lessons. Thus, having spent time with scores of teams in dozens of organizations, we would like to share the insights gained from those who were so generous in help-ing us learn why they—as teams—have made a difference.

# PART ONE

# Understanding Teams

Figure I-1

# FOCUSING ON TEAM BASICS

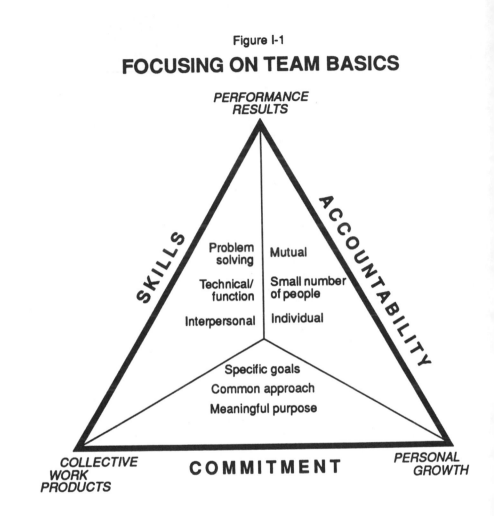

TEAMS outperform individuals acting alone or in larger organizational groupings, especially when performance requires multiple skills, judgments, and experiences. Most people recognize the capabilities of teams; most have the common sense to make teams work. Nevertheless, most people overlook team opportunities for themselves.

Confusion about what makes teams perform explains only part of this pattern of missed opportunity. More is explained by a natural resistance to moving beyond individual roles and accountability. We do not easily take responsibility for the performance of others, nor lightly let them assume responsibility for us. Overcoming such resistance requires the rigorous application of "team basics," which are highlighted in the chart in Figure I-1. The vertices of the triangle indicate what teams deliver; the sides and center describe the elements of the discipline to make that happen. By focusing on performance and team basics—as opposed to trying "to become a team"—most small groups can deliver the performance results that require and produce team behavior.

The best way to understand teams is to look at teams themselves. Their own stories reveal their accomplishments, skills, emotions, and commitment better than any abstract commentary or logical presentation. Real teams are deeply committed to their purpose, goals, and approach. High-performance team members are also very committed to one another. Both understand that the wisdom of teams comes with a focus on collective work-products, personal growth, and performance results. However meaningful, "team" is always a result of pursuing a demanding performance challenge.

# CHAPTER ONE

# Why Teams?

TEAMS have existed for hundreds of years, are the subject of countless books, and have been celebrated throughout many countries and cultures. Most people believe they know how teams work as well as the benefits teams offer. Many have had first-hand team experiences themselves, some of which were rewarding and others a waste of time. Yet, as we explored the use of teams, it became increasingly clear that the potential impact of single teams, as well as the collective impact of many teams, on the performance of large organizations is woefully underexploited—despite the rapidly growing recognition of the need for what teams have to offer. Understanding this paradox and the discipline required to deal with it are central to the basic lessons we learned about team performance.

## LESSONS WE LEARNED

Initially, we thought that executives and other decision makers could make teams work if only they understood the compelling argument for why teams make a difference to performance. We learned the challenge is more difficult than that. Most people, particularly business executives, already recognize the value in teams. Long-standing habits, demanding time schedules, and unwarranted assumptions, however, seem to prevent them from taking full advantage of team opportunities.

We also thought that people understood most of what differentiated a team from a nonteam, and, therefore, only needed a clearer definition of terms to take full advantage of teams. We discovered instead that most people simply do not apply what they already know about teams in any disciplined way and thereby miss the performance potential within existing teams, much less seek out new potential team opportunities.

There is much more to the wisdom of teams than we ever expected, which we highlight in the following summary of key lessons we have learned about teams and team performance.

**1. Significant performance challenges energize teams regardless of where they are in an organization.** No team arises without a performance challenge that is meaningful to those involved. Good personal chemistry or the desire to "become a team," for example, can foster teamwork values, but teamwork is not the same thing as a team. Rather, a common set of demanding performance goals that a group considers important to achieve will lead, most of the time, to both performance and a team. Performance, however, is the primary objective *while a team remains the means, not the end.*

Performance is the crux of the matter for teams. Its importance applies to many different groupings, including teams who recommend things, teams who make or do things, and teams who run or manage things. Each of these three types of teams do face unique challenges. Teams that make or do things often need to develop new skills for managing themselves as compared to teams elsewhere in organizations. Teams that recommend things often find their biggest challenge comes when they make the handoff to those who must implement their findings. Finally, groups who run or manage things must address hierarchical obstacles and turf issues more than groups who recommend, make, or do things. But notwithstanding such special issues, any team—if it focuses on performance regardless of where it is in an organization or what it does—will deliver results well beyond what individuals acting alone in nonteam working situations could achieve.

**2. Organizational leaders can foster team performance best by building a strong performance ethic rather than by establishing a team-promoting environment alone.** A performance focus is also critical to what we learned about how leaders create organizational environments that are friendly to teams. In fact, too many executives fall into the trap of appearing to promote teams for the sake of teams. They talk about entire organizations becoming a "team" and thereby equate teams with teamwork. Or they reorganize their companies around self-managing teams, and risk putting the number of officially designated teams as an objective ahead of performance. They sometimes loosely refer to their own small group at the top as a team when most people in the organization recognize they are anything but a team.

Real teams are much more likely to flourish if leaders aim their sights on performance results that balance the needs of customers, employees, and shareholders. Clarity of purpose and goals have tremendous power in our ever more change-driven world. Most people, at all organizational levels, understand that job security depends on customer satisfaction and financial performance, and are willing to be measured and rewarded accordingly. What is perhaps less well appreciated, but equally true, is how the opportunity to meet clearly stated customer and financial needs enriches jobs and leads to personal growth.

Most of us really do want to make a difference. Naturally, organization policies, designs, and processes that promote teams can accelerate team-based performance in companies already blessed with strong performance cultures. But in those organizations with weak performance ethics or cultures, leaders will provide a sounder foundation for teams by addressing and demanding performance than by embracing the latest organization design fad, including teams themselves.

**3. Biases toward individualism exist but need not get in the way of team performance.** Most of us grow up with a strong sense of individual responsibility. Parents, teachers, coaches, and role models of all kinds shape our values based on individual accomplishment. Rugged individualism is credited with the formation of our country and our political society. These same values carry through in our corporate families, where all advancement and reward systems are based on individual evaluations. Even when teams are part of the picture, it is seldom at the expense of individual achievement. We are taught to play fair, but "Always look out for number one!" And, most of us have taken this to heart far more deeply than sentiments such as "We're all in this together" or "If one fails, we all fail."

Self-preservation and individual accountability, however, can work two ways. Left unattended, they can preclude or destroy potential teams. But recognized and addressed for what they are, especially if done with reference to how to meet a performance challenge, individual concerns and differences become a source of collective strength. Teams are not antithetical to individual performance. Real teams always find ways for each individual to contribute and thereby gain distinction. Indeed, when harnessed to a common team purpose and goals, our need to distinguish ourselves as individuals becomes a powerful engine for team performance. Nothing we learned in looking at dozens of teams supports an argument for the wholesale abandonment of the individual in favor of teams. Nor does our book present such an either/or proposition.

4. Discipline—both within the team and across the organization—creates the conditions for team performance. Any group seeking team performance for itself, like any leader seeking to build strong performance standards across his organization, must focus sharply on performance. For organizational leaders, this entails making clear and consistent demands that reflect the needs of customers, shareholders, and employees, and then holding themselves and the organization relentlessly accountable. Out of such demands come the most fruitful conditions for teams. An analogous lesson also applies to teams. Indeed, we think of the team definition (provided in Chapter 3) not as a series of elements characterizing teams but as a discipline, much like a diet, that, if followed rigorously, will produce the conditions for team performance. Groups become teams through *disciplined action*. They *shape* a common purpose, *agree* on performance goals, *define* a common working approach, *develop*

high levels of complementary skills, and *hold* themselves mutually accountable for results. And, as with any effective discipline, they never stop doing any of these things.

## THE NEED FOR TEAMS

We believe that teams—real teams, not just groups that management calls "teams"—should be the basic unit of performance for most organizations, regardless of size. In any situation requiring the real-time combination of multiple skills, experiences, and judgments, a team inevitably gets better results than a collection of individuals operating within confined job roles and responsibilities. Teams are more flexible than larger organizational groupings because they can be more quickly assembled, deployed, refocused, and disbanded, usually in ways that enhance rather than disrupt more permanent structures and processes. Teams are more productive than groups that have no clear performance objectives because their members are committed to deliver tangible performance results. Teams and performance are an unbeatable combination.

The record of team performance speaks for itself. Teams invariably contribute significant achievements in business, charity, schools, government, communities, and the military. Motorola, recently acclaimed for surpassing its Japanese competition in producing the world's lightest, smallest, and highest-quality cellular phones with only a few hundred parts versus over a thousand for the competition, relied heavily on teams to do it. So did Ford, which became America's most profitable car company in 1990 on the strength of its Taurus model. At 3M, teams are critical to meeting the company's well-known goal of producing half of each year's revenues from product innovations created in the prior five years. General Electric has made self-managing worker teams a centerpiece of its new organization approach.

Nonbusiness team efforts are equally numerous. The Coalition's dramatic Desert Storm victory over Iraq in the Gulf War involved many teams. A team of active duty officers and reservists, for example, lay at the heart of moving, receiving, and sustaining over 300,000 troops and 100,000 vehicles with more than 7,000,000 tons of equipment, fuel, and supplies between the late 1990 build-up through and beyond the end of hostilities in 1991. At Bronx Educational Services, a team of staff and trustees shaped the first nationally recognized adult literacy school. A team of citizens in Harlem founded and operated the first Little League there in over forty years.

We do not argue that such team achievements are a new phenomenon. But we do think there is more urgency to team performance today because of the link between teams, individual behavioral change, and high performance. A "high-performance organization" consistently outperforms its competition over an extended period of time, for example, ten years or more. It also outperforms the expectations of its key constituents: customers, shareholders, and employees. Few people today question that a new era has dawned in which such high levels of performance depend on being "customer driven," delivering "total quality," "continuously improving and innovating," "empowering the workforce," and "partnering with suppliers and customers." Yet these require specific behavioral changes in the entire organization that are difficult and unpredictable for any single person, let alone an entire company, to accomplish. By contrast, we have observed that the same team dynamics that promote performance also support learning and behavioral change, and do so more effectively than larger organizational units or individuals left to their own devices. Consequently, we believe teams will play an increasingly essential part in first creating and then sustaining high-performance organizations.

Change, of course, has always been a management challenge. But, until recently, when executives spoke of managing change, they referred to "normal" change—that is, new circumstances well within the scope of their existing management approaches. Managers deal with this kind of change every day. It is a fundamental part of their job, and includes raising prices, handling disgruntled customers, dealing with stubborn unions, replacing people, and even shifting strategic priorities. Many people, however, would agree that change today has taken on an entirely different meaning. While all managers continue to have to deal with "normal" change, more and more must also confront "major" change that requires a lot of people throughout the company—including those across the broad base of the organization—to become very good at behaviors and skills they are not very good at now. The days of viewing change as primarily concerned with strategic decisions and management reorganizations have vanished.

Notice, for example, how Jack Welch, Lawrence Bossidy, and Edward Hood describe the challenge facing General Electric in their 1990 letter to shareholders.

> Change is in the air. GE people today understand the pace of change, the need for speed, the absolute necessity of moving more quickly in everything we do.... From that pursuit of speed . . . came our vision for the 1990s: a boundaryless company. Boundaryless is an uncommon word . . . one that describes a *whole set of behaviors* we believe are necessary to achieve speed. In a boundaryless company, suppliers are not "outsiders." . . . Every effort of every man and woman in the company is focused on satisfying customers' needs. Internal functions begin to blur. Customer service? *It's not somebody's job. It's everybody's job.* (Emphasis added.)

Throughout much of the 1980s, General Electric made the critical strategic, restructuring, and management changes people typically associate with top management. To achieve their goals of being either number one or number two in each of their chosen markets, Jack Welch and his colleagues divested $10 billion worth of assets and made nearly $20 billion worth of acquisitions. All of these moves were difficult and essential; yet, they represented only a portion of top management's job. The other part is in managing the kind of broad-based behavioral change described above—what our colleague Micky Huibregtsen calls "energizing" changes.

This is a much more difficult challenge and even the wisest of leaders seldom know fully what to change or how to make all the specifics happen. Jack Welch, for example, is the first to admit he developed GE's now famous "Work-Out" town meeting approach largely through trial and error. Most leaders today cannot succeed without the participation and insights of people across the broad base of the organization. Together, top management and the people who look to them for leadership must first identify and learn critical new skills, values, and behaviors, and then work to institutionalize those behaviors to sustain high performance. We believe teams are essential to such objectives because they have always induced behavioral change as both an ingredient and by-product of team performance.

Several well-known phenomena explain why teams perform well. First, they bring together complementary skills and experiences that, by definition, exceed those of any individual on the team. This broader mix of skills and know-how enables teams to respond to multifaceted challenges like innovation, quality, and customer service. Second, in jointly developing clear goals and approaches, teams establish communications that support real-time problem solving and initiative. Teams are flexible and responsive to changing events and demands. As a result, teams can adjust their approach to new information and challenges with greater speed, accuracy, and effectiveness than can individuals caught in the web of larger organizational connections.

Third, teams provide a unique social dimension that enhances the economic and administrative aspects of work. Real teams do not develop until the people in them work hard to overcome barriers that stand in the way of collective performance. By surmounting such obstacles together, people on teams build trust and confidence in each other's capabilities. They also reinforce each other's intentions to pursue their team purpose above and beyond individual or functional agendas. Overcoming barriers to performance is how groups become teams. Both the meaning of work and the effort brought to bear upon it deepen, until team performance eventually becomes its own reward.

Finally, teams have more fun. This is not a trivial point because the kind of fun they have is integral to their performance. The people on the teams we met consistently and without prompting emphasized the fun aspects of their work together. Of course this fun included parties, hoopla, and celebrations. But any group of people can throw a good party. What distinguishes the fun of teams is how it both sustains and is sustained by team performance. For example, we often see a more highly developed sense of humor on the job within the top-performing teams because it helps them deal with the pressures and intensity of high performance. And we inevitably hear that the deepest, most satisfying source of enjoyment comes from "having been part of something larger than myself."

Behavioral change also occurs more readily in the team context. Because of their collective commitment, teams are not as threatened by change as are individuals left to fend for themselves. And, because of their flexibility and willingness to enlarge their solution space, teams offer people more room for growth and change than do groups with more narrowly defined task assignments associated with hierarchical job assignments. Finally, because of their focus on performance, teams motivate, challenge, reward, and support individuals who are trying to change the way they do things.

As a result, in the kinds of broad-based change that organizations increasingly confront today, teams can help concentrate the direction and quality of top-down leadership, foster new behaviors, and facilitate cross-functional activities. When teams work, they represent the best proven way to convert embryonic visions and values into consistent action patterns because they rely on people working together. They also are the most practical way to develop a shared sense of direction among people throughout an organization. Teams can make hierarchy responsive without weakening it, energize processes across organizational boundaries, and bring multiple capabilities to bear on difficult issues.

In fact, most models of the "organization of the future" that we have heard about—"networked," "clustered," "nonhierarchical," "horizontal," and so forth—are premised on *teams surpassing individuals as the primary performance unit in the company.* According to these predictions, when management seeks faster, better ways to best match resources to customer opportunity or competitive challenge, the critical building block will be at the team, not individual, level. This does not mean that either individual performance or accountability become unimportant. Rather, the challenge for management increasingly becomes that of balancing the roles of individuals and teams versus displacing or favoring one over the other. In addition, the individual's role and performance will become more a matter for teams, instead of hierarchies of managers, to exploit; that is, in many cases teams, not managers, will figure out what the individuals on those teams should be doing and how they are performing.

# RESISTANCE TO TEAMS

Such predictions about teams, however, induce a lot of skepticism. We believe the argument for greater focus on teams is compelling, and most people we have interviewed agree. Yet when it comes to using the team approach for themselves or those they manage, most of these same people are reluctant to rely on teams. Notwithstanding the evidence of team performance all around us, the importance of teams in managing behavioral change and high performance, and the rewards of team experiences in everyday lives, many people undervalue, forget, or openly question the team option when confronting their own performance challenges. We cannot fully explain this resistance; there probably are as many reasons and emotions as there are people. Moreover, we do not suggest that such resistance is either "bad" or "good." We do, however, think that it is powerful because it is grounded in deeply held values of individualism that neither can nor should be entirely dismissed.

Three primary sources for people's reluctance about teams stand out: a lack of conviction that a team or teams can work better than other alternatives; personal styles, capabilities, and preferences that make teams risky or uncomfortable; and weak organizational performance ethics that discourage the conditions in which teams flourish.

**1. Lack of conviction.** Some people do not believe that teams, except in unusual or unpredictable circumstances, really do perform better than individuals. Some think that teams cause more trouble than they are worth because the members waste time in unproductive meetings and discussions, and actually generate more complaints than constructive results. Others think that teams are probably useful from a human relations point of view, but are a hindrance when it comes to work, productivity, and decisive action. Still others believe that concepts of teamwork and empowerment applied broadly to an organization supersede the need to worry or be disciplined about the performance of specific small groups of people.

On the one hand, most people share a lot of constructive common sense about teams but fail to rigorously apply it. People know, for example, that teams rarely work without common goals; yet far too many teams casually accept goals that are neither demanding, precise, realistic, nor actually held *in common*. On the other hand, the very popularity of the word "team" courts imprecision. People rarely use "team" with much concern for its specific meaning to them in the context they face. As a consequence, most people remain unclear over what makes a real team. A team is not just any group working together. Committees, councils, and task forces are not necessarily teams. Groups do not become teams simply because someone labels them as teams. The complete workforce of any large and complex organization is never a team. Entire organizations can believe in and practice teamwork, but teamwork and teams differ.

Most executives outspokenly advocate teamwork. And they should. Teamwork represents a set of values that encourages behaviors such as listening and constructively responding to points of view expressed by others, giving others the benefit of the doubt, providing support to those who need it, and recognizing the interests and achievements of others. When practiced, such values help all of us communicate and work more effectively with one another and, therefore, are good and valuable behaviors. Obviously, teamwork values help teams perform. They also promote our performance as individuals and the performance of the entire organization. In other words, teamwork values—by themselves—are not exclusive to teams, nor are they enough to ensure team performance.

*Teams are discrete units of performance, not a positive set of values.* And they are a unit of performance that differs from the individual or the entire organization. A team is a small group of people (typically fewer than twenty) with complementary skills committed to a common purpose and set of specific performance goals. Its members are committed to working with each other to achieve the team's purpose and hold each other fully and jointly accountable for the team's results. Teamwork encourages and helps teams succeed; but teamwork alone never makes a team. Consequently, when senior executives call for the entire organization to be a "team," they really are promoting teamwork values. However well intended, such ambiguities can cause unproductive confusion. Moreover, those who describe teams as vehicles primarily to make people feel good or get along better not only confuse teamwork with teams, but also miss the most fundamental characteristic that distinguishes real teams from nonteams—a relentless focus on performance.

Teams thrive on performance challenges; they flounder without them. Teams cannot exist for long without a performance-driven purpose to both nourish and justify the team's continuing existence. Groups established for the sake of becoming a team, job enhancement, communication, organizational effectiveness, or even excellence rarely become real teams, as demonstrated by the bad feelings left in many companies after experimenting with quality circles. While quality represents an admirable aspiration, quality circles often fail to connect specific, achievable performance objectives with the collaborative effort of those in the circle.

Ignoring performance, we suspect, also explains much of the evidence about apparent team failures. Peter Drucker, for example, has cited the difficulties GM, P&G, and Xerox, among others, have had in overshooting the mark with "team-building" efforts. Without question, teams and team efforts sometimes fail. But more often than not, such failures lie in not adhering to the discipline of what makes teams successful. In other words, unclear thinking and practice explain more about such disappointments than whether teams are appropriate units of performance to get something done. Regardless of their cause, however, such unrewarding personal experiences in groups labeled as teams weaken people's conviction about teams even further. Many of us who have observed, participated in, or watched the best intentions at team-building exercises get quickly forgotten or scorned have grown cynical, cautious, or even hostile to teams.

**2. Personal discomfort and risk.** Many people fear or do not like to work in teams. Some are true loners who contribute best when left to work quietly on their own. Some research scientists, university professors, and specialized consultants fit this pattern. Most people's discomfort with teams, however, is because they find the team approach too time-consuming, too uncertain, or too risky.

"My job is tough enough," goes one recurring comment, "without having to worry about meeting and getting along with a bunch of people I don't even know that well, or I do know and I'm not sure I like all that much. I just don't have that kind of time to invest."

In this view, teams represent a risky extra burden that can slow down individual accomplishment and advancement. Some people are uncomfortable about speaking up, participating, or being otherwise conspicuous in group settings. Some are afraid of making commitments that they might not be able to keep. And many people just do not like the idea of having to depend on others, having to listen or agree to contrary points of view, or having to suffer the consequences of other people's mistakes. These concerns particularly afflict managers who find it difficult to be part of a team when they are not the leader.

Few people deny the benefit of teamwork values or the potentially useful performance impact of teams. But, at their core, most people have values that favor individual responsibility and performance over any form of group, whether it be a team or otherwise. Our parents, teachers, ministers, and other elders emphasize individual responsibility as paramount from our earliest days onward. We grow up under a regimen that measures (academic grades), rewards (allowances), and punishes (trips to the principal's office) individual—not collective—performance. Whenever we want to "get something done," our first thought is that of holding an individual responsible.

It is hardly surprising, then, to discover strong anxieties among individuals faced with joining a team. It is not that teams and teamwork are absent from our culture. From *The Three Musketeers* through *The Dirty Dozen* and *Star Trek,* we have read about, listened to, and watched stories of famous teams accomplishing the improbable. Most sports we follow are team sports. And our parents and other teachers have also instructed us in, and expected us to practice, teamwork values. But for most of us, these admirable notions, however potentially rewarding, forever remain secondary to our responsibilities as individuals. Individual responsibility and self-preservation remain the rule; shared responsibility based on trusting others is the exception. A reluctance to take a risk and submit one's fate to the performance of a team, therefore, is almost inbred.

**3. Weak organizational performance ethics.** The reluctance to commit one's own fate to a team pervades most organizations with weak performance ethics. Such companies lack compelling purposes that appeal rationally and emotionally to their people. Their leaders fail to make clear and meaningful performance demands to which they hold the organization and, most important, themselves accountable. To the organization at large, such behavior manifests more concern about internal politics or external public relations than a commitment to a clear set of goals that balances the expectations of customers, shareholders, and employees. At the worst, such environments undermine the mutual trust and openness upon which teams depend. There is a built-in expectation that any decision of consequence must be made at the top or, at a minimum, be approved by enough other layers that the implementor of that decision is well-covered. Politics displace performance as the daily focus. And, inevitably, those politics play on individual insecurities that, in turn, further erode the conviction and courage to invest in a team approach. Bad team experiences become self-fulfilling prophecies.

Modifying the strong natural emphasis on individual accountability will, of course, be necessary as teams become more important. Yet *replacing individually focused management structures and approaches with team-oriented designs will matter little, or even do damage, unless the organization has a robust performance ethic.* If it does, then shifting the organization's emphasis away from individual toward team can enrich both the number and performance of teams—particularly if management also is disciplined about how it deals with team situations. But all the team-promoting policies in the world will fall short if the teams are not convinced that performance truly matters. Some teams, of course, will always emerge—beyond all reasonable expectation. But they will remain the exception. Because of the all-important link between teams and performance, companies with weak performance ethics will always breed resistance to teams themselves.

## CONCLUSION

Teams are *not* the solution to everyone's current and future organizational needs. They will not solve every problem, enhance every group's results, nor help top management address every performance challenge. Moreover, when misapplied, they can be both wasteful and disruptive. Nonetheless, teams usually do outperform other groups and individuals. They represent one of the best ways to support the broad-based changes necessary for the high-performing organization. And executives who really believe that behaviorally based characteristics like quality, innovation, cost effectiveness, and customer service will help build sustainable competitive advantage will give top priority to the development of team performance.

To succeed, however, they and others must also pay a lot of attention to why most people approach teams cautiously. In large part, this resistance springs from undeniable experiences and convictions about individual responsibility and the risks involved in trusting other people. Teams, for example, do demand a merging of individual accountability with mutual accountability. Teams also do require lots of time together; indeed, it is folly to assume that teams can perform without investing time to shape and agree upon a common purpose, set of goals, and working approach. Moreover, few groups become real teams without taking risks to overcome constraints imposed by individual, functional, and hierarchical boundaries. And team members do depend on one another in pursuit of common performance.

No wonder, then, that many of us only reluctantly entrust critical issues to team resolution. We all fool ourselves if we think well-meaning aspirations to "work better as a team" will be enough to dispel the resistance to teams. Building the performance of teams throughout an organization that needs to perform better, we argue, is mandatory. But doing so also poses a far more serious challenge than any of us would like to admit.

The good news is that there is a discipline to teams that, if rigorously followed, can transform reluctance into team performance. Moreover, while some of the elements of this discipline are counterintuitive and must be learned—for example, that "becoming a team" is not the primary goal—most of it builds on commonsense ideas like the importance of goal setting and mutual accountability. Furthermore, this discipline applies equally well to teams that run things, teams that recommend things, and teams that make or do things. What works at the front lines also works in the executive suite.

The bad news is that, like all disciplines, the price of success is strict adherence and practice. Very few people lose weight, quit smoking, or learn the piano or golf without constant practice and discipline. Very few small groups of people become teams without discipline as well. Extracting team performance is challenging. Long-standing habits of individualism, rampant confusion about teams and teamwork, and seemingly adverse team experiences all undercut the possibilities teams offer at the very moment that team performance has become so critical. Groups do not become teams just because we tell them to; launching hundreds of teams will not necessarily produce real teams in the right places; and building teams at the top remains among the most difficult of tests. Yet the fact remains that potential teams throughout most organizations usually can perform much better than they do. We believe this untapped potential literally begs for renewed attention, especially from the top. We also believe the key to such performance is in recognizing the wisdom of teams, having the courage to try, and then applying the discipline to learn from the experience.

# CHAPTER TWO

# One Team: A Story of Performance

THE team is a basic unit of performance for most organizations. It melds together the skills, experiences, and insights of several people. It is the natural complement to individual initiative and achievement because it engenders higher levels of commitment to common ends. Increasingly, we find management looking to teams throughout the organization to strengthen performance capabilities.

Yet "team" is a term that produces very different images among people. Most of us have in mind a team that is a reflection of our personal experiences, good and bad. Some of us picture a special task force, others might think of a military attack squad, while many focus on their favorite sports analogy; unfortunately, these examples seldom provide a consistent or clear picture of what a real team is. Nor do they reflect a disciplined recognition of why some teams far outperform others in similar circumstances. In this book we will be drawing on a variety of actual team and nonteam experiences to demonstrate how a more consistent and disciplined view of teams can lead to high levels of performance.

Successful team experiences are memorable because of both what is accomplished and what each member learns in the process. Moreover, no two experiences are the same. Each has its own unique blend of people, work products, and performance results. No two teams ever approach a performance challenge in the same way, nor do they produce the same result. Yet all teams that perform have much in common. It is the recognition and application of these commonalities across different team settings that constitute the primary learning opportunity in this book.

This chapter features a unique and memorable story of one team that achieved unexpected levels of performance—largely through the disciplined application of team basics that most of us already accept. We believe it helps set the tone for understanding the elements of team performance that cut across different kinds of teams, as well as illustrating the remarkable results teams achieve. As the story unfolds, you will undoubtedly recognize many of the elements that made this team successful; other elements may be less obvious. While the specifics of this example are unique, the commonalities of team performance that it highlights will recur throughout the book. Perhaps the most intriguing question that this story raises is: Why are the conditions for team performance so much easier to recognize than they are to create?

## BURLINGTON NORTHERN INTERMODAL TEAM

The deregulation of the railroad industry in 1981 gave rise to the opportunity for established railroads like Burlington Northern to build a new business in intermodal transportation. "Intermodal" means combining different modes of transportation—in this case trucks and trains—to speed delivery and minimize the costs of complex shipments that are not efficiently handled by one mode alone. It was a different business concept not ideally suited to railroads' traditional way of operating.

### Background
The term "piggybacking" captures the now familiar intermodal image of caravans of truck bodies or containers traveling across the country on special railroad flatcars. The concept enables a single-shipment contract to cover goods carried, for example, by truck

from Hartford, Connecticut, to New York City, then by train to San Francisco, and finally by truck to the final destination in Watsonville, California.

Prior to deregulation, piggybacking was rare and seldom offered. Trains were mostly boxcars, moved across complex logistical networks by powerful engines and professional engineers. Railroaders were engineers, logisticians, and mechanical operators whose long history and traditions had created deeply ingrained operating patterns. They were constrained to and by their rail networks. If shippers needed trucks to complete their journey, they made separate contracts. Ed Jordan, founding president of Conrail, semifacetiously maintains that prior to deregulation the organization charts of major railroads had remained unchanged for nearly 100 years. So did their service patterns for customers.

Railroaders basically disliked truckers and viewed them as competitive upstarts, even though since mid-century truckers had been taking away substantial amounts of railroad business. They were seen as "fly-by-night" entrepreneurs, unconstrained by regulation, tradition, networks, or historical operating patterns. The idea that truckers and railroaders might cooperate to serve common customers was heresy within the major railroads. Yet that was the theory behind the intermodal opportunity.

On the eve of deregulation in March 1981, Burlington Northern's head of marketing asked Bill Greenwood, an operations manager, to take over the recently formed intermodal business unit within marketing. Greenwood accepted because he believed deregulation promised an opportunity to move intermodal from obscurity to prominence. Deregulation, he knew, meant competition; competition meant newfound power for customers; and customers, he sensed, would demand far more innovative and responsive products, services, and prices. In Greenwood's mind, the coming changes would shift business away from boxcars to the more flexible and effective containers and trailers offered by intermodal. He believed Burlington Northern intermodal could lead the way, so he quickly set about putting together a team to make it happen. He vastly underestimated, however, the range and difficulty of the obstacles that would crop up along the way.

## The Performance Challenge

In 1981, Burlington Northern typified railroading's reluctant approach to intermodal. At best it grudgingly considered it a necessary evil, not a real business opportunity. In the words of one observer, the railroad's intermodal infrastructure was pitiful. Burlington Northern had more than 160 truck-to-train connecting ramps spread around the country in a patchwork that bore no relation to customer needs or operational effectiveness. Each of these ramps received stepchild treatment from the boxcar-oriented, trucker-resistant railyard managers who operated them. In addition, Burlington's intermodal equipment was old, poorly maintained, and poorly operated. Most people associated with intermodal responsibilities tended to be undistinguished performers in dead-end careers. The company's intermodal results mirrored these efforts, and in 1981 Burlington Northern ranked at the bottom of the industry.

This situation represented a "performance challenge," to say the least. But it is exactly this kind of performance challenge that often gives rise to a real team effort. Such teams are seldom designated, anointed, or even recognized; they simply happen because that is what it takes to get the job done. So it was with the Burlington Northern Intermodal Team, which by the end of the 1980s had moved the company from last to first in intermodal business in the industry, and had created a billion-dollar business.

Together, the seven men who eventually formed this team set a daunting purpose for themselves—to create an entirely new business concept within the railroad—one that would not only transform Burlington Northern but, in some ways, the railroad industry itself. They did so, moreover, in the face of what they perceived as extreme hostility from much of Burlington Northern's established power structure. Each of the seven knew he was taking on the establishment. Yet they also believed in their chance to innovate and redefine how the railroad served its customers. Over time, all this inspired a profound sense of mission or cause in the team members. To them, no obstacle seemed overwhelming. Ultimately, their depth of commitment to their purpose and to each other as well as their level of achievement set them apart as a truly extraordinary team.

## Getting Started

The Intermodal Team actually came together during 1981 and 1982. Greenwood knew that few people, including his new boss, shared his optimism or enthusiasm. Yet he also knew he could not build intermodal by himself. Not only were existing resources insufficient but, in an attitude critical to a potential team leader, he knew he did not have all the answers. He needed help and began by recruiting Mark Cane, a young, financially astute manager, to come with him from operations. Greenwood discovered another enthusiast in Emmett Brady, who had been in intermodal for many years. Unlike some of his more lackluster colleagues, Brady immediately caught onto Greenwood's vision and demonstrated his readiness and energy to help in any way possible. Quite by accident, Greenwood hired a third man, Ken Hoepner, from outside the company. Shortly after taking his new job, Greenwood received a call from Hoepner, an old friend with both operations and strategic planning experience, who wanted to use Greenwood as a job reference. Bill had other ideas.

> "I was telling Bill about the new job I wanted," recalls Hoepner, "when there was this big silence at the other end of the phone. I thought, 'Jeez, he's hung up.' So I said, 'Bill, are you still there?' "

> "He said, 'Yeah, I'm here.' Then he went on. 'Listen, forget about that new job. Let me tell you about this intermodal opportunity. We want to do something that has never been done before. I don't know a lot about this we're going to have to define it from day one. But we're putting together a team and I'd like you to join us.' "

Sensing a rare opportunity as well as the chance to join his old friend, Hoepner said okay. He joined Greenwood, Brady, and Cane, he remembers with a chuckle, on April Fool's Day, 1981. The four men immediately turned their attention to a number of priorities. They set out to transform their business unit from a dumping ground of low performers to a more proactive, talented group of people— hardly an easy task. In addition, they methodically sought and used external and internal speaking engagements to counter intermodal's poor image. Finally, they set up an intermodal task force with representatives from across the railroad to study the intermodal opportunity and develop a truly cross-functional strategy for seizing it.

> "I was assigned as the transportation function's representative to the task force," says Dave Burns, who joined Greenwood's team from the task force in early 1982. "The intermodal guys had this smart idea that if what they thought was going to happen to the railroad was stuff coming out of boxcars and going into trailers, they'd be much better off if they could get the rest of Burlington Northern to say it rather than the intermodal business unit sounding like the prophets of doom."

In addition to Burns, more than forty people from every function and business unit of the railroad participated in the task force, which lasted throughout most of 1981. The task force agreed with and elaborated on Greenwood's vision. They predicted, for example, that nearly one half billion dollars of freight business would shift out of boxcars, an amount exceeding one-tenth of Burlington Northern's total business at that time.

The first element of the task force's three-pronged strategy focused on consolidating the railroad's 160 ramp connections into a system of 22 intermodal hubs that could connect Burlington Northern's freight lines into the heavily trucked interstate highway system. Second, they recommended replacing outmoded intermodal stock with new equipment. Third, the task force pinned hopes of success to the railroad's skill and willingness to develop a full set of products and prices that would meet customer needs.

It is important to note that the task force was not a team. For one thing, forty people were too large a group to function as a real team. As a result, it could not develop the shared sense of accountability that teams have for their common performance objectives. This does not mean the task force did a poor job; quite the contrary. Inspired by the Intermodal Team's dedication, the task force delivered an excellent set of recommendations.

Greenwood, Hoepner, Cane, and Brady were thrilled with the task force's white paper. After nearly a year in intermodal, they had a sound plan to match their growing enthusiasm and ambitions. Moreover, in Burns from transportation and Bill Dewitt, corporate planning's task force representative, they recruited two additional true believers to join their team that, by spring of 1982, also numbered Bill Berry, a top operations manager from the field.

Interestingly, while Greenwood clearly had tapped Cane and Hoepner to join him and, as boss of the unit, had to "hire" the others, each man also effectively selected himself as a team member. Each saw a significant challenge he wanted to tackle. Greenwood, in turn, recognized in each of them the same excitement that he had about getting something done. As with most teams, membership was more a personal than a personnel matter. Each man, including Greenwood, earned his spot on the team every day. None relied on his formal designation or job title. Their roles were a function of their basic skills relative to team needs at the time.

## Overcoming Obstacles

All seven men on the team recognized that what had been mostly organizational indifference to intermodal prior to 1981 had grown into active hostility by 1982. The increasingly outspoken and aggressive Intermodal Team challenged others at Burlington Northern by recommending that capital dollars, customers, freight, people, and resources be shifted away from boxcars to flatcars. The team made no secret of their desire to build a new kind of cross-functional organization that would knock down the traditional barriers between marketing, operations, accounting, information systems, and so on. And they aggressively pursued ways of cooperating with truckers. Such possibilities distressed those comfortable with "business as usual"; the team became a real threat to the status quo.

> "There was this terrible dichotomy between the external world and the internal world," says Greenwood. "The external world knew we were onto something. Inside, however, there was this terrible misunderstanding and resistance. Even my own boss was out to get us and was virtually drumming up support from the rest of his marketing organization to bury us."

Many people in addition to Greenwood's boss were antagonized by the maverick personalities and brash dreams of the Intermodal Team. Whenever possible, these naysayers loudly criticized intermodal, and they made it tough to get resources, information, people, and permissions. At times the hostility verged on sabotage. According to the team, for example, one executive rigged an equipment bid to prevent intermodal from working with a preferred vendor on a critical new generation of flatcar. All of which made the Intermodal Team into a tighter, more self-sufficient unit.

> "Every time you walked into the building," remembers Ken Hoepner, "you looked around and saw howitzers aimed at you. To us it meant only one thing: 'Guys, we're in this together!'"

## Shaping the Working Approach

Togetherness characterized the team's approach, beginning with the sheer amount of time they spent with each other. They met every morning—as a team—from 8:00 to 8:20 A.M. They interacted constantly throughout the working day, which for them lasted far closer to eighteen hours than the usual eight. Even today, each of the men recalls who among them went to bed late or got up early to pursue their round-the-clock phone conversations. During that first year or so, for example, Greenwood and Hoepner, who are night owls, spoke with each other nearly every night between eleven and midnight. Whenever an issue arose that they could not resolve through their morning meetings or other ad hoc interactions, the full team gathered on Sunday afternoons at Greenwood's house. They demanded candor and objectivity from each other.

> "If you would take an idea to this team," summarized Dewitt, "you would get a wealth of testing on any relevant issue. Everyone knew about the marketplace and knew about operations and knew about equipment and so on. You didn't blow smoke by anybody in this group. That was part of why we trusted each other so much. You knew that if there was something missing in your logic or application, the others would say, 'Wait a minute. Come again.'"

> Greenwood agrees: "There was always a lot of disagreement, different ideas, different areas of emphasis. But there was always self-respect and respect for others."

Like all truly effective teams, however, these seven exploited their mutual candor and respect by never losing sight of their common performance challenge. All of their activities pointed in the same direction: What would it take to build an intermodal business at Burlington Northern? What did each of them alone and together need to do—that day, that week, that month—to make it happen?

> "In my mind," says Dave Burns, "the key word to this team was 'shared.' We shared everything. There was a complete openness among us. And the biggest thing that we shared was an objective and a strategy that we had put together jointly. That was our benchmark each day. Were we doing things in support of our plan?"

## Galvanizing Events

The team's single-minded concentration, dedication, and work ethic infected the entire intermodal business unit, which had grown to forty-five people by mid-1982. That spring and summer, everyone in the unit contributed to the hub proposal that put Burlington Northern's interest in intermodal to the ultimate test: Would the railroad approve the capital and operating changes necessary to take the first real step toward implementing the task force's recommended strategy?

The outcome of the hub proposal was very much in doubt. First, the organization's resistance to intermodal reached into the highest offices of the railroad. Second, in asking for capital to close down the 160 ramps and open up the new hubs, the team's request sought to tap the railroad's most critical resource. Third, in a move that shocked people throughout the railroad, the team wanted to hire truckers to operate each of the hubs and to bring them in at a job grade high enough to merit bonuses.

> "People were still in the mind-set of regulation," says Bill Dewitt, "where truckers are the absolute worst enemy you could possibly think of. And here we want to go hire truckers to run operations right in the heart of the railroad!"

Everyone on the team vividly recalls the day the hub proposal went to the chairman and the president. The entire intermodal business unit had worked for months on this proposal and their anticipation was high. Greenwood was to be the spokesperson and, notwithstanding the enormity of their request and the well-known resistance to it, the team had every confidence Bill would somehow carry the day.

The meeting was scheduled for early afternoon. At first, everyone in intermodal went about their jobs as best they could. But there was no doubt about the anxiety level in their modest quarters in the Ft. Worth headquarters building. As the afternoon wore on, people began wandering between cubicles and offices, clustering around coffee machines, speculating and worrying more and more. All semblance of normal work came to a halt. By late afternoon, people were openly asking each other, "What could be taking so long?"

The actual meeting was even worse than Greenwood had expected. Instead of an hour, it lasted almost four. One of the senior executives clearly opposed the hubs from the beginning, and no amount of fact or emotion would budge him. Luckily, the other executive who had done some intermodal work earlier in his career was nervously supportive. But he did not want to take any big risks.

For hours, they went back and forth on the merits and risks of the proposal, with Greenwood doing his best to counter objections, ameliorate fears, collect on old favors, and promise them anything to get the go-ahead. His best efforts failed.

> "In the end," says Greenwood, "the two men said they would not approve the proposal until Intermodal proved it could do what it said. They wanted us to pilot the hub concept. *And* they picked the two worst possible locations to let us try."

> "One guy didn't believe we could hold onto all of our existing business while closing down the ramps and constructing the new hubs. So he picked Midway in Minnesota, which involved closing the greatest number of hubs. The other didn't think we could build the business like we projected. So he picked Portland, where we faced the strongest railroad competition."

> "It was a test," Greenwood believes, "to see us fail."

When the meeting finished, Greenwood was exhausted and discouraged. It was not what he had hoped for, and certainly not what the team or the business unit were expecting. Still, he knew it was better than nothing.

That evening, when Bill returned, the anxious group packed into the only space that would hold them all. The anticipation on their faces made it even more difficult for Bill to break the news. "It's not what we hoped," he said, "but we do have the okay on two hubs. I think we should give it a shot."

In some ways, Bill had underestimated the heart in his group. Sure they were disappointed and there was a momentary silence. Everyone instantly recognized the difficulties associated with the two chosen hubs. In addition to the number of ramps to be closed at Midway, Minnesota, and the competition in Portland, Oregon, the hubs were scheduled to open the winter of 1982–1983, when construction would be stalled by cold weather and business slowed by the country's deep recession. A less committed and self-sufficient group might have given up in discouragement, frustration, or a pending sense of failure. Not the Intermodal Team. They had a green light; not the one they hoped for, but still a green light. So within seconds of Bill's announcement, the room began to buzz with statements of support, resolve, excitement, and determination.

> "We had all this coiled energy," remarks Bill Dewitt. "I had never participated in anything where we had so thoroughly thought out all the interrelated issues needed to get things done. We already knew how we were going to handle the ramp closings, where we would get the new equipment from, and how we were going to run it. To us, this was the go-ahead to finally do something."

The team tightened its belt and worked virtually around the clock to launch the Midway hub in October 1982 and the Portland hub in November. Talk about bad timing! The winter was even colder than normal, the country was in recession, and the freight business did slow after Christmas as it always does. But to teams like Intermodal, all that is just more grist for the mill. The two new Burlington Northern hubs exceeded all the predictions made for them, and with their success came the full maturation of the Intermodal Team into an extraordinary team.

## Commitment and Fun

All real teams share a commitment to their common purpose. But only exceptional team members like Intermodal's also become deeply dedicated to each other. The seven men developed a concern and commitment for one another as deep as their dedication to the vision they were trying to accomplish. They looked out for each other's welfare, supported each other whenever and however needed, and constantly worked with each other to get done whatever had to get done. Furthermore, they genuinely enjoyed each other's company. Greenwood speaks for the team when he says, "There were things we had to do with the rest of the company that were not fun. But it was always fun inside the team. You could really let your guard down. We always really liked being around each other."

The combination of commitment to each other and commitment to their cause provided powerful meaning to the team. Says Bill Berry, "We were really fanatical in our belief of what we were trying to accomplish. Not only would this thing have an impact on ourselves, but it would also have an impact on the company. We really believed we would make a big difference."

### Capability and Confidence

A variety of strengths characterized the team. Each of the men brought with him a reputation as a renegade within the railroad; each believed strongly in Greenwood. Interestingly, none of them had ever had marketing experience while all of them had operating experience. But Greenwood had not insisted on a proven marketing track record; instinctively he picked people with the potential to develop the skills needed to meet the team's performance challenge—and they did.

> "We were coming into a marketing group," says Mark Cane, "but none of us had ever been in marketing before. I think that worked to our advantage because we brought fresh perspective and didn't carry any baggage. Moreover, it was clear to all of us that we had to restructure the way the business operated in order to make it marketable."

Each of the men did assume individual roles. Dewitt emerged as the best marketer, Burns, Brady, and Berry focused on operations, Greenwood on sales, and Cane and Hoepner on strategy, finance, and planning. Yet, given their common operating backgrounds and recent introduction to marketing, the team also developed interchangeable skills in these critical disciplines—all of which reinforced their mutual confidence and capability and gave them greater flexibility than they would otherwise have had.

Leadership was also shared across the entire team. Greenwood characterizes his own role as fostering a creative environment within the team while focusing primarily on selling Intermodal to the rest of the company and its customers. Much of the team's intellectual leadership came from Dewitt, Cane, and Hoepner. Burns emerged as the critical social leader who provided constant positive feedback and reinforcement.

"I never worked *for* Bill Greenwood," comments Hoepner. "I worked *with* Bill Greenwood."

## Performance and Reward

Following the successful hub pilots, nothing stopped this powerful team. When finance refused to give them an existing cost model with which to build a pricing structure, the team "borrowed" it. When they could not get much needed information or computer support to construct an intermodal profit and loss statement, the team violated company policy and got their own personal computers. When they needed communications equipment to stay in touch with each other and the expanding hub network, they circumvented the communications department and bought voicemail. The team played fair, but by their own rules. And rule number one was "whatever it takes to achieve performance."

Burlington Northern had a long-standing practice of maintaining a low profile in the press; Intermodal advertised heavily. To appeal to truckers, they consciously, and to the rest of the railroad heretically, excluded trains from their ads. Everyone in the industry painted their cars white; Intermodal ordered theirs painted green. They lined up first to try out every piece of new equipment, including one time when they ordered trailers not yet approved by the Interstate Highway Commission.

In one of the many phrases that had special meaning to the team, Dave Burns summarized all this activity by describing what he calls the "Jesuit principle" of management: "It is much easier to ask for forgiveness than for permission."

Given the team's performance, however, they rarely had to ask for forgiveness. Within eighteen months, Burlington Northern became number one in intermodal among railroads, and then started measuring itself against truckers. They broke record after record, going from five thousand trailers per week to seven thousand to twelve thousand without increasing the number of trailers themselves. "We far exceeded what this network ought to have produced," exclaims Greenwood. "The numbers would just blow our minds."

To a man, they are deeply proud of what they built. Burlington Northern's performance exceeded even the team's most optimistic expectations. Members of the Intermodal Team went on to powerful positions within the railroad that fought them so hard for so long. Bill Greenwood became chief operating officer; Mark Cane took over a four-billion dollar equipment division; Bill Dewitt became vice president of automotive marketing.

Yet, in speaking with each of these men, the greatest reward seems to have been the team itself. Echoing sentiments expressed by the others, Ken Hoepner said with great emotion, "Most people don't have this opportunity to ever work on a team like this. I had never been on one before and I haven't been on one since. But I sure do want to do it again."

## CONCLUSION

Many team aspects in the Burlington Northern Intermodal Team story are quickly recognizable. Their dedication to a common purpose and performance challenge, their sense of mutual accountability, the candor and mutual respect in their interactions, and even the affection that developed among them are things each of us have observed or experienced in teams. Our common sense tells us that when these conditions exist, a real team and the kind of performance it can deliver are more likely to happen.

Other important elements of the Intermodal Team are perhaps less obvious. We first heard about this team, for example, in an unrelated discussion with Greenwood. Like many senior executives, he tended to think about teams rather narrowly as special projects or task forces. But when we began describing the characteristics of real teams, the Intermodal Team immediately sprang to his mind, along with a big grin across his face. Neither Greenwood nor any of the others ever set out to become a team; and none of them really thought about themselves in team terms.

Their team effort was not an "add-on" or "extra" in the sense of time and attention diverted from individual responsibilities. The team approach they actually followed was simply the way they did their jobs, period. The team work ethic certainly demanded a lot from all members, but in service of, not diversion from, their performance challenge. Many people, from executives through supervisors, stumble over this distinction. They too often assume team efforts will generate excess cost, diverted resources, and unclear responsibilities. Unfortunately, such assumptions preclude them from gaining the upside potential of integrated team efforts and commitment where mutual accountability transcends individual roles.

Greenwood also overlooked another subtlety in the story. He suggested quite strongly that the most critical factor in the development of a high-performance team lies in the initial selection of its members. Yet, the Intermodal Team experience illustrates that, while Bill did "hire" each of the others, this team also selected itself—both at the beginning and, more important, throughout its effort. Brady, DeWitt, and Burns, for example, wanted to join Greenwood's effort as much, if not more, than Greenwood wanted them. Moreover, membership in the team had far more to do with ongoing contributions than with selection itself. Like members of all effective teams, the Intermodal players had to earn their membership every day. Thus, while initial selection is important to team performance, it is more important to foster the conditions after selection that will allow members to continually develop and earn their membership in the team.

Finally, the Intermodal Team illustrates some unexpected points about the number of people who can be part of a team as well as the influence of teams on those around them. In discussing the story with those involved, it became clear that the seven key men were the only members of the team. They did not, however, in any way want to minimize the crucial contributions of their colleagues by suggesting the others were not part of the team. So each of them kept using expressions like "inner group" or "core team" in describing themselves. Still, instinctively, they knew something distinguished their roles from the those of the rest of the forty-five people in the intermodal business unit.

In fact, the story exemplifies the underappreciated influence a real team can have on the "extended team" around them. By their attitude and behaviors, teams like Intermodal energize and focus the efforts of others, thereby extending their performance impact beyond the direct results the team produces itself. This extended team phenomenon goes well beyond teamwork and supportiveness by clarifying and deepening the direction, motivation, values, and performance standards of the broader group. It is why we believe cultivating a few real teams is one of the best ways of upgrading the overall performance ethic of an organization.

We think the Intermodal Team story is remarkable. These seven men and the extended team around them converted a meaningful opportunity into a billion-dollar business and did so in the face of much adversity. As people, each of them experienced something special, truly memorable, and much bigger than themselves. Clearly, their level of commitment and achievement both stand out. But the very success of their efforts, when compared with less effective team opportunities in all of our lives, begs a number of questions: If teams offer such attractive performance upside, why do we so often overlook or underutilize the team option? Why are the conditions that make teams work much easier to recognize than to apply? What are the attitudes, assumptions, and habits we have that get in the way? Frankly, we have become convinced the answers to these questions, like the untapped potential in teams all around us, lie mostly in first understanding and then rigorously applying the proven principles of team performance.

# CHAPTER THREE

# Team Basics: A Working Definition and Discipline

WHY define "team"? The primary reason is to clarify what *we* mean by team because the word conveys different things to different people. Some think entirely of sports, where coaching, "individual bests," and practicing hard to win matter most. Some think about teamwork values like sharing, cooperating, and helping one another. Some think that any group that works together is a team; some believe any management grouping is a team; and some think primarily of two-person pairings like those found in marriage and partnership.

In addition, we encounter many views on the benefits and costs of teams. Like us, some believe teams are a powerful vehicle for performance. Some believe their main value is to support and build self-confidence in their members, or to promote involvement, empowerment, and broad-based teamwork. Some believe teams add value only to short-term project work. On the other hand, many people believe teams waste time, squander resources, and get in the way of decisive individual action and performance. Still others believe teams expose them to unpleasant personal risks like the loss of hierarchical control.

Because of these differences, we need to provide a clear definition for interpreting the stories and lessons in our book. We also want to clarify what we are *not* trying to do. We are not debating the semantics of what "team" should mean to other people. The groups described in this book could be labeled in many ways. We could have called them "effective groups" or "performance cadres." Or we might have invented a new term. We chose instead to call them teams (actually "real teams," as you will see). Readers should feel free to use whatever terminology is most helpful. Our rationale for supplying a definition is to convey the *meanings* most relevant for this book, not to advocate particular labels. We want to focus on what teams do, not what they are called.

At the heart of our definition of team lies our fundamental premise, namely that teams and performance are inextricably connected. We believe that the truly committed team is the most productive performance unit management has at its disposal—*provided there are specific results for which the team is collectively responsible, and provided the performance ethic of the company demands those results.*

Yet most potential teams, as well as the companies they are part of, pay too little attention to either the company's performance standards or the purpose and goals of individual teams. As a result, too many teams fall short of their potential. Within teams, there is nothing more important than each team member's commitment to a common purpose and set of related performance goals for which the group holds itself jointly accountable. Each member must believe the team's purpose is important to the success of the company, and collectively they must keep each other honest in assessing their results relative to that purpose. It is not just that "the monkey is on the back" of every individual member, but that the *same* monkey is on *all* their backs together. Without this internal team discipline, the team's potential accomplishments will come up short.

Within an organization, no single factor is more critical to the generation of effective teams than the clarity and consistency of the company's overall performance standards—or "performance ethic." Companies with meaningful, strong performance standards encourage and support effective teams by helping them both tailor their own goals and understand how the achievement of those goals will contribute to the company's overall aspirations. A company's performance ethic provides essential direction and meaning to the team's efforts.

The crucial link between performance and teams is not our invention. Rather, it is the most significant piece of wisdom we learned from the teams and nonteams who helped us with this book. In thinking about the subject of teams, we read dozens of excellent articles and books to find out what experts had to say on the topic. These were very helpful, and we have included them in the section "Selected Readings" at the end of the book. But it was really only by listening to people who are or have been part of teams and potential teams that we developed our definition that distinguishes a team from a mere group of people with a common assignment:

*A team is a small number of people with complementary skills who are committed to a common purpose, performance goals, and approach for which they hold themselves mutually accountable.*

We will emphasize this definition throughout the book because it is all too easy for potential teams to overlook it. In fact, we think of it less as a definition than an essential discipline that, if applied, will produce both teams and performance.

## SMALL NUMBER

Virtually all the teams we have met, read, heard about, or been members of have ranged between two and twenty-five people. The majority of them, like the Burlington Northern Intermodal Team, have numbered less than ten. Consequently, we have included "small number" in our team definition.

We admit size differs from meaningful purpose, specific performance goals, common approach, complementary skills, and mutual accountability. Those five aspects of teams are absolute necessities. "Small number" is more of a pragmatic guide. A larger number of people, say fifty or more, can theoretically become a team. But groups of such size more likely will break into subteams rather than function as a single team.

Why? Because large numbers of people—by virtue of their size—have trouble interacting constructively as a group, much less agreeing on actionable specifics. Ten people are far more likely than fifty to successfully work through their individual, functional, and hierarchical differences toward a common plan and hold themselves jointly accountable for the results.

Large groups face logistical issues like finding enough physical space and time to meet together. They also confront more complex constraints, like crowd or herd behaviors, that prevent the intense sharing of viewpoints needed to build a team. As a result, large groups tend to settle on less clear statements of purpose that, typically, get set by the hierarchical leaders, and they look to teamwork values as their working approach. Then, when teamwork values break down, the groups revert to formal hierarchy, structure, policies, and procedures.

Even small groups of people fail to become teams on teamwork values alone. Listen, for example, to Sandy Charlap, a teacher at the Dutchess Day School in Millbrook, New York. Like other faculty and staff, Sandy went through team training in the hopes of improving her effectiveness as a teacher and counselor to the kids. For several months following the training, the teamwork values practiced among the teachers and administrators improved and positively influenced the school environment.

But when asked if she and others became a team, Sandy says, "No. We treat one another somewhat better. And we meet periodically to keep the team topic alive. But beyond some general notion of wanting 'things to improve,' we don't really know why we're doing this. In fact, I've noticed that our meetings lately have become a chore—something we do more because we think we have to than because we want to."

When meetings become a chore, it is a sign that most of the people in the group are uncertain why they have gathered, beyond some notion of getting along together better. Most people consider this a waste of time. Large groups usually reach this breaking point much sooner than small numbers of people.

Thus, groups much bigger than twenty or twenty-five have difficulty becoming real teams. As the Burlington Northern story illustrates, however, sizable groups can function as extended teams whose performance is stimulated well beyond what one would expect in a hierarchy because of the influence of a real team in their midst. The most powerful extended teams occur when the real team operates at the top, as in Burlington Northern Intermodal. But other teams can have the same kind of effect. In the next chapter, for example, we tell the story of a frontline team called "ELITE" who stimulated many of their colleagues to behave as an extended team that, in turn, significantly enhanced the performance of their company.

Still, the distinctions here are critical because of the limits to the team concept. Extended teams, powerful as they are, are not real teams. For all the reasons discussed above, large numbers of people usually cannot develop the common purpose, goals, approach, and mutual accountability of a real team. And when they try to do so, they usually produce only superficial "missions" and well-meaning intentions. As a result, and perhaps counterintuitively, extending the benefits of a team to a large group is better accomplished by challenging subsets of the group to tackle significant performance goals and then helping those subgroups to become real teams. One real team in the midst of a large group will influence overall group performance more effectively than any number of mission or teamwork statements.

## COMPLEMENTARY SKILLS

Teams must develop the right mix of skills, that is, each of the complementary skills necessary to do the team's job. These team skill requirements fall into three categories:

- **Technical or functional expertise.** It would make little sense for a group of doctors to litigate an employment discrimination case in a court of law. Yet *teams* of doctors and lawyers often try medical malpractice or personal injury cases. Similarly, product development groups that include only marketers or engineers are less likely to succeed than those with the complementary skills of both.

- **Problem-solving and decision-making skills.** Teams must be able to identify the problems and opportunities they face, evaluate the options they have for moving forward, and then make necessary trade-offs and decisions about how to proceed. Most teams need some members with these skills to begin with although many will develop them best on the job.

- **Interpersonal skills.** Common understanding and purpose cannot arise without effective communication and constructive conflict that, in turn, depend on interpersonal skills. These include risk taking, helpful criticism, objectivity, active listening, giving the benefit of the doubt, support, and recognizing the interests and achievements of others.

Common sense tells us that it is a mistake to ignore skills when selecting a team. A team cannot get started without some minimum complement of skills, especially technical and functional ones. And no team can achieve its purpose without developing all the skill levels required. Still, it is surprising how many people assemble teams primarily on the basis of personal compatibility or formal position in the organization.

Interestingly, however, an equally common error is to *overemphasize* skills in team selection. Much of the popular literature on teams, for example, stresses skill mix as a prerequisite to selection, almost like recipes—particularly for interpersonal skills. Yet, in our research, we did not meet a single team that had all the needed skills at the outset. We did discover, however, the power of teams as vehicles for personal learning and development. Their performance focus helps teams quickly identify skill gaps and the specific development needs of team members to fill them. The shared commitment in teams encourages a healthy fear of failure as opposed to debilitating insecurity among those challenged to learn. Finally, each team member's sense of individual accountability to the team promotes learning. Once harnessed to a common purpose and set of goals, natural individualism motivates learning within teams. Except for certain technical and functional skills, most of us have the potential to learn the skills needed in teams. And individualism drives the majority of us to find some way to make our own distinctive and individual contribution to the team. Accordingly, as long as the skill *potential* exists, the dynamics of a team cause that skill to develop.

Not a single person on Burlington Northern's Intermodal Team, for example, had a specific marketing background for what, in some respects, was a classic marketing challenge. Yet, as that story illustrates, many of the advantages and rewards of a team come in the opportunities for personal growth after people join the team. Other teams have experienced similar growth. For example, a plant manager who was part of a team at Weyerhaeuser charged with developing a business strategy felt he was holding back the team because of his inexperience with computers. But he wanted to be part of the team so much that he spent hours on his own developing his computer skills. General Electric routinely trains new members in interpersonal and problem-solving skills as a foundation for what they will need to become effective team members. At Motorola, when a member of one self-managing team who could not read asked to be replaced so she would not slow down the rest of the team, the team insisted on teaching her to read and went on to achieve its goals. Thus, the challenge for any potential team lies in striking the right balance between selection and development as the means for building the full set of complementary skills needed to fulfill the team's purpose over time.

## COMMITTED TO A COMMON PURPOSE AND PERFORMANCE GOALS

A team's purpose and performance goals go together. Indeed, we have yet to find a real team without both. The team's near-term performance goals must always relate directly to its overall purpose; otherwise, team members become confused, pull apart, and revert to mediocre performance behaviors.

1. **A common, meaningful purpose sets the tone and aspiration.** Teams develop direction, momentum, and commitment by working to shape a meaningful purpose. Building ownership and commitment to team purpose, however, is not incompatible with taking initial direction from outside the team. The often-asserted assumption that a team cannot "own" its purpose unless management keeps completely away from the team actually confuses more potential teams than it helps. In fact, it is the exceptional case—for example, entrepreneurial situations—when a team actually creates a purpose entirely on its own.

Most teams shape their purposes in response to a demand or opportunity put in their path, usually by management. The team of

Xerox scientists who invented personal computing developed their purpose after the chairman of Xerox called for the creation of an "architecture of information." The Rockingham Dri-Loc Team at Sealed Air Corporation began shaping its purpose with the instruction from management to cut waste and reduce downtime. The Deal-to-Steel Team at Enron Corporation created its purpose to vastly improve Enron's pipeline construction deals in response to senior management's expressed frustration over barriers and bureaucracy.

Direction from management helps teams get started by broadly framing the performance requirements of the company. This is what Bob Waterman and Tom Peters call "solution space"; that is, defining the boundaries and scope of authority clearly enough to indicate direction, but flexibly enough to allow the modification required for commitment to develop. Figure 3-1 is one of the best illustrations we found of a management guideline for teams. It was developed at Procter & Gamble during its impressive major change and performance turnaround between 1985 and 1991. It makes clear the charter, the rationale, and the performance challenge for the team, but leaves plenty of solution space for the team to set specific goals, timing, and approach.

The best teams invest a tremendous amount of time and effort exploring, shaping, and agreeing on a purpose that belongs to them both collectively and individually. In fact, real teams never stop this "purposing" activity because of its value in clarifying implications for members. With enough time and sincere attention, one or more broad, meaningful aspirations invariably arise that motivate teams and provide a fundamental reason for their extra effort.

Listen, for example, to how three people describe the purpose and implicit values of the Kodak "Zebra Team," which manages fifteen hundred Kodak employees responsible for producing seven thousand different black and white film products:

"Black and white, black and white. Everybody's a partner."
"We're so pleased with what we're doing and the results we're getting that we want the rest of the company to learn from us."
"We're crazy. We'll do anything."

**FIGURE 3-1**
**Initiative Team Charter**

Mission:             Launch XYZ new product by March 5, 1993
Basis for interest:  (Consumer, customer, competitive, cost, etc.)
Input targets:       (Product design and reliability, cost, product cube,
                     pricing, capital, etc.)
Output targets:      (Revenue, volume, consumer preference, start-up time
                     and cost, etc.)
Team members:
Team process:
Sponsors:

| Key challenges | How to overcome |
|---|---|
| • Different equipment in each plant<br>• Reducing color changeover time<br>• Availability of critical raw material<br>• Ensuring rapid distribution with minimal obsolete inventories | |

| Key milestones | Timing | Throwaway ($) | Data availability |
|---|---|---|---|
| • Capital initiation<br>• Start of construction<br>• Start of production<br>• Start of shipments | | | |

These comments, like those of most teams, have more meaning to the team than to a casual, first-time observer because of the time invested by the team in understanding what it is trying to do and why. If you ask the Zebra Team members to interpret, however, they will say they are describing their collective aspirations of leading broad-scale corporate change throughout Kodak, building values of partnership and risk taking, and proving the worth of black and white film at Kodak, where color has been in the limelight.

Make no mistake—the Zebra Team set clear performance objectives aimed at increasing profits, reducing cycle-time along with work-in-progress inventory, cutting production costs, increasing customer satisfaction, and improving on-time deliveries. Without such goals, it would not have become or remained a team. Yet a few years into continual team discussions, decisions, actions, and more discussions, the three people quoted here are describing a mission that goes well beyond operational economics.

Groups that fail to become teams rarely develop a common purpose that they own and can translate into specific and actionable goals. For whatever reason—an insufficient focus on performance, lack of effort, poor leadership—they do not coalesce around a challenging aspiration. The Executive Committee of a leading financial services company provides a good example. After many years of industry leadership, this company's competitive position began to erode in the late 1980s. As with most entrenched industry leaders, it took awhile before the Executive Committee ever talked about, much less recognized, the threat.

By 1991, however, the company had crafted a credible competitive strategy that, by any standard, promised to put it back on course. Unfortunately, the Executive Committee did not convert the strategy into an effective team purpose. Its deep-seated habits of individualism, reinforced by strong, articulate personalities and, probably, ignorance about the need for a team purpose prevented it from developing a specific team purpose and, hence, from becoming a team. Without mutual commitment to a broader team purpose, groups like this Executive Committee are forced to operate without a sense of direction *that they understand in common.*

But what makes purposes like that of Kodak's Zebra Team so powerful? First, a team purpose is a joint creation that exists only because of the team's collaborative effort. As such, it inspires both pride and responsibility. The better teams often treat their purpose like an offspring in need of constant nurturing and care. Naturally, they spend relatively more time in the beginning shaping their purpose; but, even after the team is operative, the members periodically revisit the purpose to clarify its implications for action. They continue such "purposing" activity indefinitely.

Next, because of the intense discussions that mold a team's purpose, the purpose itself conveys a rich and varied set of meanings to guide what the team needs to do, particularly in meeting its goals. Scores of scenarios get painted about customer needs, competitor capabilities, governmental or other requirements, and external as well as internal constraints. Consequently, when challenges arise, team members can respond, confident that they have the trust and support of their teammates—so long as the actions taken make sense in light of the team purpose. In other words, risks that otherwise might not be taken get done as a matter of course.

Most important, team purposes give teams an identity that reaches beyond the sum of the individuals involved. This team identity keeps conflict—something both necessary and threatening to teams—constructive by providing a meaningful standard against which to resolve clashes between the interests of the individual and the interests of the team. Armed with team purpose, everyone on the team knows when an individual may be getting out of line and must put the team first or else risk breaking it apart.

**2. Specific performance goals are an integral part of the purpose.** Transforming broad directives into specific and measurable performance goals is the surest first step for a team trying to shape a common purpose meaningful to its members. Specific goals—like getting a new product to market in less than half the normal time, responding to all customers within twenty-four hours, or achieving a zero defect rate while simultaneously cutting costs by 40 percent— provide clear and tangible footholds for teams for several reasons.

First, they define a *team work-product* that is different from both an organizationwide mission and the summation of individual job objectives. To be effective, team work-products must require roughly equivalent contributions from all the people on the team to make something specific happen that, in and of itself, adds real value to company results.

Second, the specificity of the performance objectives facilitates clear communications and constructive conflict within the team. For example, one of Sealed Air Corporation's* plant-level teams set a goal of averaging two hours for machine changeover. The clarity of that goal forced the team to concentrate on what it would take to achieve it—or, alternatively, to seriously reconsider whether the goal should be changed. When such goals are clear, team discussions can focus on how to pursue them or whether to change them; when goals are ambiguous or nonexistent, such discussions are much less productive.

Third, the attainability of specific performance goals helps teams maintain their focus on getting results. A product development team at Eli Lilly's Peripheral Systems Group set definite yardsticks for the market introduction of an ultrasonic probe to help doctors locate deep veins and arteries in patients. The probe had to have an audible signal through a specified depth of tissue, be manufacturable at a rate of 100 per day, and have a unit cost less than a pre-established amount. Moreover, the team committed itself to develop the product in less than half the usual time frame for its division. Because each of these objectives was attainable and measurable, the team knew throughout the development process where it stood. Either it had achieved its goals or it had not.

Fourth, as Outward Bound and other team-building programs illustrate, specific objectives have a leveling effect conducive to team behavior. When a small group of people challenge themselves to get over a wall or up a mountain or through a desert—or to reduce cycle time by 50 percent—their respective titles, perks, and other "stripes" fade into the background. Instead, the teams that succeed evaluate what and how each individual can best contribute to the team's goal and, more important, do so in terms of the performance objective itself rather than a person's status or personality.

Fifth, specific goals should allow the team to achieve small wins as it pursues its purpose. *Small wins are invaluable to building members' commitment* and overcoming the inevitable obstacles that get in the way of achieving a meaningful long-term purpose.

---

*Sealed Air is a high-performing producer of packaging materials and systems. Its efforts to develop world-class manufacturing skills through extensive use of teams is described in Chapter 10.

Last, performance goals are compelling. They challenge the people on the team to commit themselves, as a team, to make a difference. Drama, urgency, and a healthy fear of failure combine to drive teams who have their collective eye on an attainable goal. The Eli Lilly medical probe team, for example, put its pride on the line when it committed to getting the new product to the market in record time. Nobody beyond the team could make it happen. It was *their* challenge.

**3. The combination is essential to performance.** A team's purpose and specific performance goals have a symbiotic relationship; each depends on the other to stay relevant and vital. The specific performance goals help a team track progress and hold itself accountable; the broader, even nobler aspirations in a team's purpose supply both meaning and emotional energy. For example, the combination of the Zebra Team's aspirations, such as "putting black and white film back on Kodak's map," and specific goals, such as reducing cycle-time and improving on-time delivery, provide a terrific example of what it takes to sustain teams over time—namely, purposes and performance goals that are both economic and social, rational and emotional, performance-focused and meaningful.

Usually, a team's aspirations and purpose will grow out of a persistent pursuit of specific performance goals. The *Tallahassee Democrat*'s ELITE Team described in the next chapter transformed its initial goal of reducing advertising errors into the more meaningful purpose of providing overall better customer service. Sometimes, however, a team starts with a compelling and noble aspiration and works hard to translate it into specific and attainable performance objectives. For example, the PBS program "Schools in America"* described four economically hard-pressed schools whose faculty leadership teams were determined "to prove that our youngsters could be as successful as affluent youngsters in public education in America." Only later did the teams shape measurable goals having to do with test scores, attendance, and graduation. Some teams begin with clear performance objectives, others

---

*More detail is given in Chapter 7.

only get there after stumbling around for awhile. Whatever the sequence, the directional intensity so necessary for successful team performance comes from the continuing integration of purpose and performance goals.

## COMMITTED TO A COMMON APPROACH

Teams also need to develop a common approach—that is, how they will work together to accomplish their purpose. Indeed, they should invest just as much time and effort crafting their working approach as shaping their purpose. A team's approach must include both an economic and administrative aspect as well as a social aspect. To meet the economic and administrative challenge, every member of a team must do "equivalent" amounts of real work that goes beyond commenting, reviewing, and deciding. Team members must agree on who will do particular jobs, how schedules will be set and adhered to, what skills need to be developed, how continuing membership is to be earned, and how the group will make and modify decisions, including when and how to modify its approach to getting the job done. Agreeing on the specifics of work and how it fits together to integrate individual skills and advance team performance lies at the heart of shaping a common approach. It is perhaps self-evident that a working approach that delegates all the real work to a few members (or staff outsiders) and thus relies on review and discussion meetings for the only "work together" aspects of the approach cannot sustain a real team.

Often many teams treat the social aspect of work as unrelated to performance. But effective teams always have team members who, over time, assume important social as well as leadership roles such as challenging, interpreting, supporting, integrating, remembering, and summarizing. These roles help promote the mutual trust and constructive conflict necessary to the team's success. In the best teams, each member assumes different social roles, depending on the situation. As a result, teams develop their own unique processes for energizing and supporting one another and for keeping each other honest and on track. We emphasize, however, that such roles evolve over time to meet performance needs. People make a mistake if, upon reading a description of useful social roles, they think they must assemble a team at the beginning with "all the right parts."

The three-man team who led the Irvington Division of Garden State Brickface from last to first in terms of division performance never stopped discussing and improving its approach to becoming number one—just as it never stopped discussing the importance of being number one. Garden State is a small construction company specializing in applying decorative brickface and stucco for clients ranging from middle-class homeowners to world-famous architects. Each job is a custom effort in which hundreds of slip-ups ranging from cracking, to color or texture deficiency, to damaging the house or building can disappoint customers.

When Charlie Baum, Doug Jimmink, and John Patterson set their sights on turning around Irvington, the division had a history of poor performance. Projects ran too long, costs were out of control, and quality was spotty. Dissatisfied customers often refused to pay. Stealing, accidents, and drug and alcohol abuse were common. Sales blamed production for all the problems and vice versa.

Each man brought his own strengths and weaknesses to the team. Charlie, the general manager, was an Ivy League graduate and former consultant with strong process and analytic skills and a deep faith in the value of fairness and integrity. Charlie, however, neither looked like a brickface guy nor knew much about the complicated job of doing brickface work. Nor did he have much in common with Irvington's workers.

Doug, the vice president of sales, was a born salesman who knew all the con games. Though he had a fiery personality that inspired the sales force, he had little interest in the administrative details of his job.

John, the vice president of production, was an up-from-the-ranks leader who understood brickface work inside out and the lives of the men who did it. Unlike Charlie and Doug, he had no formal management experience, and lacked broad understanding of the business of brickface—that is, what really produced bottom-line results.

As these three men worked out their approach to make Irvington the number one division of Garden State, their job titles faded into the background as more relevant roles, skills, and practices emerged:

- Charlie became the prime customer service contact, goal suggester, educator, arbitrator of fairness, and liaison with corporate headquarters. He was also Mr. Integrity.

- Doug motivated, challenged, and inspired the team as well as his sales force. With John, he figured out how best to keep sales and production working constructively to meet the goals Charlie suggested.

- John promoted Charlie's belief in fairness with the men, kept Charlie practical, and became the prime challenger and supporter of the work force. He was also Charlie's "lead student" in learning about the business economics of brickface, providing a critical role model to the division at large.

- They used customer expectations, job-by-job "brickface" economics, and employee skill development as the yardsticks for planning and problem resolution.

- All three men played games (e.g., basketball, softball, and darts) to provide a comfortable and open context for raising, discussing, and resolving team issues. Says Doug, "That dart board resolved more problems than you would ever believe."

Obviously, these roles, skills, and practices did not exist the first day the three men met, nor were they dictated by Charlie (the boss). They took shape out of endless conversations about how the team could achieve its purpose in the face of the challenges it faced. The power here comes from perpetually adjusting the team approach with reference to purpose and goals. As the Garden State Brickface Team carved out ways to work best together, it developed the insight and courage required to tackle many knotty obstacles; for example:

- Early on, John accepted an order from a salesman who had submitted such a low-ball bid that there was no way Garden State could make money. Previous production vice presidents had always rejected such jobs. John, however, knew the link between sales and production was more critical to Garden State's approach than the profitability of a single job. Since the commission on the order was crucial to the salesman, he wanted to demonstrate that he and the production crews would do whatever they could to make the job work.

- The team shaped new approaches to compensation, training, and information to emphasize the profitability of each job. It provided each new crew with the necessary information to influence job profitability, trained the crews in how to use the data to improve performance, and rewarded crews on the basis of job-by-job results.

- The men developed a "Brickface University," conducted during the cold, slow winter months, that was aimed at enriching everyone's understanding of the whole business—an on-the-job educational effort that later won national recognition from Congress.

- The team changed job assignments from a functional-specialty basis that mixed and matched different individuals on different days to a crew-based approach that kept crews intact. Then they conducted a crew draft along the lines of professional sports teams that put the job of forming crews in the hands of the frontline workers. As a consequence, Irvington was able to reduce its cost base significantly while simultaneously improving job quality.

Certainly, any of these men, acting as an individual in a hierarchy, might have done some of these same things. But we argue that such initiatives—both separately and cumulatively—are far more likely to emerge out of a commonly agreed on and continually updated team approach. When individuals approach a team situation, especially in a business setting, each has pre-existing job assignments as well as strengths and weaknesses reflecting a variety of backgrounds, talents, personalities, and prejudices. Only through the mutual discovery and understanding of how to apply all its human resources to a common purpose can a group really develop and agree on the best team approach to achieve its goal. At the heart of such long and, at times, difficult interactions lies a commitment-building process in which the whole team candidly explores who is best suited to each task as well as how all the individual roles will come together. In effect, it establishes a social contract among members that relates to their purpose, and guides and obligates how they must work together.

# MUTUAL ACCOUNTABILITY

No group ever becomes a team until it can hold itself accountable as a team. Like common purpose and approach, this is a stiff test. Think, for example, about the subtle but critical difference between "the boss holds me accountable" and "we hold ourselves accountable." The first case can lead to the second; but, without the second, there can be no team.

At its core, team accountability is about the sincere promises we make to ourselves and others, promises that underpin two critical aspects of teams: commitment and trust. By promising to hold ourselves accountable to the team's goals, we each earn the right to express our own views about all aspects of the team's effort and to have our views receive a fair and constructive hearing. By following through on such a promise, we preserve and extend the trust upon which any team must be built.

Most of us enter a potential team situation cautiously; ingrained individualism discourages us from putting our fates in the hands of others. Teams do not succeed by ignoring or wishing away such behavior. Mutual promises and accountability cannot be coerced any more than people can be made to trust one another. Nevertheless, mutual accountability does tend to grow as a natural counterpart to the development of team purpose, performance goals, and approach. Accountability arises from and reinforces the time, energy, and action invested in figuring out what the team is trying to accomplish and how best to get it done. When people do real work together toward a common objective, trust and commitment follow. Consequently, teams enjoying a strong common purpose and approach inevitably hold themselves, both as individuals and as a team, responsible for the team's performance.

The specific performance goals of teams also provide clear yardsticks for accountability: for example, the Sealed Air Team that wanted to reduce machine changeover time by two hours or the Eli Lilly Team that wanted to introduce its new medical device in record time. As such goals are discussed and the approaches to them developed, the people involved—over time—have a clearer and clearer choice: they can disagree with the goal and the path the team selects and, in effect, opt out of the team; or, they can pitch in and become jointly accountable with their teammates.

Accountability, then, provides a useful litmus test of the quality of a team's purpose and approach. Groups that lack mutual accountability for performance have not shaped a common purpose and approach that can sustain them as a team. The Executive Committee at the financial services firm mentioned earlier illustrates this point. Each of the individuals on that committee is an experienced professional who has shown repeatedly the readiness to sign on and follow through on any assignment. Individual accountability is familiar to each of them. Throughout the crisis, however, the members of the Executive Committee failed to demonstrate that they held themselves mutually accountable, as a team, for any aspect of the company's performance. They remained accountable as individuals only, a sure sign that they lacked a common team purpose, work-product goals, or mutual agreement on how best to proceed. By contrast, if you observe a group of people who are truly committed and accountable for joint results, you can be almost certain they have both a strong team purpose and an agreed-on approach.

## CONCLUSION

Despite the fact that most of us are familiar with teams, we are imprecise in thinking about them. For that reason, gaining a clear understanding of what a team is and is not—and particularly how teams and performance depend on each other—can provide useful insights in how to strengthen the performance of your group. Imprecise thinking about teams, however, pales in comparison to the lack of discipline most of us bring to potential team situations. Teams do not spring up by magic. Nor does personal chemistry matter as much as most people believe. Rather, we believe that by persistently applying the definition offered here, most people can significantly enhance team performance. And focusing on performance—not chemistry or togetherness or good communications or good feelings—shapes teams more than anything else.

As a starting point, we urge you to think about each of the six basic elements of teams when you assess your group's current situation: 1) Are you small enough in number? 2) Do you have adequate levels of complementary skills and skill potential in all three categories necessary for team performance? 3) Do you have a broader, meaningful purpose that all members aspire to? 4) Do you have a specific set of performance goals agreed upon by all? 5) Is the working approach clearly understood and commonly agreed upon? and 6) Do you hold yourselves individually and mutually accountable for the group's results?

While these questions are relatively straightforward, it is probably worthwhile to probe each one further to obtain practical and actionable insights for improvement. Specifically:

1. Small enough in number:
   a. Can you convene easily and frequently?
   b. Can you communicate with all members easily and frequently?
   c. Are your discussions open and interactive for all members?
   d. Does each member understand the others' roles and skills?
   e. Do you need more people to achieve your ends?
   f. Are sub-teams possible or necessary?

2. Adequate levels of complementary skills:
   a. Are all three categories of skills either actually or potentially represented across the membership (functional/technical, problem-solving/decision-making, and interpersonal)?
   b. Does each member have the potential in all three categories to advance his or her skills to the level required by the team's purpose and goals?
   c. Are any skill areas that are critical to team performance missing or underrepresented?
   d. Are the members, individually and collectively, willing to spend the time to help themselves and others learn and develop skills?
   e. Can you introduce new or supplemental skills as needed?

3. Truly meaningful purpose:
   a. Does it constitute a broader, deeper aspiration than just near-term goals?

b. Is it a *team* purpose as opposed to a broader organizational purpose or just one individual's purpose (e.g., the leader's)?

c. Do all members understand and articulate it the same way? And do they do so without relying on ambiguous abstractions?

d. Do members define it vigorously in discussions with outsiders?

e. Do members frequently refer to it and explore its implications?

f. Does it contain themes that are particularly meaningful and memorable?

g. Do members feel it is important, if not exciting?

4. Specific goal or goals:

   a. Are they *team* goals versus broader organizational goals or just one individual's goals (e.g., the leader's)?

   b. Are they clear, simple, and measurable? If not measurable, can their achievement be determined?

   c. Are they realistic as well as ambitious? Do they allow small wins along the way?

   d. Do they call for a concrete set of team work-products?

   e. Is their relative importance and priority clear to all members?

   f. Do all members agree with the goals, their relative importance, and the way in which their achievement will be measured?

   g. Do all members articulate the goals in the same way?

5. Clear working approach:

   a. Is the approach concrete, clear, and really understood and agreed to by everybody? Will it result in achievement of the objectives?

   b. Will it capitalize on and enhance the skills of all members? Is it consistent with other demands on the members?

   c. Does it require all members to contribute equivalent amounts of real work?

   d. Does it provide for open interaction, fact-based problem solving, and results-based evaluation?

   e. Do all members articulate the approach in the same way?

f. Does it provide for modification and improvement over time?
g. Are fresh input and perspectives systematically sought and added, for example, through information and analysis, new members, and senior sponsors?

6. Sense of mutual accountability:
   a. Are you individually and jointly accountable for the team's purpose, goals, approach, and work-products?
   b. Can you and do you measure progress against specific goals?
   c. Do all members feel responsible for all measures?
   d. Are the members clear on what they are individually responsible for and what they are jointly responsible for?
   e. Is there a sense that "only the team can fail"?

Answering the preceding questions can establish the degree to which your group functions as a real team, as well as help pinpoint how you can strengthen your efforts to increase performance. They set tough standards, and answering them candidly may reveal a harder challenge than you may have expected. At the same time, facing up to the answers can accelerate your progress in achieving the full potential of your team. In Part II, we will describe in more detail how potential teams actually go about improving their "scores" on these questions and, more important, their performance.

# CHAPTER FOUR

# High-Performance Teams: Very Useful Models

TEAMS occasionally emerge that outperform all reasonable expectations as well as all other similarly situated teams. These "high-performance teams" even surprise themselves. The seven men who built Burlington Northern's intermodal business were such a team. So were the *Tallahassee Democrat* ELITE and Dallas Mafia teams described in this chapter. All produced exceptional results.

Behind high-performance teams lies a story of commitment. Like any real team, a high-performance team must have a small number of people with the required skills, purpose, goals, approach, and accountability described in our working definition. What sets apart high-performance teams, however, is the degree of commitment, particularly how deeply committed the members are to one another. Such commitments go well beyond civility and teamwork. Each genuinely helps the others to achieve both personal and professional goals. Furthermore, such commitments extend beyond company activities and even beyond the life of the team itself.

Jennifer Futernick, who is part of the high-performing Rapid Response Team described in Chapter 5, calls the emotion binding her teammates together a form of love. A more typical, but not necessarily different description, comes from Ken Hoepner of the Burlington Northern Intermodal Team: "Not only did we trust each other, not only did we respect each other, but we gave a damn about the rest of the people on this team. If we saw somebody vulnerable, we were there to help." Ken obviously feels great pride about this attribute of his team.

Such strong interpersonal commitments drive a number of aspects that distinguish high-performance teams. Fueled by interpersonal commitments, team purposes become even nobler, team performance goals more urgent, and team approach more powerful. The notion, for example, that "if one of us fails, we all fail" pervades high-performance teams. In addition, mutual concern for each other's personal growth enable high-performance teams to develop interchangeable skills and hence greater flexibility. High-performance teams also share leadership within the team more than other teams. And, not insignificantly, high-performance teams seem to have a better developed sense of humor and more fun.

High-performance teams, however, are rare. Looking back on a combined fifty-five-year career of team activity, for example, the two of us can recall, as individuals, being part of only four high-performance teams. This should surprise no one, because the personal commitments we are describing are difficult to achieve and sustain. It is not obvious how people can be managed or even led into caring about one another's personal success and growth. Certainly, such bonds do not arise from team-building exercises or training programs. No rules, best practices, or secret formulas exist that ensure high-performance outcomes. Nonetheless, high-performance teams, however scarce they might be, provide terrific models for any potential team to study.

High-performance teams are also where you find them, not where you wish they were. They arise on their own and in different settings. This chapter, for example, relates the stories of a frontline team (ELITE) and a young management group (Dallas Mafia) who each became high-performance teams. The members of ELITE were all women who, with a few exceptions, held frontline jobs at the *Tallahassee Democrat* newspaper in Florida. The members of the Dallas Mafia were all highly paid professional men charged with leading a business unit in the highly competitive world of investment banking. It is hard to imagine two more disparate sets of people, challenges, and circumstances. Yet, each story illustrates how strong personal commitments transformed the people involved into high-performance teams and, in turn, enhanced the performance of the organizations around them. The commonalities are more striking than the differences.

# THE *TALLAHASSEE DEMOCRAT'S* ELITE TEAM

Knight-Ridder's *Tallahassee Democrat,* like newspapers across North America, began experiencing an unusual business challenge in the 1980s. Explosive growth in television and cable, combined with falling literacy rates and shrinking leisure time, forced so many papers out of business that most cities had only one or two left. Those that remained, like the *Democrat,* theoretically enjoyed strong bargaining positions relative to advertisers. Nevertheless, most papers hit a wall in terms of profitability. Like other embattled industries of the 1980s, they gradually recognized that customer service and continuous improvement were their best hope for growth. These, however, depended on broad-based behavioral changes that could not happen without first breaking down the barriers among the historically divided functions within a newspaper.

### The Performance Challenge

Fred Mott, the general manager of the *Democrat,* recognized this challenge earlier than many of his counterparts. In part, Mott took his lead from Jim Batten, who made "customer obsession" the central theme of his corporate renewal effort shortly after he became Knight-Ridder's CEO. But the local marketplace also shaped Mott's thinking. The *Democrat* was Tallahassee's only paper and made money in spite of its customer service record. Mott believed, however, that further growth could never happen unless the paper learned to serve customers in ways "far superior to anything else in the marketplace."

The ELITE Team story actually began with the formation of another team made up of Mott and his direct reports. The management group knew they could not hope to build a "customer obsession" across the mile-high barriers isolating production from circulation from advertising without first changing themselves. It had become all too common, they admitted, for them to engage in "power struggles and finger pointing."

Using regularly scheduled Monday morning meetings, Mott's group began to "get to know each other's strengths and weaknesses, bare their souls, and build a level of trust." Most important, they did so by focusing on real work they could do together. For example, early on they agreed to create a budget for the paper as a team instead of singly as function heads.

Over time, the change in behavior at the top began to be noticed. One of the women who later joined the ELITE Team, for example, observed that the sight of senior management holding their "Monday morning come-to-Jesus" meetings really made a difference to her and others. "I saw all this going on and I thought, 'What are they so happy about?' "

Eventually, as the team at the top got stronger and more confident, they forged a higher aspiration: build a customer focus and break down the barriers across the broad base of the paper. Like many top managers, however, their first instinct was to create a new organizational structure, in this case the Advertising Customer Service department. The goal was to liberate ad sales reps from administrative burdens that cut into their time with customers by pulling together under one umbrella all the artists, production workers, and clerical, accounting, and billing personnel involved with ads.

A year after setting up the new department, however, Mott was both frustrated and impatient. Neither the Advertising Customer Service department, a series of customer surveys, additional resources thrown against the problem in the interim, nor any number of top management exhortations had made any difference. Ad errors persisted, and sales reps still complained of insufficient time with customers. In fact, the new unit had turned into another organizational barrier.

Customer surveys showed that too many advertisers still found the *Democrat* unresponsive to their needs and too concerned with internal procedures and deadlines. People at the paper also had evidence beyond the surveys. In one instance, for example, a sloppily prepared ad arrived through a fax machine looking like "a rat had run across the page." Yet, the ad passed through the hands of seven employees and probably would have found its way into print if it had not been literally unreadable! As someone later commented, "It was not anyone's job to make sure it was right. If they felt it was simply their job to type it or paste it up, they just passed it along." This particular fax, affectionately known as the "rat tracks fax," came to symbolize the essential challenge at the *Democrat*.

No wonder Mott was mad. He had tried everything he could think of when Doris Dunlap, one of his direct reports and, later, the team leader of ELITE, told him, "Fred, the fact that you want it so bad, and you know it needs to happen, will not make it happen. You have to back off and leave it alone."

At the time, Mott was reading about Motorola's quality programs and the goal of zero defects. He decided to heed Dunlap's advice by creating a special team of workers charged with eliminating all errors in advertisements. Mott now admits he was skeptical that frontline people could become as cohesive a team as he and his direct reports. So he made Dunlap, his trusted confidante, the leader of the team that took on the name ELITE for "ELIminate The Errors."

## The Performance Results

A year later, Mott was a "born again" believer in teams. Under ELITE's leadership, advertising accuracy, never before tracked at the paper, had risen sharply and stayed above 99 percent. Lost revenues from errors, previously as high as $10,000 a month, had dropped to near zero. Ad sales reps had complete confidence in the Advertising Customer Service department's capacity and desire to treat each ad as though the *Democrat*'s existence were at stake. And surveys showed a huge positive swing in advertiser satisfaction. All of which Mott considered nothing less than a minor miracle.

The impact of ELITE, however, went beyond numbers. It completely redesigned the process by which the *Democrat* sells, creates, produces, and bills for advertisements. More important yet, it stimulated and nurtured the customer obsession and cross-functional cooperation required to make the new process work. In effect, this team of mostly frontline workers transformed an entire organization with respect to customer service.

## Shaping the Purpose and Performance Goals

ELITE had a lot going for it from the beginning. Mott gave the group a clear performance goal (eliminate errors) and a strong mix of skills (twelve of the best people from all parts of the paper). He committed himself to follow through by promising, at the first meeting, that "whatever solution you come up with will be implemented." In addition, Jim Batten's customer obsession movement helped energize the task force.

But it took more than a good sendoff and an overarching corporate theme to make ELITE into a high-performance team. In this case, the personal commitments began to grow, unexpectedly, over the early months as the team grappled with its challenge. At first, the group spent more time pointing fingers at one another than coming to grips with advertising errors. Only when one of them produced the famous "rat tracks fax" and told the story behind it did the group start to admit that everyone—not everyone else—was at fault. Then, recalls one member, "We had some pretty hard discussions. And there were tears in those meetings."

The emotional responses galvanized the group to the task at hand and to one another. And the closer it got, the more focused it became on the challenge. ELITE decided to look carefully at the entire process by which an ad was sold, created, printed, and billed. When it did, the team discovered patterns in the errors, most of which could be attributed to time pressure, bad communication, and poor attitude.

Some of this the team believed could be fixed through technical and process solutions. To relieve some of the time pressures, for example, it recommended giving cellular phones and portable fax machines to ad reps so they could send in ad orders throughout the day instead of all at once after five o'clock. To reduce communications breakdowns and increase pride of ownership, ELITE asked the *Democrat* to buy desktop computers and publishing software for production employees who, with training, could create an ad from start to finish. To fully eliminate errors, however, ELITE knew, would require people throughout the paper to work together for the benefit of customers. As one person on the team put it:

We all became focused on the customer. We didn't let other things like personality get in the way. We were focused enough on where we were going, with what we were doing, that we made a commitment to the people around us that we were going to help them see exactly what we were seeing and not let anything interfere with that.

## Personal Commitments

Commitment to one another drove ELITE to continually expand its aspirations. Having started with the charge to eliminate errors, ELITE moved on to breaking down functional barriers, then to redesigning the entire advertising process, then to defining new standards and measures for customer service, and, finally, to spreading its own brand of "customer obsession" across the entire *Democrat*. One member remarked:

How else were we going to get everyone else on the bandwagon? We could implement the plan. We could give them the tools. We could do everything but jump into their brains and give them the excitement we had. Somehow we had to get that across.

This passion led ELITE to ignore the official closing date of its assignment. It just continued to change the paper. Indeed, notwithstanding the team's respect and admiration for Mott and others, ELITE simply did not believe management would get the full benefit of its ongoing recommendations without its help. Mott was smart enough to get out of the way:

The team started attacking things I never dreamed of. They looked into every crevice that could provide service and value to customers. There was a real power that developed among them, and it affected everyone.

## The Extended Team Effort

Inspired by ELITE, for example, one production crew started coming to work at 4 A.M. to ease time pressures later in the day. For the first time, Advertising Customer Service started charting and measuring advertising quality. And sales reps did begin spending more time with customers. A new atmosphere took hold. One ELITE member said:

People in the building who get a piece of paper began to realize that that piece of paper, whether it be a bill or an ad layout or whatnot, is no longer just a piece of paper. It is the customer. I think that transformation was the hardest and the most eye-opening event to me. People cradled that piece of paper and took care of it in a way they never had before.

Customers were delighted. A notoriously demanding restaurant manager, for example, rejected one ad late enough in the day that normally it would have been killed. By deploying the new communication and computer equipment, however, an artist worked with the sales rep to turn around the ad in less than thirty minutes. The restauranteur was flabbergasted. And very pleased. "He became," said the rep, "one of our best customers."

To this day, the spirit of ELITE lives on at the *Democrat*. "There is no beginning and no end," says Dunlap. "Every day we experience something we learn from." ELITE's spirit made everyone a winner—the customers, the employees, management, and even Knight-Ridder's corporate leaders. CEO Jim Batten was so impressed that he agreed to pay for managers from other Knight-Ridder papers to visit the *Democrat* to learn from ELITE's experience. And, of course, the twelve people who committed themselves to one another and their paper had an impact and an experience none of them will ever forget.

The ELITE story shows how a commitment to one another when combined with a commitment to a team's goals broadens and deepens the purpose and achievements of a high-performance team. On the basis of their commitment, ELITE moved from being a task force with a narrow agenda to, in many respects, an unofficial leadership team who transformed the entire *Tallahassee Democrat*. The Dallas Mafia in our next example, by contrast, began as a leadership group (of a business unit we have disguised). Armed with their commitment to each other, they changed the strategy and focus of their business, built a remarkable performance ethic throughout their organization and, in the process, had a tremendously good and rewarding time.

# THE DALLAS MAFIA

The Dallas Mafia story really began with a series of strategy meetings, the essence of which several members of their team have helped us try to recreate. Imagine five young men sitting around the small conference table on the 28th floor of a Dallas office building. They are the top management group newly responsible for the Southwest region corporate finance operations of "Global Limited," an investment bank headquartered in New York. The five have been meeting on and off for several days, trying to shape a new strategy.

Bob Waldo, one of the younger men, interjects with clear emotion, "Investment bankers are what investment bankers do. If we continue to do mostly plain vanilla deals for mediocre companies, we will be plain vanilla bankers. Is that what you guys want?"

Mack Canfield, the official leader of the group, sighs. "Well, it may not be what we want, Bob. But, we can't just walk away from routine financing needs of real live customers. After all, we are not going to meet our target ROS and RORC [return on spending and return on risk capital] if we don't take this kind of business. It is all very well to talk about becoming the financial counselors to great leaders, but we are a long way from being able to advise the Bass family on their financial strategy for global expansion."

Jim Barrows and John Logan start to laugh, but Canfield glares at them. "I know you guys think this is pretty funny. But my neck in on the line here. We've barely got enough business coming in to keep the staff busy, and you are still talking about becoming the financial counselors of tomorrow. I've got to worry about today. New York believes we're all too wet behind the ears anyway, and if we start turning down reasonable deals because of some grand idea about changing our image, they'll replace us next week. Annual ROS and RORC is how they think this game is played."

"What New York doesn't know won't hurt them," rejoins Logan. "Those guys have their heads in the sand anyway. What's more, if I have to be a plain vanilla deal doer for the next five years, I'd just as soon be replaced next week. As far as I'm concerned, we either pull up our socks here and make something different out of this office, or we're all better off pursuing other careers."

## The Performance Challenge

As Logan would later recall, the group was committed to "either change or leave." They changed. Four years after first getting together, the team had upgraded a stagnating mix of business, lengthened the duration of active customer relationships, and increased Dallas's profitability to among the highest at Global. They also had strengthened the Dallas professional staff so much that other regions routinely looked to them to fill key positions. Finally, and a significant aspect of the Dallas story that characterizes most high-performance teams, they had a great deal of fun that they will never forget.

Canfield had been a controversial choice to lead Dallas because he lacked any prior office management experience. He was to replace John Elders, the native Texan who founded the Dallas office and ran it successfully for more than twenty years. At the time, not only Elders but also the three other most senior bankers were due to retire within a year of one another. Given the youth, inexperience, and brash reputations of the remaining Dallas professionals, many at Global headquarters argued that Canfield, at 38, and the other young men in Dallas were not up to exploiting the growing corporate finance markets in the Southwest. This attitude, it turned out, posed both an obstacle and a rallying point for the Dallas Mafia.

Les Walters, Global's chief executive, nonetheless decided to give the nod to Canfield. When Mack arrived, as we saw in the opening vignette, he found a frustrated group. To them, the retirement of Elders and the others meant a terrific opportunity. They all had been hired by Elders and admired him a great deal. Still, they believed the traditionally plain vanilla work of the office increasingly fell short of more complex client needs and their own capabilities.

Canfield later observed that the group's aspirations were so high that they probably were destined to become a team with or without him. None of them, however, were certain how to make their dreams happen. And Canfield, who at first only wanted to make the office more profitable, knew he needed their help. "I didn't have the answers," he said. "But I did believe we could somehow figure it out together."

## Setting the Performance Goals

Their early strategy discussions produced a collective set of performance goals based on three key elements:

- To shift the business mix from standard plain vanilla debt underwriting, lending, and investing (a volume-oriented business) to merger and acquisition advising and restructuring (a quality- and service-oriented business)

- To discourage one-shot deals in favor of lasting relationships with major corporate leaders who valued the office's superior execution and problem-solving capability

- To sustain an increasingly balanced and diverse group of highly talented professionals

Moreover, notwithstanding Canfield's financial concerns, the team agreed to seek "growth in quality, not growth in size or profits alone." They also converted each element of their strategy into specific performance goals. For example, the team relentlessly reviewed their mix of business, the duration of active involvements with major accounts, and the quality of the staff.

## Shaping the Working Approach

Over the first year, the team also forged a special set of values and approach that each followed religiously. Although they seldom worked directly with one another on specific customers, they openly shared experiences, insights, issues, and frustrations. They kept each other true to their common aspirations and rigorous about the quality of work negotiated, transaction teams assembled, and customer relationships built.

Unlike the more easily measured goals of some teams (for example, reduced cycle-time), the Dallas Mafia had set objectives that, while attainable, required mutual vigilance to assess. They watched each other closely with caring eyes. As one later described, "There was no way any of us wanted to have to explain to the others his lack of courage in turning down a plain vanilla debt underwriting. In fact, we took almost as much pride in losing business for the right reasons as we did in winning it."

The team stressed heavily the merit of ideas proposed rather than the position in the hierarchy of those advancing them. Without the safety net provided by senior, well-connected men like Elders, the new team concentrated on finding just the right mix of customer knowledge, problem-solving skill, and creativity to meet each opportunity. This forced them to take greater than normal risks on younger people who, for example, now regularly joined in negotiating arrangements with even the most senior of customer executives.

## Developing Personal Commitment

As the commitment to each other, their purpose, and their business unit grew, the team fostered a performance-driven and risk-seeking environment. Everybody was learning together and having fun doing it. Canfield recalls one episode that captured the essence of the approach and values the team had spread throughout the office: quality work, mutual trust, taking risks on people, giving talent the chance to grow and fail, being there for one another, and having a good time. Bob Waldo had just returned from the final Texas Instruments (TI) competitive negotiation with TI's chief financial officer (CFO) to which he had taken a particularly talented junior professional named Allen Duckett.

"So how did it go?," asked Canfield.

"Oh we won the mandate, all right," responded Waldo. "But you'll never believe what happened. I took Allen along both for the experience and because he really knows more about TI's business than any of us. But you know how eager and intense Allen is. Obviously, I was a little worried about how Dan Kelly [the CFO of TI] would react to him. So I told Allen to let me handle the discussion until I specifically asked for his comments.

"We got off to a great start. So I asked 'Mr. Intensity' to give Dan our view of the capital needs of the industry. Since there was only one extra seat in Dan's office, Allen had been leaning against the wall near the window. Allen started off okay. But—I still can't believe this—pretty soon his feet started to slide slowly out from under him on the hardwood floor in Dan's office. I learned afterward he had purchased a new pair of shoes the day before, and they were still slick on the bottom. Well, Allen was so intent on what he was saying that he doesn't even realize his feet are slipping, or that he is slowly sliding down the wall! Dan and I, of course, are so spellbound by this scene that we didn't think to warn Allen in time to prevent him from sliding all the way to the floor. Fortunately, he didn't hurt himself."

"You mean he went clear to the floor before realizing what was happening?" asked Canfield, starting to laugh.

"Not only that," exclaimed Waldo. "He never stopped talking the whole time! He actually went right on with his comments while sitting on the floor in front of Dan's desk until I helped him back to his feet—still talking. It was all I could do to keep from breaking up completely. I'm sure Dan must have been thinking, 'Did I really see that?' The good news is that Dan was so impressed with Allen's obvious concern for TI that he gave us the mandate on the spot! I'm thinking of building this act into all of my negotiations."

Just like the Burlington Northern Intermodal Team, the Dallas Mafia followed its own rules and approach instead of Global's. For example, Global normally would expect Canfield, the office manager, to cover the important Shell Oil account. Instead, the team handed that responsibility over to their youngest member, Jim Barrows, because of his industry experience. Barrows was not yet a full partner, but the team still asked Canfield to "report" to him on Shell—a fact Global interpreted as a typo until Canfield persisted in explaining that no mistake had been made.

## The Extended Team Effect

Counter-culturally, the team actively sought to transfer good people out of Dallas to other parts of Global. They thought such moves enriched the individuals, usually young people with high potential. They also believed Dallas would benefit when those transferred returned with best practices, new ideas, and fresh approaches. By contrast, many other units of Global at the time would transfer only unneeded, undesired performers.

Sometimes Dallas's own rules were reversed by Global corporate. A year after taking over the office, for example, Canfield decided everyone on the team should receive equal pay. Global refused. And Global refused again when Canfield tried the same thing a year later.

These "failures," however, only reinforced the team's commitment to one another's growth and success, as measured by their own standards instead of Global's.

The impact of their dedication to one another spread throughout the office. It is a classic illustration of the extended team effect of high-performance teams. According to one of the professionals who was not part of the core team: "Dallas simply had no commercial feel to it. We had supreme quality. Even the customer was not the final judge. We were. As a result, people were willing to stick their necks out, confident that they would never be criticized for doing what they thought was right."

The office assumed the classic work hard, play hard atmosphere of a large group led by a high-performance team. As Bob Waldo's story about Allen Duckett illustrates, the team found a lot of fun at work—something we have often observed in real teams and even more in high-performance teams. People on the Burlington Northern Intermodal Team spoke of fun; so did the women of ELITE. Significantly, all of them described the fun and the sense of humor of the team in contexts that related directly to performance. We would suggest that fun, just like teamwork values, is only real and sustainable if it feeds off the team's purpose and performance aspirations.

In the Dallas story, this atmosphere spread beyond the office as well. Scheduled social events under Elders had reflected a formality commensurate with his age, social position, and style. People enjoyed themselves, but also attended out of a sense of obligation. Under the influence of the Dallas Mafia, partying was far more spontaneous. In the annual touch football game, for example, everyone let the decidedly unathletic Canfield score the winning touchdown each year, then roundly roasted him for months about whatever illegal move helped him across the goal.

An after-hours group emerged, the members of which made their own wine called "Chateau Desenex" (in honor of a well-known foot powder) from grapes shipped to Texas from California. This led on one occasion to an episode that people from the office have never forgotten. Canfield had been assigned to check the temperature of the grapes fermenting in large plastic garbage cans in his garage. He knew little about wine and less about fermentation. But his more knowledgeable colleagues had told him to signal the alert if the temperature rose above 80 degrees. His instructors, however, had failed to mention that, to get a proper reading, he must insert the thermometer well below the top crust (where the fermentation was most active and hottest).

Just before going to bed, Canfield and his wife took a reading of the ten 30-gallon garbage cans—right at the crust level, of course. With visions of spoiled wine and disappointed friends, Canfield immediately started racing up and down the stairs with ice cubes, while his wife got everybody that she could reach by phone out of bed with cries of "Over 90 degrees and climbing! Bring ice!" Within minutes, cars began arriving in the Canfields' driveway, and more people joined the ice bucket brigade. About thirty minutes later, Tim Crown, the office vintner, arrived. He surveyed the madness, raised his hands in the air, and shouted: "Hold it people! Hold everything! Stop and think how many ice cubes it's gonna take to cool 300 gallons of fermenting squashed grapes! Are you all crazy?"

Dead silence. Then Canfield's wife started laughing, and soon the whole crowd collapsed on the garage floor in hysterics over the foolishness of their midnight rescue. As Crown said many years later, "No wonder Canfield needed a team!"

# CONCLUSION

Strong personal commitments to one another's growth and success distinguish high-performance teams from real teams. Energized by this extra sense of commitment, high-performance teams typically reflect strong extensions of the basic characteristics of teams: deeper sense of purpose, more ambitious performance goals, more complete approaches, fuller mutual accountability, interchangeable as well as complementary skills. You can both see and feel these differences.

The ELITE Team's performance ambitions and sense of purpose seemed literally to grow with their increasing commitment to one another. Each of the men on the Burlington Northern Intermodal Team learned marketing skills to add to their operations experience. This made them interchangeable and even more confident in their dependence on one another. In the Dallas example, each man's concern for the others and their purpose emboldened them to say no to plain vanilla deals and, thereby, to deepen and clarify their sense of mutual accountability to the kind of investment bankers they wanted to become. And all had a disproportionate amount of fun in the process.

Furthermore, leadership is shared in high-performance teams. The formal leadership role remains, but is mostly ceremonial or for the benefit of outsiders. We observed this in the Dallas, ELITE, and Burlington Northern Teams. Each team had a formal leader: Canfield, Dunlap, and Greenwood. Yet once each group had become a high-performance team, leadership emerged from many members as they took whatever initiatives necessary to remove obstacles or seek opportunities. In fact, in the Dallas case, Canfield tried to persuade Global to formalize the shared leadership arrangement. It responded, however, like most outsiders who try to understand leadership patterns inside high-performance teams—with confusion.

Though related, this shared leadership phenomenon goes beyond empowerment. Members of real teams usually feel empowered to make their common purposes happen. Having continually discussed the team's purpose, goals, and approach, and developed rich understandings, team members take initiatives comfortably. Nevertheless, people on real teams more often than not will check with the team leader either before or right after taking action. And the best team leaders, of course, typically applaud. High-performance team members go further. They still check their initiative either before or after taking it. But, and this is the essential difference, they do so primarily with other team members instead of the leader. The formal leader's comments matter. But the balance of approval is in favor of the team.

The extended team effect is evident with all high-performance teams, and many other real teams. We described it in detail in the Burlington Northern story. It was equally evident with ELITE, as they energized most other parts of the paper to focus on customer service. It was even more evident in the impact the Dallas Mafia had on the rest of the office.

When combined, the intense commitments to one another and their mutual cause plus their shared leadership and interchangeable skills make high-performance teams entirely self-sufficient. They move ahead by their own rules. Rejection does not get in their way. Nor does organizational hostility or indifference, limited resources, insufficient compensation, or, as we saw in Intermodal, even "freezing weather" stop these powerful teams.

They achieve beyond any measure of reasonableness, and they have fun doing it. The finely developed sense of humor in these groups seems to distinguish them as well. Not everything they do is laced with fun, and there may be some humorless high-performance teams out there. But we doubt it. Here again, however, is an element that cannot be managed. People cannot be made to have fun. Rather, in high-performance teams, like so much else, fun seems to be a by-product of, and an ingredient in, the team's sense of commitment to each other and performance.

Every high-performance team member we met described their teams as special and their experiences as having participated "in something bigger and better than myself." Furthermore, each such team positively influenced the performance ethic of the larger groups, or extended teams, around them. They created an aura of excitement and focus that sustained the growth of new capabilities and openness to change. Still, such teams are rare. They cannot be created on purpose. As a result, executives must understand them if they are to recognize and take advantage of them. And the wisest leaders will do whatever it takes, from providing recognition or additional challenges to just getting out of the way, to keep these valuable teams—and all they represent and influence—alive.

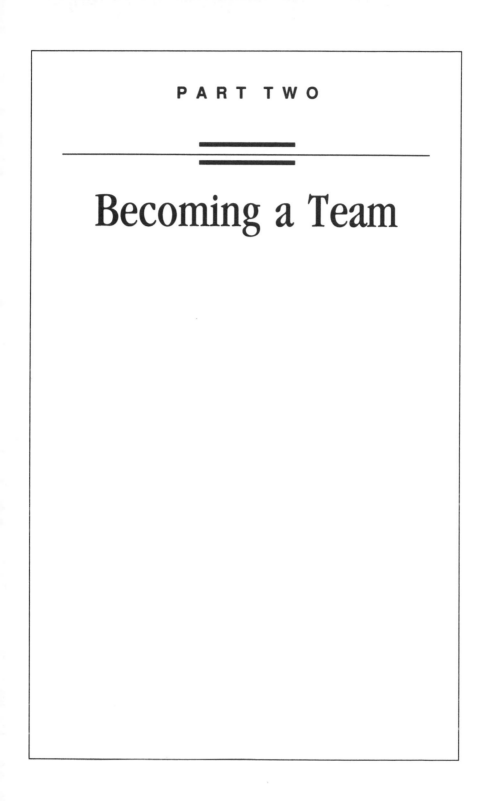

PART TWO

# Becoming a Team

Figure II-1
# THE TEAM PERFORMANCE CURVE

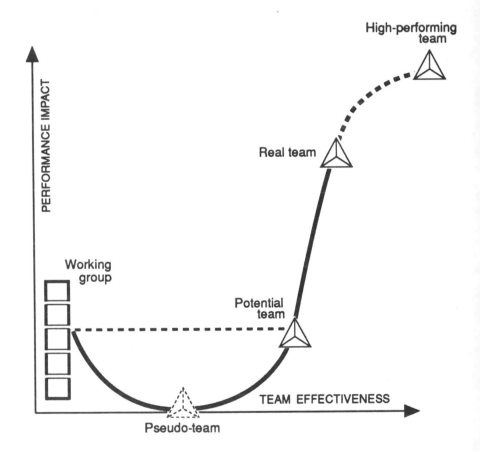

THE "team performance curve" (Figure II-1) illustrates that how well any small group of people performs depends on the basic approach it takes and how effectively it implements that approach. Unlike teams, working groups rely on the sum of "individual bests" for their performance. They pursue no collective work products requiring joint effort. By choosing the team path instead of the working group, people commit to take the risks of conflict, joint work-products, and collective action necessary to build a common purpose, set of goals, approach, and mutual accountability. People who call themselves teams but take no such risks are at best pseudo-teams.

Potential teams that take the risks to climb the curve inevitably confront obstacles. Some teams overcome them; others get stuck. The worst thing a stuck team can do, however, is to abandon the discipline of the team basics described in Part I. Performance, not team building, can save potential teams or pseudo-teams, no matter how stuck.

All teams come to an end. Endings, however, do not need to sacrifice continued performance. The handoff of recommendations to others, arrival of new members, departure of old ones, and changes in team leaders—if seen as transitions calling for a renewal of team basics—enable most teams to exploit the performance potential even further, whether or not the team itself comes to an end.

Most team leaders must develop skills after they take the job. Those who succeed have an attitude that they do not need to make all key decisions nor assign all key jobs.

Effective team leaders realize they neither know all the answers, nor can they succeed without the other members of the team. The wisdom of teams lies in recognizing that any person, whether previously an autocrat or a democrat, who genuinely believes in the purpose of the team and the team itself can lead the team toward higher performance.

CHAPTER FIVE

# The Team
# Performance Curve

Those kinds of comments are pretty hard to ignore. Obviously, the people in this company don't think we're a very cohesive team. I guess we don't work together as well as we might. But I didn't realize it was of that much concern to the rest of the organization. What should we do about it?

THE president of Cosmo Products Inc. was talking informally with his top executive group. They had just finished listening to excerpts of taped interviews with more than one hundred employees who had been asked for their views about the progress of the company's recently launched change effort. It was a major effort aimed at changing the behavior of literally thousands of people throughout the company.

Many of the comments were to be expected. The employees understood that Cosmo Products' strategy and performance had declined significantly over the previous five years. The company no longer consistently beat the competition to the market with the right products at the right time. Nor did its sales force perform as well as it once had. The employee responses offered many explanations, including product proliferation, quality problems, shifting consumer preferences, more aggressive competitors, and demographic changes in the sales force. They also understood the consequences: the overall market had leveled, sales and share were down, and so were prof-its—so much so that analysts and the business press openly criticized the company. Morale and confidence were clearly shaken, and ev-eryone knew that a great deal of change was required.

So, it was painful though not surprising to the executives, to hear the employees recount earlier failures to correct the situation. Those interviewed were saying that the current effort to change had better be different. Yes, they understood and agreed with the company's new vision. Yes, they expressed a sense of urgency. And yes, they were ready to participate in the various change strategies being de-veloped in the company's key functions and operating units. "But," the taped comments insisted, "something had better be different this time!"

What most startled the president and other top executives was the repeated admonition: "You guys are all pulling in different direc-tions; you are not a team! If you don't get your act together, nothing will change." After listening to this message, the executive group knew that Cosmo Products' problems would require more than a team at the top. But they also realized that a real team effort on their part could help a great deal.

## THE CRITICAL CHOICE

The Cosmo executives faced a critical choice: Should they con-centrate on improving their effectiveness as a working group, or should they try to become a team? Though phrased in the language of "team," the comments of Cosmo's employees really argued that the top executives were working at cross purposes. Clarifying the direction and roles of a group, however, does not require a team. In fact, in many situations, particularly at the top of multibusiness companies, the structured working group option can make more sense. Too often, however, the choice between working group and team is neither recognized nor consciously made.

The basic distinction here turns on performance. A working group relies primarily on the individual contributions of its members for group performance, whereas a team strives for a magnified impact that is incremental to what its members could achieve in their individual roles. The choice depends largely on whether individual achievements can deliver the group's performance aspirations, or whether collective work-products*, skills, and mutual accountability are needed.

Working groups are both prevalent and effective in large organizations. They thrive in hierarchical structures where individual accountability counts the most. The best working groups come together to share information, perspectives, and insights, to make decisions that help each person do his or her own job better, and to reinforce each other's individual performance standards. But the focus is always on individual performance goals and accountabilities.

An effective working group, like a team, benefits from a clear purpose and common understanding of how performance will be evaluated. The Cosmo executives, as we will see, failed in part because they never clarified their purpose even with a view to being a more effective working group. Unlike teams, a working group uses its purpose solely to delineate individual roles, tasks, and responsibilities. Those roles typically match formal organizational positions. To get their assigned tasks done, working group members, especially at senior levels, usually delegate the real work to others beyond the group. Working groups pay attention to individual outcomes and results. Members of effective working groups constructively compete with one another in their pursuit of individual performance targets. They also provide counsel and insights to each other and become concerned when any among them falters. But working group members do not take responsibility for results other than their own. Nor do they try to develop incremental performance contributions requiring the combined, real work of two or more group members.

Teams differ from working groups. They require both individual *and* mutual accountability. Teams rely on more than group discussion, debate, and decision; on more than sharing information and best practice perspectives; on more than a mutual reinforcing of

---

*We use the phrase "collective work-products" to call to mind the need for any team to produce something of incremental performance value that is more than the sum of each member's individual efforts—and that requires a real work contribution from each. It is the basic idea of everyone rolling up their sleeves and working together to get something tangible accomplished.

performance standards. Without discrete team work-products produced through the joint, real contributions of team members, the promise of incremental or magnified performance impact goes untapped.

The team option promises greater performance than the working group. But it also brings more risk. Because of deep-seated values of individualism and a natural reluctance to trust one's fate to the performance of others, the team choice demands a leap of faith. Rugged individualists—and there are many, especially at the top—cannot contribute to real team performance without taking responsibility for their peers and letting their peers assume responsibility for them. Yet they instinctively believe that "if you want a job done right, do it yourself." It is against their nature to rely on others for the really important tasks in life.

Moreover, the price of "faking" this leap of faith is also high. When the team approach fails, members do get diverted from their individual goals, work-products do not add significant value, costs do outweigh benefits, and people do resent the imposition on their time and priorities.

Working groups present fewer risks. Effective working groups need waste little time in shaping their purpose, objectives, and approach since the leader usually establishes them. Meetings are run against well-prioritized agendas. They are efficient in the use of members' time. And decisions are implemented through specific individual assignments and accountabilities. Most of the time, therefore, if performance aspirations can be met through individuals doing their respective jobs well, the working group approach is more comfortable, less risky, and less disruptive than trying for more elusive team performance levels. Indeed, if there is no performance need for the team approach, efforts spent to improve the effectiveness of the working group make much more sense than floundering around trying to become a team.

## THE TEAM PERFORMANCE CURVE

To help understand the choice confronting groups like the top managers of Cosmo Products as well as the risks and performance potential involved, we find it useful to apply a simple framework we call the "team performance curve" (see Figure II-1). On it are five key points, each of which uses the definition of a team described in Chapter 3 as the primary reference. To avoid confusion, we call this a "real team" on the curve.

1. **Working group:** This is a group for which there is *no significant incremental performance need* or opportunity that would require it to become a team. The members interact primarily to share information, best practices, or perspectives and to make decisions to help each individual perform within his or her area of responsibility. Beyond that, there is no realistic or truly desired "small group" common purpose, incremental performance goals, or joint work-products that call for either a team approach or mutual accountability.

2. **Pseudo-team:** This is a group for which there could be a significant, incremental performance need or opportunity, but *it has not focused on collective performance and is not really trying to achieve it*. It has no interest in shaping a common purpose or set of performance goals, even though it may call itself a team. Pseudo-teams are the weakest of all groups in terms of performance impact. They almost always contribute less to company performance needs than working groups because their interactions detract from each member's individual performance without delivering any joint benefit. In pseudo-teams, the sum of the whole is less than the potential of the individual parts.

3. **Potential team:** This is a group for which there is a significant, incremental performance need, and *that really is trying to improve its performance impact*. Typically, however, it requires more clarity about purpose, goals, or work-products and more discipline in hammering out a common working approach. It has not yet established collective accountability. Potential teams abound in organizations. As our performance curve illustrates, when a team approach makes sense, the performance impact can be high. We believe the steepest performance gain comes between a potential team and a real team; but any movement up the slope is worth pursuing.

**4. Real team:** This is a small number of people with complementary skills who *are equally committed to a common purpose, goals, and working approach for which they hold themselves mutually accountable.* Real teams are a basic unit of performance, and were defined in detail in Chapter 3.

**5. High-performance team:** This is a group that meets all the conditions of real teams, and has *members who are also deeply committed to one another's personal growth and success.* That commitment usually transcends the team. The high-performance team significantly outperforms all other like teams, and outperforms all reasonable expectations given its membership. It is a powerful possibility and an excellent model for all real and potential teams. It was described in detail in Chapter 4.

The curve in Figure II-1 illustrates important relationships and options with regard to these five points. First, it shows that working groups have a wide range of potential performance outcomes, and suggests the working group option remains sensible in many situations. The curve also shows that, for most groups, the largest performance gain occurs between the potential team and the real team, and that the possible performance impact for the real team is significantly higher than for the working group. The dotted line between real team and high-performance team indicates the exceptional personal commitment required for high performance. Finally, the dotted line connecting the working group and the potential team symbolizes the leap of faith involved in making that choice. Beneath that line lie the risks and disappointments of pseudo-team performance. One hopes to avoid them at all costs since the performance impact of pseudo-teams is lowest, and overcoming pseudo-team dynamics can be very difficult, as we will illustrate with the conclusion of the Cosmo Products story.

Cosmo's senior managers certainly had the reason and potential to become the team their employees hoped for. First, the performance challenge they faced called for a team: *multiple negative forces at work, no clear-cut answer for dealing with them, repeated failure of hierarchical approaches to achieve performance aspirations, and a crying need for leadership to pull together in a unified way.* In addition, they were a small number of people with the right skill mix. Given the challenge facing Cosmo Products, we believe they could have established a common purpose, performance goals, and approach for which they could have held themselves mutually accountable as a team. Moreover, the incremental performance promise of a team was badly needed.

Prior to listening to the tapes that the president described as "pretty hard to ignore," however, the senior managers were not even a good working group. They were a pseudo-team; that is, they referred to themselves as a team but made no serious effort to establish a team purpose, meet performance goals, or define their team approach. Political concerns almost always overshadowed performance considerations. In fact, they were even denying themselves the chance to get better as a working group by improving their individual performance standards, clarifying and coordinating individual activities, and making sure individual results added up to the necessary corporate performance results.

The employee feedback session spurred the Cosmo senior group to want to move from pseudo-team to potential team to real team. The top executives decided that becoming a team was important if they were to have any chance of leading a transformation at Cosmo. Interestingly, and all too typically for such groups, however, they gave little serious consideration to a more rigorous working group option before leaping to the team performance curve. Also, when they met, they did so with the express purpose of becoming a team, not attacking a specific performance challenge.

Most of their meetings were marked by the candor necessary to team building. They worked hard raising and grappling with many issues critical to managing broad-based change at Cosmo, including:

"The vision is too abstract. We've got to be clearer on what we want the vision to mean to employees and customers."

"Everything has become a priority around here. We have to find a way to get things into better focus before we create a system overload."

"Leadership at the holding company doesn't understand our problem here. We need them to buy into the change program we are trying to implement."

"Our people don't really understand what is expected of them. We need to communicate specifically what and how we want them to change, and then get them working on it."

"We still don't really trust one another. We need to keep having these meetings, maybe even a special retreat, to work on that issue."

Discussions like these went on sporadically for a few months following the employee feedback session. Out of them, the group emerged with a stronger sense of the vision and purpose for the company—but not for the group itself. It also developed a better understanding of how to set company priorities, an intention to try to communicate more clearly with employees, and a firmer basis for trust among the members. They began to work more collaboratively than before; and, for a while, their effectiveness as a management group improved.

Regrettably, however, the group never agreed on any specific performance goals to pursue as a team. Such objectives were possible. For example, as both the employees and executives knew, Cosmo Products was introducing far too many products of varying quality every year. The senior executive group might have taken on the challenge as *an ad hoc team,* to cut the number of new offerings by 50 percent while simultaneously designing a process to get to the market on time and within established quality standards. Or, in light of the well-understood demographic changes wreaking havoc on the sales force, the group might have committed itself *as a team* to shape and lead initiatives aimed at strengthening the account relationship skills of the traditionally part-time sales force.

Had the group defined such goals, it would have had something concrete to do *as a team,* that is, something specific to advance its aspirations to turn around the company. This would have given it the chance to advance from potential team to real team based on concrete accomplishments. Without any agreed-on performance objectives, however, the Cosmo Products executive group found no way to engage as a team in pursuit of its nobler aspirations. It did discuss and debate at length the urgency of the situation as well as the desire to do something about it. But the group never translated its desire into specific team goals and work-products. Eventually, the team-building sessions deteriorated into nothing more than talk.

When this happened, instead of confronting the need to establish a specific team performance objective, the team became frustrated. Once again, it fell back into the weak performance pattern of a pseudo-team.

Three years after the launch of the major change program, Cosmo Products still had not developed the fundamentally different skills, values, and behaviors required for competitive success. Instead, the company endured continuing financial disappointments, major take-over battles, key business divestitures, disturbing top management changes, and wrenching cost-cutting drives, all of which over-whelmed everyone in the company, including the senior executives.

The employee warnings had been right: the performance potential in the top managers becoming a team was as enormous as its ultimate failure was disastrous. More subtly, the executive group's failure to choose consciously between the working group and team options, like its failure to move ahead with a disciplined eye on performance, left the group and its employees, customers, and shareholders well short of the performance they were entitled to expect.

Most of us have belonged to pseudo-teams like the Cosmo Products executives; they exist in many parts and levels of most organizations. Many behaviors characterize such groups, including confusion over purpose, an inability to focus, unbridled personal animosity or ambition, ignorance of the benefits of a team approach, and hierarchical rituals used to avoid instead of engage one another. The net result is always the same: the group makes no serious effort to find a common path for moving ahead together.

The pseudo-team is a sad paradox. It refers to itself publicly as a "team" even though privately its members will admit otherwise. People throughout the organization recognize these self-proclaimed labels for the sham that they are. The Cosmo Products executive group, for example, often spoke about itself as a team before the taped employees emphatically contradicted them.

Often, when individuals on pseudo-teams lament their failure to act like a team, they describe yet another irony. Each person faults the other people on the pseudo-team, especially the leader. The remedy prescribed inevitably sounds like "we would do much better as a team if only the *rest of them* would work as a team in the way *I think* makes the most sense."

# COMTECH CELLULAR

A group of nine regional general managers from "ComTech Cellular" helps to demonstrate the distinction between working group and potential team. ComTech Cellular is a division of ComTech, a large, regulated telecommunications company. In the 1980s, ComTech created Cellular to go after opportunities presented when cellular telephones burst into the marketplace. The division quickly entered four key markets through wholly owned subsidiaries and five others through joint ventures with nonregulated cellular companies. One of the complexities of the cellular business is that some of ComTech's joint venture partners in certain markets actually compete with ComTech subsidiaries in other markets.

ComTech's cellular division has both the advantages and disadvantages of being part of a large, regulated company. On the plus side, it has marketplace clout, name recognition, and significant organizational, technological, and economic resources. On the negative side, ComTech is hamstrung by its link to the still-regulated basic telephone business. ComTech's competitors can act far more quickly and aggressively because they are neither regulated by government nor slowed by the bureaucratic constraints that victimize most large organizations.

The nine general managers all report to Cameron Daly, a seasoned executive known for his people management skills and orientation toward team building. Daly puts a high priority on the nine becoming a team—believing that if they were a team, they would bring multiple skills and perspectives to bear on some of the division's more vexing problems. But the image of a team held by Daly and the nine general managers is of a group that communicates well, gets along together, and shares ideas. It does not extend to doing real work together in pursuit of joint goals.

Even if they had more of a performance focus, however, the team approach is probably unrealistic and counter-productive for them. Indeed, for a number of reasons, the nine general managers represent a classic working group instead of a potential team. First, ComTech has joint venture partners in some markets that compete with ComTech in other markets. This makes the mutual trust required in teams even more difficult than usual to build. As the New York general manager of ComTech's largest market put it, "I'm not going to give my time, attention, and other resources to help our Chicago operation come up with some innovation that their joint venture partner will then use to bite me in the behind back here in New York!"

Second, the unique competitive circumstances of each of the nine markets demand individual insight and responsibility. "When the head of Chicago comes forward with some idea," says Dave Mars of Cleveland, "my thought process is how is that going to affect my world in Cleveland because I'm not convinced he's spent any time thinking about it. That's not his job. His job is to think about Chicago." While the general managers all see value in sharing information and best practices that will not create indirect problems like the New York–Chicago example, they do not have the capacity or incentive to produce joint work-products in real time. None of them sees any credible reasons why he should commit valuable resources to solving anything other than problems in his own market areas.

Third, the disproportionate size of New York makes it practically impossible for the group to identify a common purpose, set of performance goals, and approach. Objectives that center on New York alienate the other general managers; but New York's general manager as well as others recognize that ignoring New York is unrealistic. There is little or no common interest being served here.

In creating a distinction between a working group and a potential team, we are not making a "good" or "bad" value judgment. We are simply arguing for a conscious choice that considers the alternatives and trade-offs in a disciplined manner. The ComTech general managers are not somehow deficient as executives because their circumstances preclude the team option. Clearly, for example, they can help one another, their customers, their employees, and their company by adopting and practicing teamwork values and sharing best practices. But, as we have argued before, teamwork and sharing are not synonymous with teams.

In theory, all groups have the potential to find some common team purpose and approach to fill an important performance need; and, in theory, the ComTech general managers might do so. In practice, however, people like Cameron Daly and the ComTech general managers must ask whether any common performance goals and collective work-products credibly demand their mutual attention, active and equal participation, extra effort, and shared accountability. When the practical answer is no, then asking or expecting such a working group to become a team simply creates confusion and unproductive activity. It also diverts the individuals from moving up the performance range as a working group.

## RAPID RESPONSE TEAM: MOVING UP TO A HIGH-PERFORMANCE TEAM

The Rapid Response Team at McKinsey & Company provides an example of a team that moved up the performance curve from potential team to real team to high-performance team. We should note that Rapid Response is atypical within McKinsey because it is not a client project team. Rather, it is a support function, and in that sense, the challenges it faced resemble those of potential teams in many other companies.

Rapid Response emerged out of McKinsey's organization practice, which, like other practice and industry groups within McKinsey, faced a dilemma at the end of the 1980s: how to share knowledge and experience across an increasingly global professional firm. In earlier times, a consultant could seek out the best current thinking and practice by relying on personal knowledge of what other people were doing plus word of mouth. By 1989, however, McKinsey's two thousand-plus professionals who worked in more than fifty offices spread across five continents no longer could depend on informal personal networks for knowledge sharing.

This problem particularly vexed the organization practice because the demand for organization knowledge and experience cuts across nearly every important client relationship regardless of industry. As one partner put it, "While only 20 percent of our work starts out as an 'organization' project, over 70 percent of it ends up that way." In view of this, when the leaders of the practice gathered in September 1989, they resolved to find a more effective approach to sharing and managing the firm's cumulative knowledge. After much discussion they agreed on an ambitious aspiration: to respond to all requests for best current thinking and practice by providing access to both documents and experienced consultants within twenty-four hours of the request.

## A Potential Team Is Launched

The practice leaders then looked for volunteers to make it happen. Six people signed up, including Jennifer Futernick, a practice librarian, and Joe Miles, an organization specialist, both from San Francisco; Lynn Heilig, a practice specialist, and Ed Michaels, a partner, both from Atlanta; Paul David, a senior associate from Chicago; and Doug Smith, a partner from New York.

These six were now a potential team; that is, they had the potential and desire to shape a common purpose, performance goals, and working approach for which they could hold themselves mutually accountable. By the time they first got together several weeks later, however, the picture had changed. Joe Miles had decided to leave McKinsey for another job, and Paul David could not make it to the meeting because of a client scheduling conflict. The other four met anyway. After much debate, they replaced the virtually impossible twenty-four hour turnaround standard with a more realistic commitment to get requestors what they needed as "rapidly" as possible. They christened the new hot-line service the "Rapid Response Network," and they agreed to a more specific near-term performance objective: to have a Rapid Response system designed and launched by July 1, 1990. This was aggressive because each of them could work on the project only in his or her spare time.

Two central design challenges stood in the way of the target date. First, Rapid Response needed a new computer system to manage the library of documents and experience profiles of consultants as well as be user-friendly to both Lynn and Jennifer, who would answer the phone requests. Second, to provide personal contact with experts in addition to relevant documents, the group had to ensure that busy McKinsey professionals would call back requestors in a "rapid" manner. This latter task is similar to getting your teenage son to answer the telephone during the Super Bowl.

Like all potential teams, the members also faced a number of subtler challenges. For example, Lynn, who had recently made the transition from general consultant to practice specialist, believed Rapid Response provided her the rare opportunity to enhance her own job. However, she was worried because the July launch commitment coincided with her baby's due date.

Meanwhile, Jennifer was apprehensive about the changes implied for her job. For nearly a decade, she had relied on her extensive knowledge of the practice as well as her extraordinary service orientation to provide what was universally acknowledged as excellent help. Jennifer seemed to focus many of her concerns on the prospective computer system. She had never used computers and admitted she did not like them. Lynn, Doug, and Ed, however, suspected that computers only symbolized her uneasiness about the unknown changes that lay ahead.

In addition, the leadership of the core team was unclear. While Ed remained supportive, other demands on his time would allow him to act only as a sounding board and senior sponsor. That left Doug and Paul David to handle the supervision of the project itself, and Paul was in a difficult situation because of heavy client demands. Not surprisingly, all these issues raised anxieties in the group.

Nevertheless, the discussions, decisions, and identified next steps helped the group move up the performance curve, although it was still more of a potential team than a real team. It had agreed on a purpose and set of goals; and Lynn, Jennifer, and Doug were all prepared to do real work. Moreover, the subtler obstacles had been at least brought to the surface and discussed.

## The Potential Team Becomes "Real"

The group started resolving its uncertainties over the next few months as it carved out its working approach. Doug and Lynn agreed to focus on gaining the commitment of consultants to support the network. Meanwhile, Lynn, Jennifer, and, hopefully, Paul David were supposed to work on the computer system, with Jennifer thinking mostly about the topical organization of the data base as opposed to the actual computerization aspects. But Paul continued to miss meetings. When he and the others realized he could not contribute—that is, do the real work required of all team members—there was some awkwardness. But the team instinctively had the good sense to let Paul withdraw without making it a big deal.

Lynn and Jennifer engaged Scott Ehmen, a computer professional in the Atlanta office, as well as an outside computer design firm to help work on the system.

By spring, Lynn, Jennifer, Doug, and Scott had the complementary skills, agreed-on purpose and approach, and shared sense of accountability that characterizes a real team. They were confident the computer support system would be ready to meet the July launch date. Their most difficult challenge had become how best to use a worldwide meeting of organization practice consultants in April to gain active support for the Rapid Response Network.

That support was essential to the design of the network. In theory, someone wanting the best current thinking and practice on organization issues would call Rapid Response and reach either Lynn or Jennifer, who would help identify the most pertinent documents and the best experts. If Lynn or Jennifer felt the requestor's issues went beyond her own expertise, she could put that person in touch with an "on-call consultant," a member of the organization practice group who was supposed to respond rapidly to the requestor—on the same day if possible.

Getting documents and experts' names to requestors was straightforward enough. But getting the experts and the on-call consultants to actually make or receive follow-up phone calls was no small task. Good intentions were not the problem; it was the logistical and other difficulties of busy people, multiple time zones, and the very newness of Rapid Response's promise and approach that stood in the way. The toughest task by far would be to convince enough experienced consultants to add one more "to do" to already overloaded priority lists.

The team knew they had to use the April meeting to build understanding, enthusiasm, and support for Rapid Response. They decided on a combination of fun and hard selling. At every opportunity, the team provided promotional give-aways (e.g., coffee mugs, stickers, T-shirts) embossed with the Rapid Response logo and telephone number. By the end of the second day, the sixty-plus people at the conference had begun to enjoy and look forward to these "interruptions."

Rapid Response made its final pitch to the group following dinner on the last night. Lynn, Doug, and Jennifer had asked everyone to wear Rapid Response T-shirts to the dinner, and by ten o'clock, when they made their presentation, Lynn and Doug faced a black-and-silver clad audience filled with wine and ready for a good time. They explained the design of the network, stressed the important role of the experts and on-call consultants, and poked fun at themselves for the folly of launching a new system when one of the key people was about to have a baby. To laughter and applause, Doug asked random individuals to stand up, close their eyes, and try to repeat the Rapid Response telephone number seen and heard so often over the previous two days. The next morning nearly everyone signed up to be an expert or an on-call consultant, putting in place the critical missing piece for the July launch.

The team then turned their attention to the thorny issues of what to do during Lynn's pregnancy leave and Jennifer's anxieties over computers and change. Fortunately, a new team member emerged to help. Nancy Taubenslag, a former associate and part-time organization consultant in New York, was intrigued enough by the April meeting to volunteer as a back-up while Lynn was on pregnancy leave. Nancy, however, soon learned she had underestimated the amount of work involved. When she and Jennifer joined Lynn in Atlanta in early June to get trained on the new computer system, all three discovered it still required a lot of debugging. With Lynn's baby and the official launch of Rapid Response imminent, Nancy and Jennifer had to quickly figure out how they would work together to make the system do what was promised.

By this time, a real affection and commitment to one another began to develop within the team. In particular, Lynn and Nancy were determined to help Jennifer overcome her concerns. They liked working with her and had tremendous regard for her knowledge about organization. Jennifer also knew that, with the arrival of Lynn's baby, much of the success of the project depended on her. Furthermore, she understood that Lynn hoped Rapid Response would be her main job when she returned from pregnancy leave, and she did not want to let Lynn down.

Nancy took on the computer debugging job and spent extensive time on the phone with Jennifer nearly every day to help her enter data and otherwise become more familiar and comfortable with the system. Prior to her baby's arrival, Lynn led the effort to respond to requests; afterward, she pitched in from home whenever she could. Finally, Doug agreed to act as an on-call consultant of last resort to ensure that all requestors received a timely response. And, to relieve some of the pressure, the whole team agreed to postpone any active promotion of the Rapid Response service until after the computer problems had been resolved and Lynn was back full time. They hoped that word of mouth would generate enough requests to keep the service alive, but not overwhelm it in its infancy.

For most of July and August, Jennifer continued to work in her traditional way, albeit consulting Nancy and Lynn for help. Then, late in the summer, Jennifer received a particularly complex request over the phone and decided to try the system out on her own. To her surprise, it not only supplied answers she expected but also yielded ideas she would not have identified otherwise. Jennifer immediately phoned Lynn and Nancy to express her delight and gratitude for their unceasing help and confidence—and to announce that, finally, she was a full-fledged convert!

When Lynn returned to work full time in November, the three women had developed an intensely collaborative approach to Rapid Response, the unexpected rewards of which were both exciting and fulfilling to each of them. They enjoyed tremendously providing requestors with the best possible response, learning from one another on a daily basis, and sharing a lot of personal experiences and challenges. A strong ethic developed within the team that equated each person's own success with the success of Rapid Response. "We really believe," says Nancy, "in the 'if you look good, I look good' approach."

## A High-Performance Team Emerges

By the end of 1990, the team's commitments went well beyond their common purpose and approach to include a deep concern for one another's growth and success. The system was debugged, the on-call consultants and experts had followed through, and all three women had mastered the librarian, consulting, and computer skills required by their jobs. The team agreed to put itself and the Rapid Response Network to a major test by mounting an extensive marketing campaign throughout the firm. In January 1991, it sent out advertising flyers, phone stickers, and coffee mugs to consultants around the world, arranged for an internal magazine to do a feature article, and asked organization practice consultants to talk about Rapid Response in their respective offices around the world. Then the members sat back to see if the phone would start ringing.

And ring it did! The next month's demand was triple any previous month's. Requests came from every office around the world and from professionals of every level. By the end of the year, Rapid Response had answered more than a thousand requests and assisted nearly a quarter of the firm's consultants and clients throughout the entire world. Users who at first were skeptical about receiving timely help from on-call consultants and experts soon learned that the Rapid Response promise was dead serious. The system elicited positive comments ranging from thanking the team for quickly answering questions to praising Rapid Response for fundamentally redirecting the approach to meeting client needs. Unsolicited testimonials kept coming in. In addition, other practices began to take notice; several contacted Rapid Response to see what they could learn.

Interestingly, and quite unusually for a team situation, this team rarely could get together in person because of the expense and geography involved. But the unpredictable, busy, and, difficult job of helping McKinsey professionals across the globe pulled its members together by phone and fax every day. In fact, the more difficult the assignment, the more fun they had figuring out how best to respond.

The quality of the team's efforts as well as the members' commitment to each other continued to grow throughout the year until, by the end of 1991, they were promising each other and their customers to treat every request for help as though the future of the specific client involved and McKinsey itself entirely depended on the effectiveness and speed of the response. To outsiders, such an all-encompassing sense of importance might seem farfetched or overblown. For the high-performing Rapid Response Team members, however, this deep personal commitment to one another and their shared mission keeps them operating at the upper reaches of the team performance curve.

# CONCLUSION

"What will it take for us to achieve significant performance results?"

This is the most important question members of a group assigned to work together can ask themselves. The answer depends on the specific nature of the performance challenge at hand. For example, if we were among the ComTech general managers asking ourselves, "What will it take for us to build a cellular business in nine different markets around North America?," we would answer, "It will require us to do our individual jobs the very best we can, including sharing best practices, insights, and other relevant information with each other." In the terminology of this chapter, this means becoming an effective working group. If, on the other hand, we were part of a group like ELITE (Chapter 4) and asked ourselves, "What will it take for us to eliminate all advertising errors in the newspaper?," we would answer, "It will require us to work together as a team to deliver joint work-products in addition to individual contributions. It may also require us to increase customer service values across the entire paper." In short, "We need to work as a team."

If people pursue the team option, how can they evaluate where they stand on the team performance curve? We believe two different sets of indicators, or "vital signs," can help them. The indicators of the first set relate to the elements in our team definition—the team basics. By asking the series of questions at the end of Chapter 3 about small number, complementary skills, common purpose, performance goals, working approach, and mutual accountability, most groups can figure out whether they are operating like working groups, pseudo-teams, potential teams, or real teams.

In addition, however, we have observed a second set of five vital signs that are helpful to monitor. These include:

**1. Themes and identity:** Teams inevitably rally around a favorite set of themes that convey meaning about their basic purpose and identity. The map of the interstate highway system, for example, symbolized the Burlington Northern Intermodal Team's commitment to building a fundamentally different approach to intermodal, one that cooperated with instead of antagonized truckers. The Kodak Zebra Team mentioned in Chapter 3 adopted a variety of black and white logos, apparel, and songs to communicate their aspirations to raise the performance and status of black and white film. Even the dart board in the Garden State Brickface example in Chapter 3 became a theme as well as a meeting place that took on special meaning for how that team approached its job.

The key to these themes lies in the richness of their meaning to the team. Like a special language or code words, team themes reflect shorthand ways to communicate what is important and why it is important inside the team. Such critical and deeply shared meaning, however, cannot be manufactured; T-shirts and coffee mugs do not make teams. But where there is meaning behind the logos, you will find teams.

2. **Enthusiasm and energy level:** Teams work hard and enthusiastically. They also play hard and enthusiastically. No one has to ask them to put in extra time; they just do it. No one has to remind them not to delegate jobs to others; again, they just do the work themselves. To outsiders, the energy and enthusiasm levels inside teams are unmistakable and even seductive. When you enter the team room you instantly feel the difference. For example, once the Burlington Northern Intermodal Team got going, even though they were controversial, many people from other parts of the railroad surreptitiously called to enlist. The energy and enthusiasm that characterizes a team, however, cannot be mandated from on high—it must derive from the interactions of the members.

3. **Event-driven histories:** As teams evolve, their stories often progress through a series of galvanizing events—often unplanned and sometimes "failures"—that propel team performance. The professional sports draft of frontline workers in Garden State, the approval of the two horrible hubs in Burlington Northern, the response to the "rat tracks fax" advertisement by the ELITE Team, Global's rejection of the Dallas Mafia's pay proposal, and the after-dinner sales pitch by Rapid Response each served to mobilize and advance the teams involved.

**4. Personal commitment:** As illustrated in the Intermodal, ELITE, Dallas, and Rapid Response stories, members' strong personal commitment to one another's growth and success is what distinguishes a high-performance team. When this commitment exists, it always enriches the team's sense of purpose, stretches its performance aspirations, and makes its members' approach to working with one another more powerful. Once again, however, this vital sign is either present or absent—people cannot be ordered to care about one another.

**5. Performance results:** In the final analysis, performance is both the cause and effect of teams. Real teams almost always outperform similarly situated and challenged individuals acting as individuals. High-performance teams, in addition, outperform all reasonable expectations for the group, including those of the team members themselves. Without specific, tangible performance results, in fact, little else matters. Groups like the Cosmo Products executives that fail to focus on specific performance objectives and the collective team work-products to produce them cannot become teams. If you want to know whether any particular group is a real team, look first at its performance results.

To summarize, we think two sets of vital signs indicate whether any specific group of people is a real team. The first set of signs includes the elements in the definition of a team—the team basics. Whenever any are missing or not quite right, the group can and should confront them directly, and work on getting them right. The second set of vital signs—themes and identity, energy and enthusiasm, event-driven histories, personal commitments, and performance results—includes equally powerful indicators of whether any particular group is a team. With the exception of performance results, however, groups usually cannot advance against these indicators by working directly on them. The rich meaning in team themes does not necessarily spring forth from the creation of a team logo; the energy or enthusiasm characteristic of a team and the level of personal commitment found in high-performance teams cannot be mandated through edict or decision.

Significantly, if a review of either set of vital signs suggests a group is not a team, there may be reasons to try improving performance as a working group instead of pursuing the team option. The upside potential gain in performance may not be worth the risk, or the group may not be ready to make the leap from working group to team. Evaluating these trade-offs carefully can prevent a premature decision one way or the other. In any case, the important thing is to rigorously consider both options and then be disciplined about pursuing whichever choice is made.

Assuming, however, that unlike ComTech Cellular, a team approach makes sense, and that unlike Cosmo Products, the people involved are willing to try for team performance, then they should periodically continue to consult both sets of vital signs to track their progress up the team performance curve. Each time they do so, hopefully they will develop new insights about what stands between them and their team performance opportunity as well as deepen their commitment to the common purpose, performance goals, and approach necessary to moving ahead.

# CHAPTER SIX

# Moving up the Curve: From Individual to Team Performance

W HAT do potential teams need to do to move up the team performance curve? There is no best answer to this question. Each of the scores of teams we have researched, read about, or been a part of has applied a unique blend of actions, events, and decisions to achieve higher performance. Among them all, however, we have observed an underlying pattern: real teams do not emerge unless the individuals on them take risks involving conflict, trust, interdependence, and hard work.

Of the risks required, the most formidable involve building the trust and interdependence necessary to move from individual accountability to mutual accountability. People on real teams must trust and depend on one another—not totally or forever—but certainly with respect to the team's purpose, performance goals, and approach. For most of us such trust and interdependence do not come easily; it must be earned and demonstrated repeatedly if it is to change behavior. Our natural instincts, family upbringing, formal education, and employment experience all stress the primary importance of individual responsibility as measured by our own standards and those to whom we report. We are more comfortable doing our own jobs and having our performance measured by our boss than we are working and being assessed jointly as peers.

Consequently, team performance demands that most of us adjust our attitudes as well as our normal behavior. Moreover, the adjustment must come primarily through action, not words. In the Dallas Mafia story (Chapter 4), for example, it was fairly easy for each man to announce his intention to say no to plain vanilla investment banking deals. Actually turning down such deals, however, was riskier. Each had to trust that the others would back up the decision and share any related financial burden. Moreover, each man depended on the others and knew they were depending on him, to find, negotiate, and complete the more innovative deals the team wanted. As in any potential team situation, the Dallas men could build a sense of mutual accountability only through taking a series of risky actions over time and thereby prove to each other that interdependence could work.

Conflict, like trust and interdependence, is also a necessary part of becoming a real team. Seldom do we see a group of individuals forge their unique experiences, perspectives, values, and expectations into a *common* purpose, set of performance goals, and approach without encountering significant conflict. And the most challenging risks associated with conflict relate to making it constructive for the team instead of simply enduring it.

The most obvious contentions in a potential team arise from functional differences. For example, the ELITE Team, charged with eliminating errors in the newspaper advertising process, included people from sales, production, art, accounting, and customer service departments. Conflict within the group began, as it often does, with people blaming departments other than their own. This kind of conflict, however unpleasant, rarely involves much risk. The far riskier conflict, and the formative event for ELITE, was when individuals chanced the personal exposure and disappointment that came with admitting that they, not only "others," were at fault. At that point, all cards were on the table—face up—and the group could engage in the constructive conflict necessary to move forward.

Other sources of conflict involve individual personalities, attitudes, and expectations as varied and as common as people themselves. Certain concerns almost always exist among the people entering a potential team situation. They include: "Why will it be different this time?," "What are the real agendas here?," "What is this going to mean for me?," "How can I make this person realize that he really does need to do things differently?," and "How long is this going to last?"

Real teams learn how to deal with such concerns through frank and open communication. That, however, is easier said than done. Most people, particularly in large companies, have learned to speak carefully and within accepted boundaries. The conditioned response emphasizes impressing and respecting your superiors, not letting your subordinates see your weaknesses, supporting the party line to avoid appearing disloyal, and offering blinding insights without advancing wild ideas. These behaviors make constructive conflict difficult and risky. Yet only when someone opens up a conflict—and one or more other people respond constructively—can individual differences and concerns be discussed and molded into common goals. Only then does the potential team give itself the chance to move ahead. But such conflicts are risky—they can produce crippling animosities, hurt feelings, misunderstanding, and disappointments.

Dealing with the issues of trust, interdependence, and conflict requires hard work that, because it might not bear fruit, poses yet another risk. Not all potential teams become real teams. Individual differences, threats of being personally disadvantaged, actions that destroy instead of build mutual trust and interdependence, unconstructive conflict, the inertia of business as usual—these and other forces can block team performance and can even produce pseudo-teams with worsening performance. When this happens, anyone who has worked hard to invest in the team suffers lost time and disappointment.

## DEAL-TO-STEEL

The story in this chapter illustrates how one potential team, a task force called "Deal-to-Steel" at the Enron Corporation, took the risks necessary to move up the team performance curve. Enron is a natural gas company that, in addition to other things, constructs and operates pipelines that connect gas reservoirs to gas users. The Deal-to-Steel Task Force looked at ways Enron could improve the construction process in terms of both customer service and profitability. That process actually begins when a customer contracts with Enron to lay pipe—the "deal." The challenge is to construct the pipeline—

the "steel"—in accordance with the contract, the customer's expectations, and Enron's own operating and financial requirements. Because of significant post-merger challenges plus a demanding new vision for Enron, identifying and recommending ways to improve the process represented a major performance challenge for the Deal-to-Steel Task Force, that is, how to dramatically improve customer service. This required the potential team to work hard to get themselves and others at Enron—an organization built on individual accountability and functional differences—to approach the Deal-to-Steel process in new ways.

## The Performance Challenge

In August 1990, the Enron Corporation Deal-to-Steel Task Force met in a Houston hotel conference room to figure out what to do about their assignment. Two months earlier, they had been asked to identify and eliminate the inefficiencies plaguing natural gas pipeline projects from the time Enron contracted with a customer until the pipeline construction was completed and the gas turned on. So far, they had not progressed very much.

Deal-to-Steel was among the first initiatives of "Project 1990s," a corporate effort launched by Ron Burns, chief executive of the pipeline group, to help transform Enron into "the most innovative and reliable provider of clean energy." The task force knew Enron faced a number of challenges if it was to make that exciting vision happen. Enron had become the largest natural gas company in the United States through a series of mergers and acquisitions in the mid-1980s. The resulting pipeline group, headed by Burns, actually consisted of five separate companies, each of which had its own way of doing business, ranging from cautious to aggressive. By 1990, the five companies still acted like a group of independent siblings rather than a single family dedicated to serving customers in a reliable, innovative, and environmentally sound manner.

If the five companies reporting to Burns agreed on anything, it was that they had a common complaint within Enron itself. Following all the merger and acquisition activity, Enron had established a sixth stand-alone operating company that did not report to Burns. This separate organization controlled the operations, construction, engineering, and technical support on which the five companies in Burns's group depended. The goal in setting up the operating company had been to gain efficiencies from shared resources. Along with efficiency, however, had come tension and infighting. None of Burns's five companies, now reduced to performing marketing and regulatory roles, were happy with being stripped of so many critical functions. They believed the operating company had too much power and that it too often failed to act in the best interests of their customers.

The growing dissension within Burns's five marketing companies and the operating company had so frustrated Enron's employees that, by the late 1980s, some had left and many more were talking about quitting. Several explanations were offered: they did not want to move to the new headquarters in Houston; they thought their own pipeline's CEO should have been named head of the group; they thought the operating company had too much power; they did not understand Enron's overall direction and purpose; or they just did not like Enron. It all added up to a level of employee discontent so pervasive that Kenneth Lay, Enron's chairman, asked Ron Burns and other top executives to join him at a special two-day meeting away from the office to address the companywide dissatisfaction.

From those high-level discussions came some important insights. Enron had done a good job persuading its shareholders and the financial community about the advantages of its expanded size and scope. It also had convinced most customers that these advantages would benefit them. The executives agreed, however, that they had failed to inspire confidence, across the broad base of Enron's people, that it was both good and promising to work for the largest U. S. natural gas company.

To remedy the situation, the senior management group developed what they called a "Vision and Values" program. The vision was to make Enron into "the first natural gas major" and "the most innovative and reliable provider of clean energy worldwide for a better environment." The values, aimed squarely at converting employee discontent into customer-oriented employee involvement, included "Your Personal Best Makes Enron Best"; "Communicate—Facts Are Friendly"; and "Better, Simpler, Faster."

## Working Out Team Basics

Burns left the off-site meeting determined to make both the vision and the values a reality. Enemy number one, he believed, was turf. So, in order to begin "blowing away all the hierarchical and organizational barriers," Burns asked Stan Horton, president of one of the five marketing companies, and James Prentice, a vice president of engineering and construction from the operating company, to set up the Deal-to-Steel Task Force. For this, Burns and Prentice had to get the okay from the head of the operating company. Horton and Prentice asked people from construction, engineering, marketing, accounting, auditing, and finance to figure out how to clean up the pipeline deal-making and construction process. Other than diversity, according to Horton, there was only one criterion for selection to the group: were people willing to speak their minds and to try to come together across organizational lines to find better ways to serve the customer? In this, however, Burns, Horton, and Prentice were asking a lot because of Enron's strong functional orientation, as well as the bias toward individual accountability and the continuing effects of the separate company identities within the recently formed Enron.

Horton and Prentice appointed William Janacek, a manager from the operating company, to lead the task force. Janacek immediately divided the task force into two groups: one to look at project economics and the other to investigate responsiveness and turnaround. Each group, however, had trouble getting a real handle on their assignment during their first several meetings. Some people held back, not wanting to risk conflict. Those who did speak out only reiterated what everyone knew, namely that the marketing companies blamed the operating company for inefficient construction while the operating company blamed the marketing companies for bad deals. People readily found excuses to step in and out of the meetings to attend to other business.

Six weeks of this left Janacek more than a little frustrated. People in each group seemed overly inhibited, parochial, and far too easily distracted. When issues did surface, they were no different despite each group's unique assignment. So Janacek decided to try something unusual. He asked both groups to join him at a hotel for the next meeting. As it turned out, this simple move was pivotal in actually getting Deal-to-Steel off the ground.

As often happens with potential teams, spending time together away from the office helped the Deal-to-Steel Task Force relax, have more candid, open discussions, and get to know each other. When the subgroups discovered they had each been talking about the same problems, it sparked a constructive dialogue about the common performance challenge before them. It also reminded them they had an important assignment that management expected them to focus on and carry out.

Task force members began to see things differently. Janacek himself, for example, credits the meeting with triggering new insights about his full-time job in the operating company as well as his job as task force leader.

> I had never fully appreciated that the people in the operating company, from technical services, construction, engineering, and so on, really should be service providers to the marketing people in the pipeline companies. And that included me. When I did realize this, I knew that somehow I had to help other people on the task force to see it too. That's when I started guiding the group. I finally became the facilitator.

## Taking the Necessary Risks

The natural instinct of managers like Janacek in companies built on individual accountability is to identify, divide up, and assign tasks to individuals instead of letting a group figure out a common purpose, set of goals, and a working approach to optimize collective skills. The latter was risky because, as Janacek knew, his superiors still held him individually accountable for the task force. Nevertheless, Janacek started to behave in ways that lessened his control but allowed a mutual accountability to grow among his group. According to other team members, for example, he encouraged freewheeling discussion while prohibiting finger pointing. "We're looking at the process, not the people" became a common refrain. He also started to step back and let others take charge when they could apply a special skill or offer a new insight.

Following the off-site hotel meeting, the task force decided to take another risk. Instead of assuming it already knew what caused all Deal-to-Steel process problems, it asked Enron's auditing department to analyze in detail one of many projects that had run amok. This project, which we will call "Table Top," was originally expected to cost $240,000 and take less than five months to complete. It finally came in at $1.2 million after ten months.

When the task force gathered to discuss Table Top, the auditors had to wrap all four walls of a conference room three times around to present the complete paper trail of mishaps. The team worked all day reviewing Table Top, detail by wretched detail. Seeing the walls covered with irrefutable mistakes by every part of the organization—not just operations and not just marketing—once again opened up a lot of eyes. "We found that from the first moment the deal was conceived," remembers someone from operations, "that we didn't have enough fingers and toes to count all the potential problems." "Before seeing Table Top," admits one marketer, "in my mind, every change I ever made to a project was warranted, and every change that engineering made was unnecessary. Once I got over that initial feeling, however, everything really jelled."

The task force continued challenging itself with fresh information. It discovered how poorly Enron performed on key measures in comparison to other pipeline companies. It was a bit frightening. Enron, for example, took more time and spent more money laying pipe than did its key competitors. Not only could Enron do better, the group started to realize, but the company probably would have to do better to survive. And as these performance problems came into clearer focus, the team became more committed.

The task force also took risks in the form of actions necessary to build mutual trust and interdependence. Perhaps the most effective of these risks actually was a failure. Early on, the task force concluded that the operating company's control over budgeting posed a significant obstacle to the coordination required across functional boundaries to improve the time, cost, and quality of the Deal-to-Steel process. Everyone agreed that the marketing companies should have more budgetary freedom since they could best understand customer needs. Accordingly, the task force asked three of their members, including Janacek, to approach the head of the operating company about the possibility of his giving up some capital budget control. Control over budget, however, means power in companies like Enron where individual accountability is the norm. Asking someone to give up part of his budget was like asking someone to voluntarily demote himself. Making this request was also particularly risky for Janacek because, when not on the task force, he reported directly to the head of the operating company.

As it turned out, the operating company rejected the request. Nevertheless, the credibility of Janacek and his two colleagues—as well as the mutual sense of trust and accountability of the whole task force—shot up because, as Janacek describes, "Everyone saw we were trying to deal with the biggest issue."

### Building Commitment

By the time this had happened, all but a few of the task force members were set on finding ways to improve the whole process of deal making and construction. The few stragglers did not get in the way since the rest of the team pretty much ignored them. Determined people often circumvent the less committed in their ranks, in effect redesigning the real team without them. Indeed, this is the least disruptive way to modify team membership.

Having developed a common sense of purpose and approach, the team once again split into smaller groups to develop recommendations that could be discussed by the full team. One group, for example, discovered that Enron was investing too much financial and engineering talent in making accurate project estimates. By eliminating steps for certain kinds of projects, accuracy might suffer, but Enron could cut its total project completion time and still meet overall financial goals. Another subgroup suggested using thinner pipes, another suggested reducing on-hand inventories, and still another suggested easing Enron's own right-of-way purchasing requirements. Like most of the team's best recommendations, each of these posed a threat to one or more people on the task force. Engineers and financial analysts worried that eliminating certain project steps would reduce the need for their services. Operations people worried that thinner pipes would make field people insecure and nervous. Pipeline company people worried that lower on-hand inventory levels would reduce the flexibility required to meet schedules.

Instead of being torn apart, however, the team worked hard to deal with such individual biases, risks, and concerns. By this time, there was a well-developed sense of mutual accountability. The focus was completely on the team's purpose and what was best for Enron's customers and Enron as a whole. In fact, even before its recommendations were finalized, the task force members asked people they knew at Enron to try out some of their new ideas. One construction crew, for example, saved more than a half million dollars by using thinner pipes on one project.

By December, when the recommendations were due, the team's common purpose had evolved beyond just recommending how to fix the broken Deal-to-Steel process. The team now believed it was an integral part of Burns's drive to change Enron. They wrote and produced a videotape to present their recommendations and began an ambitious schedule of presenting the tape and personally answering questions in front of small groups throughout the company. They also appointed a small implementation subteam to develop scorecards to measure how effectively the team's recommendations would be carried out.

Throughout the life of the task force, its senior sponsors—Burns, Horton, and Prentice—actively supported the team. These senior executives regularly appeared at team meetings and took every opportunity to draw favorable attention to the team's work in public settings, all of which helped members of the task force take the risks needed to do their job. Once the recommendations were in, however, Burns decided to hold the presidents of each of the marketing companies individually accountable for implementation. Accordingly, the team's own implementation subteam disbanded after Burns assigned the presidents to a new Deal-to-Steel Council.

This frustrated some of the Deal-to-Steel Team members who, having experienced the power and promise of a team built on mutual accountability, believed an opportunity was being missed. To them, the return to individual accountability for implementation seemed premature, if not risky. Unlike when they had first gathered six months earlier, however, the team's frustrations now grew from a desire to make its recommendations happen rather than individual turf concerns or parochial biases.

The Deal-to-Steel Task Force set in motion changes that, once fully implemented, would mean millions of dollars for Enron by reducing construction times, cutting costs, and increasing levels of customer service and satisfaction. The team also became a model for Burns's major change effort and it helped encourage others to energize change across the company. It also knew that—as a team—it accomplished more than would have been possible as individuals working through the existing organizational hierarchy.

# COMMON APPROACHES TO BUILDING TEAM PERFORMANCE

There is no guaranteed "how-to" recipe for building team performance. Deal-to-Steel, for example, first came together as a potential team and it might have stayed that way—or even shifted to a working group mode—but for a few key turns of events, new insights, and wise choices. Like many other team stories, Deal-to-Steel illustrates that the difference between potential team and real team can be as subtle as whether a group capitalizes on a key formative event or as fundamental as ignoring performance over an extended time period.

Still, we found a variety of common approaches that can help potential teams take the risks necessary to move the team up the performance curve. These are summarized below, using Deal-to-Steel and other examples to highlight them.

**1. Establish urgency and direction.** All team members need to believe the team has urgent and worthwhile purposes, and they want to know what the expectations are. Indeed, the more urgent and meaningful the rationale, the more likely it is that a real team will emerge. The best team charters are clear enough to indicate performance expectations, but flexible enough to allow teams to shape their own purpose, goals, and approach. However, this is not always as easy as it sounds.

Ron Burns, the head of Enron's pipeline group, made it clear that he considered both the task force's work and the overall company change program urgent priorities. Moreover, his actions demonstrated his support; for example, he spent more than a third of his time personally trying to "blow away barriers." He chose two key executives, Horton and Prentice, to put together and oversee the task force. These two plus Burns spent ample time with the team and repeatedly supported the team's work in public. As a result, Burns, Horton and Prentice helped set both the direction, credibility, and urgency of the Deal-to-Steel effort. Says Janacek of Burns, "He was really pushing and motivating. He really wanted to see things change."

**2. Select members based on skills and skill potential, not personalities.** Teams must have the complementary skills needed to do their job. Three categories of skills are relevant: 1) technical and functional, 2) problem-solving, and 3) interpersonal. The key issue for potential teams is striking the right balance between members who already possess the needed skill levels versus developing the skill levels after the team gets started.

Far too many leaders overemphasize selection, believing that without "just the right set of people at the start," an effective team will not be possible. Yet, with the exception of some advanced functional or technical skills, most people can develop needed skills *after* joining a team. All of us have the capacity for personal growth and need only be challenged in a performance-focused way. Accordingly, instead of focusing solely on whether candidates already have the needed skills, it can be more pertinent to ask whether the team, including its leader, will invest the time and effort to help potential team members grow. If the answer is no, then putting, or keeping, such people on the team probably makes no sense.

Selection, by the way, is not only an issue for task forces or special project teams. Ongoing groups, whether they are managers who run things or others who make or do things, also must assess which individuals will be part of the team. Too often there is a presumption that existing job status automatically warrants team membership. Instead, when groups are still potential teams, skill and skill potential must be carefully considered. This, for example, is exactly what happened when the Garden State Brickface Team (Chapter 3) asked the supervisors to "draft" their job crews. By doing so, the supervisors had to take a fresh look at the skills and skill potential of the men they selected to be on their teams.

Once the membership of a group is settled, the question of training often arises. Formal training helps, although it is not always the best or only way to build team skills. Training works best when it is supplied "just in time" and is customized to meet specific performance needs of the group in question. General Electric, for example, provides frontline worker teams early training in problem solving, decision making, and interpersonal and teamwork skills. Motorola encourages anyone who wants training to contact experts for immediate help. In this way, Motorola tries to ensure that the timing and content of training relates to the specific performance challenge of the person or team requesting help.

Horton and Prentice selected people from across Enron to ensure that the Deal-to-Steel Task Force had the range of technical and functional skills necessary to tackle its charter. They also instinctively considered interpersonal skills by picking people they thought would speak their minds. While the task force did not resort to any official training programs, they did use outside expertise in a just-in-time fashion to help enhance the quality of their problem solving and decision making.

**3. Pay particular attention to first meetings and actions.** Initial impressions always mean a great deal. When potential teams first gather, everyone alertly monitors the signals given by others to confirm, suspend, or dispel going-in assumptions and concerns. They particularly pay attention to those in authority: the team leader and any executives who set up, oversee, or otherwise influence the team. And, as always, what such leaders do is more important than what they say.

Burns, Horton, and Prentice, the sponsoring executives in Deal-to-Steel, effectively communicated their seriousness from the beginning largely by how much time they devoted to the team. So did Fred Mott when he convinced the ELITE Team of his commitment to implement their recommendations ("whatever you come up with"), and when he freed up the best people for this assignment. In another example developed later, a plant manager at Sealed Air Corporation began a world-class manufacturing effort by holding a series of education sessions about the operational economics of the business—during the working day. As one employee said later, "I found out right quick that he was an honest man who cared about this."

As the Deal-to-Steel Team discovered, meetings away from the work site can facilitate the looser, less inhibited interactions that help potential teams get off to a good start. The advantage of such off-site locations, obviously, is the extra time it provides for informal interaction in a less pressured setting. But other teams we know have performed well and have never gone off-site.

First meetings and actions are not necessarily limited to a single event; indeed, in Deal-to-Steel, the "first meeting" stretched across a handful of get-togethers near the beginning of the project. Moreover, for ongoing groups like potential management or worker teams, first meetings usually are not the first time the people in them have ever met as a group. More often, such "first meetings" occur upon or after the arrival of a new leader, the declaration of a new program or initiative, or the establishment of a different performance objective. The Cosmo Products executives (Chapter 5), for example, had their first meeting after they listened to their employees' taped remarks on the problems facing Cosmo—notwithstanding the fact they had been meeting together for years. Too many potential teams fail to approach such meetings as "first meetings" and instead allow existing habits and operating styles to dominate, including an overemphasis on individual instead of mutual accountability. As a result, they lose the chance to tackle performance challenges in a fundamentally different way.

Even more critical than settings is how the team leader acts. Janacek, for example, was far more effective off-site than in the earlier headquarters meetings. By combining the subgroups, he indicated both flexibility and the willingness to admit mistakes. By sharing the floor with others, he showed that he intended to listen as well as talk. By expressing his own recognition that, as an operating company manager, he had to learn to treat the marketing companies as his customers, he demonstrated the courage to deal with personal bias and habit. The key to Janacek's success was in the attitude, flexibility, and focus that his actions reflected, allowing an open enough discussion to deal with individual concerns while simultaneously setting a tone for how the whole team should behave.

Whatever triggers first meetings, the leader must be sensitive to the potential impact of his or her actions at such gatherings. One new leader we know was introduced to his potential team at a special dinner after being transferred into the group from another division of the company. Only a few of the people knew him personally, but his reputation for hard work—and hard play—had preceded him. The group had gone to great lengths to prepare a special welcoming skit, and at the end of a fun evening for all, he was asked to comment. Instead of seizing the chance to communicate a few key themes or directions, all he said was, "I'm really glad to be joining this group." It turned out to be a missed opportunity that he never regained.

**4. Set some clear rules of behavior.** All real teams develop rules of conduct to help them achieve their purpose and performance goals. The most critical early rules pertain to attendance (for example, "no interruptions to take phone calls"), discussion ("no sacred cows"), confidentiality ("the only things to leave this room are what we agree will leave this room"), analytic approach ("facts are friendly"), end-product orientation ("everyone gets assignments and does them"), constructive confrontation ("no finger pointing"), and, often the most important, contributions ("everyone does real work").

Such rules promote focus, openness, commitment and trust—all oriented toward performance. In Deal-to-Steel, for example, the task force effectively adopted the rule of "focusing on the process, not the people," thereby helping to keep conflicts constructive. These rules do not have to be written down; some emerge implicitly from the group. The founding team of the New York City Partnership described in Chapter 7 had a rigorous rule forbidding the executives involved from sending staff people as substitutes to meetings. The team never formally adopted the rule, but they never broke it either.

However they arise, such rules test a group's own credibility. For example, if everyone agrees to make team meetings a top priority and then members fail to show up, it signals that the group may not be able to manage even the simplest of details, let alone conquer its performance challenge. The rules must be enforced. One team we know decided on total confidentiality to encourage open discussion.

Early on, a member violated the rule by talking to outsiders. When the rest of the team learned that the leader had gently, but firmly, reprimanded the offender, team discussions became even more open, free-wheeling, and, ultimately, creative.

**5. Set and seize upon a few immediate performance-oriented tasks and goals.** Most teams trace their advancement to key performance-oriented events that forge them together. Potential teams can set such events in motion by immediately establishing a few challenging yet achievable goals that can be reached early on. Potential frontline worker teams, like those we observed at Motorola, Sealed Air Corporation, and General Electric, set numerically measurable goals for cycle-time, on-time deliveries, reject or error rates, machine set-up times, and other similar measures. Other teams set goals that, although not subject to numerical measurement, still could be assessed. The Dallas Mafia, for example, had to judge themselves against a nonnumerical goal of replacing plain vanilla investment banking deals with more innovative financing.

Whether quantitatively or qualitatively assessable, the performance goals must include a clear "stretch" component. Several years ago, a leading financial services company analyzed several of its biggest business successes around the world to identify commonalities. The company discovered that, in every case, the leadership group of the unit in question had established specific performance goals that other people in the company regarded as "virtually impossible, if not crazy." Moreover, in most cases, the leadership groups became teams in the process and accomplished their goals.

Significantly, *the events generated by such stretch goals do not have to be successes.* The refusal by the chief of Enron's operating company to relinquish some budgetary control helped galvanize the Deal-to-Steel Task Force. So did the rejection by Global headquarters of the Dallas Mafia's equal pay proposal. The wise team recognizes the value of performance-oriented events and takes advantage of them regardless of how they turn out.

**6. Challenge the group regularly with fresh facts and information.** New information causes a potential team to redefine and enrich its understanding of the performance challenge, thereby helping the team shape a common purpose, set clearer goals, and improve on its common approach. When the Deal-to-Steel Task Force reviewed all the mishaps in the Table Top project, it positioned itself both to learn and to focus as a team.

Conversely, potential teams err when they assume that all the information needed exists in the collective experience and knowledge of the members. Task forces like Deal-to-Steel are less likely to victimize themselves in this manner than workers or managers trying to use a team approach in their regular, ongoing jobs. After all, task forces and special projects often must develop new information as an explicit part of their charter. Potential teams with more permanent, ongoing assignments, on the other hand, easily develop habits that shut out new information and perspective. Indeed, new facts often startle such groups into action, as we saw with the impact of the taped employee comments on the executives of Cosmo Products.

**7. Spend lots of time together.** Common sense tells us that teams must spend a lot of time together, especially at the beginning. Yet potential teams often fail to do so. The time spent together must be both scheduled and unscheduled. Indeed, creative insights as well as personal bonding require impromptu and casual interactions just as much as analyzing spreadsheets, interviewing customers, competitors, or fellow employees, and constantly debating issues. Somewhat surprising, we found that the time need *not* always be face-to-face. Increasingly, team members are using telecommunications to bring them together, as we saw in the Rapid Response illustration in Chapter 5.

Busy executives and managers too often intentionally minimize the time they spend together. In fact, even when physically together, they often limit their interactions by design. Meetings get scheduled for the shortest possible time to cause the least disruption to other tasks. Agendas are strictly adhered to as the group pushes to get on with it. Purposing discussions, in particular, are often cut off in the interests of meeting arbitrary agenda constraints. Too often, as happened at the start of Deal-to-Steel, people find reasons to step out to take a phone call, or they avoid attending at all. All of this yields poor results: the potential team never gives itself the time to *learn* to be a team. The occasional open-ended meeting or three-day off-site is one of the best ways to break this pattern because it allows free time for informal interaction and problem solving. But off-sites are not enough if, upon returning to work, the potential team reverts to agenda-driven, noninteractive sessions.

One potential team of executives we encountered used a series of off-sites to give it a promising start. They soon had an inspiring purpose, a set of specifically agreed-on performance goals, an approach that capitalized well on their complementary skills, and even the solid beginnings of mutual respect and trust. Regrettably, they assumed they could carry out their assignment with a minimum of meeting time. Yet, by reducing the time they spent together, they unwittingly diminished the mutual priority and clarity of the team's purpose and goals. They also eroded strong initial levels of trust and respect. Within six months, the individuals began interpreting the group's purpose in varying and conflicting ways. By then, unfortunately, they had lost their desire to get together to learn from their differences. What had begun as a potentially powerful team ended as a pseudo-team that eventually had to be completely reformed.

By contrast, the more successful teams always find a way to spend extra time together, particularly when things go awry. The Burlington Northern Intermodal Team scheduled daily morning meetings and interacted constantly throughout the day and the night as well. When they needed to, they even got together on Sunday afternoons. The Rapid Response Team, whose members were located thousands of miles apart, spent hours on the phone with one another every day. The people on Deal-to-Steel found themselves working together so much that the task force assignment became, in effect, a second job. Interestingly, as with most successful task force or special project teams, this second job and the time spent on it ultimately seemed far more satisfying than their regular jobs.

**8. Exploit the power of positive feedback, recognition, and reward.** Positive reinforcement works as well in a team context as elsewhere. "Giving out gold stars" helps to shape new behaviors critical to team performance. If people in the group, for example, are alert to a shy person's initial efforts to speak up and contribute, they can give him or her the positive reinforcement that encourages continued contributions. Similarly, when someone risks opening up a sensitive, conflict-ridden issue, the others on the team and especially the leader can use positive feedback to powerfully signal their openness to further such challenges.

The benefits of positive feedback and recognition extend to people at all levels. David Rockefeller masterfully used positive reinforcement to transform a group of volunteer chief executives into the highly successful New York City Partnership (see Chapter 7). At every meeting, Rockefeller singled out each executive for praise, always tying the compliment to a specific contribution the executive had made to the group's objective. Some suspected that Rockefeller used his staff to help him prepare such comments. But it did not matter. To a person, each of the chief executives involved recognized both Rockefeller's passion for the group's mission and the fact that he, a very busy man himself, genuinely appreciated the time and effort they were contributing. Even the strongest egos respond to positive feedback—when it is real.

There are many ways to recognize and reward team performance, of which direct compensation is only one. Executives, for example, provide immediate rewards for participation when, like Ron Burns of Enron, they describe to the team and others the urgency of the group's effort. Sometimes, companies have existing pay, bonus, or other reward programs that a team can exploit. Other times, the potential team must develop its own approaches. The Kodak Zebra Team described in Chapter 3, for example, gave dinner certificates to people who made special contributions. Ultimately, the satisfaction in the team's performance becomes the most cherished reward. Until then, however, potential teams must find other ways to recognize and reinforce their individual and team contributions and commitment.

## CONCLUSION

Most potential teams can become real teams, but not without taking risks involving conflict, trust, interdependence, and hard work. For example, a common team purpose, set of performance goals, and approach rarely arise without conflict. Indeed, quite the contrary—the most successful teams recognize their members' conflicting views and experiences as a source of strength. Similarly, mutual accountability requires trust and interdependence, which usually do not grow without risk taking. And, finally, most potential teams include members who must develop the skills needed by the team after they have joined the team itself. This, too, implies risks and hard work for everyone on the team.

The eight "best practices" summarized in this chapter can facilitate the risks teams need to take. But each of the eight—like any team-building approach you or others might try—will only add value if it is employed in pursuit of performance. For example, we have noted that successful potential teams spend lots of time together. Yet, in the Deal-to-Steel story, each of the two initial subgroups *wasted time together* over the first several weeks. Not until the off-site, when they risked opening up conflicts and dealing with them constructively in light of their performance challenge, did they begin to spend *productive time together*. Similarly, by adopting the rule of "focusing on the process, not the people" and by asking the operating company chief to relinquish some budgetary control, the Deal-to-Steel group took performance-oriented risks that helped it build mutual trust and interdependence. Moreover, Deal-to-Steel provides an exellent example of how the continual search for fresh facts and information (e.g., the painful review of the Table Top disaster and the benchmarking against industry performance) can spur team performance.

When potential teams, as well as managers and executives who care about their results, lose sight of this all-important connection between risk taking and performance, they get easily lost and frustrated. People then start looking for recipe-like design cures such as "all teams need a 'challenger,' an 'integrator,' and an 'arbitrator,' " or "all teams need up-front training in interpersonal skills." Too often, under such schemes, team-like characteristics, such as building togetherness for its own sake, tend to replace performance as the focus of the potential team's attention.

Such cookie-cutter approaches miss the principal point of teams, namely performance and the specificity with which teams deliver it. *Each team must find its own path to its own unique performance challenge.* This is why we emphasize that the team basics of number, skills, purpose, performance goals, approach, and accountability are more of a discipline than a definition. This discipline, and the performance focus at its heart, provide the essential compass to potential teams that must navigate through all the risks inherent in moving up the team performance curve. Joining a team is a career risk, giving up individual control is a performance risk, acknowledging personal responsibility for needed change is a self-esteem risk, allowing others to lead is an institutional risk, and abandoning hierarchical command and control is a stability risk. Taking such risks makes sense only if it unleashes a team's capabilities in pursuit of performance. Only then can people avail themselves of the wisdom of teams.

# CHAPTER SEVEN

# Team Leaders

COLONEL Randy Geyer began the first day of his new job by signing in, "I am not John Carr."

Geyer had just assumed command from Carr of a U. S. Army planning unit, called a logistical cell (or log cell for short), that was responsible for devising how best to move, receive, and sustain the soldiers, equipment, and supplies involved in the Gulf War. Five months earlier, Geyer, who describes himself as "just a reservist from Indianapolis," had been marketing furniture. He knew a lot about logistics, but not nearly as much as Carr, a career logistician who had performed brilliantly at the planning task during the war. But the hostilities were now over, and Geyer had to lead the log cell as they tackled the less life-threatening but no less difficult job of orchestrating the swift and safe return home of soldiers, equipment, and supplies—an effort Geyer later likened to moving the entire state of Wyoming to a new location.

Geyer knew he could not meet the challenge at hand without the fullest possible contribution of everyone in the log cell. "I didn't have Carr's expertise and doctrine," says Geyer. "He was the best guy, the 'smart guy.' I wasn't that guy." So, by defining himself in the negative from the very beginning, Randy Geyer made it clear to his people that he wanted and needed their help. He also instinctively revealed an attitude critical to team leadership: putting team performance first and recognizing that he needed help.

Successful team leaders instinctively know that the goal is team performance results instead of individual achievement, including their own. Unlike working groups, whose performance depends solely on optimizing individual contributions, real team performance requires impact beyond the sum of the individual parts. Hence, it requires a complementary mix of skills, a purpose that goes beyond individual tasks, goals that define joint work-products, and an approach that blends individual skills into a unique collective skill—all of which produces strong *mutual* accountability.

Getting people to work together as a team toward a common goal, we have observed, depends on attitudes like Geyer's more than personality, reputation, or rank. The belief that "only the team can fail" begins with the leaders. Team leaders act to clarify purpose and goals, build commitment and self-confidence, strengthen the team's collective skills and approach, remove externally imposed obstacles, and create opportunities for others. Most important, like all members of the team, *team leaders do real work themselves.* Yet, in each of these aspects, team leaders know or discover when their own action can hinder the team, and how their patience can energize it. Put differently, team performance almost always depends on how well team leaders like Geyer strike a critical balance between doing things themselves and letting other people do them.

In this too, attitude is the key. Team leaders genuinely believe that they do *not* have all the answers—so they do not insist on providing them. They believe they do *not* need to make all key decisions—so they do not do so. They believe they *cannot* succeed without the combined contributions of all the other members of the team to a common end—and so they avoid any action that might constrain inputs or intimidate anyone on the team. Ego is *not* their predominant concern.

Such behaviors are neither difficult to learn nor practice; most of us can do it, and at various times in our lives, most of us have. But few of us practice such things automatically, especially in business contexts where authority typically means the ability to command and control subordinates and to make all the tough decisions. This is sometimes called the "divine right of managers." Such managers believe they must have all the answers—or be perceived as losing control or being unreliable. To them, only individuals can be heroes.

Such attitudes can effectively support working groups. But they cripple potential team leaders. It is not that decisiveness or control are bad; all teams need both. Team performance levels, however, ultimately require the *team* to be decisive, the *team* to be in control, and the *team* to be the hero. As we discussed in Chapter 6, this requires the team to take risks involving conflict, trust, interdependence, and hard work. None of that happens when the leader alone calls every shot and has the final comment on every action. None of it happens either if the team leader "never makes a mistake." Moving a group from potential team to real team, therefore, demands that a leader give up some command and some control—and that means he or she too must take some real risks.

Simply abandoning all decision making to a potential team, however, rarely works either; the team leader's challenge is more difficult than that. He or she must give up decision space only when and as much as the group is ready to accept and use. Indeed, this is the essence of the team leader's job—striking the right balance between providing guidance and giving up control, between making tough decisions and letting others make them, and between doing difficult things alone and letting others learn how to do them. Just as too much command will stifle the capability, initiative, and creativity of the team, so will too little guidance, direction, and discipline. But, because of managerial habits learned in working groups and hierarchies, most potential team leaders err on the side of too much guidance and leave too little room for team decision making and growth.

This delicate balancing act differs from team to team, each of which has its own unique characteristics. No two teams have the same mix of people and skills, choice of purpose and goals, best approach, and hurdle of mutual accountability. Rarely does a leader's experience with one team match the needs of another, and we encountered a number of situations where successful team leaders in one situation were unsuccessful in another. Certainly, patterns exist from which we all can learn, but there are no standard approaches or recipes that guarantee how to lead a team.

Even within the same team, a leader's role practically never ends up in the same place it started. As the potential team grows into a real team, and possibly even a high-performance team, the leader's job changes markedly. His or her formal authority may go unchanged; but when, whether, and how to use it shifts. The key to the leader's evolving role always lies in understanding what the team needs and does not need from the leader to help it perform. In one sense, the team leader is the ultimate utility infielder or substitute player; he or she must be there to deliver *only* as needed. Fortunately for most team leaders, the team will help identify what the leader needs to do—or not do—at any point in time so long as the leader listens carefully to what is going on and how it relates to the team's performance challenge.

Nobody undervalues the importance of a team leader to a team's success or failure. In fact, most people overestimate the leader's role and responsibilities, creating unrealistic expectations and conditions for team leadership. Many people, for example, confuse the team leader's task with leadership in general. Yet, while being a good team leader is a worthy test for any of us, it does not require, as one executive opined, "having the patience of Job, the courage of Napoleon, the insight of Pasteur, and the wisdom of Churchill." This overblown estimation illustrates the all-too-common assumption pervading many organizations that leadership is a mysterious accident of birth that people either have or do not have and certainly cannot learn.

Too many people also mistakenly think the basic requirements of leading an effective team are the same, if perhaps less fully developed, as those needed to lead a successful corporation. In fact, leading a team pales in comparison with the challenge of leading a large, complex organization. Corporate leaders must orchestrate the performance-driven pursuit of long-term visions and strategies by hundreds, thousands, or even hundreds of thousands of people spread across geographic, functional, cultural, hierarchical, and business boundaries. Commonly cited characteristics of such leaders include being visionaries, communicators and motivators, keen evaluators of talent, insightful decision makers, unassuming role models, and wise and courageous judges in the face of uncertainty and change.

General Norman Schwarzkopf, who oversaw the conduct of the Gulf War, surely was such a leader. And so was William Pagonis, the three-star general who commanded the tens of thousands of people in the U. S. Army's Support Command that provided logistical support to 300,000 troops and 100,000 vehicles with more than seven million tons of equipment, food, fuel, and supplies. Pagonis had seven generals and a chief of staff through whom he could direct the efforts of all the traditional logistics functions like transportation, engineering, police, ammunition, communications, quartermaster, and so on. But he also wanted a group—the log cell—to stand apart from this normal military hierarchy and act as his private think tank to help him ensure that the entire Support Command had the best, most effective plan for moving, receiving, sustaining, and, ultimately, returning all the troops and equipment. To succeed, this fifteen-person unit had to be cross-functional and combine the talents and experience of both career officers and reservists. Thus, Carr's and then Geyer's job in getting the log cell to perform, while obviously critical, differed in scale, scope, and kind from Pagonis's own leadership job.

Unlike Schwarzkopf and Pagonis, Geyer was essentially a player-coach who had to get his team to perform one day at a time. Among other things, this required him to champion the log cell's cause, listen attentively to what people were saying and not saying, and interpret the meanings and feelings of fifteen people from a variety of backgrounds and orientations. In addition, he had to encourage, counsel, and support both individuals and the whole team, continually help the team balance and rebalance assignments, and have the courage to take on the system whenever it threw an otherwise insurmountable obstacle in the log cell's path. To make a difference, moreover, he had to do all these things with an unswerving eye on the team's purpose, goals, and approach.

Geyer did a terrific job. But that does not mean he could have done Pagonis's job. Nor does the fact that Pagonis performed so well at the top of a large and complex organization mean he could have, like Geyer, been an effective team leader. Corporate leadership, business unit leadership, and team leadership differ. While some people can do all three well, either equating or inadvertently assuming that the capacity to lead large enterprises is a prerequisite for team leadership artificially limits the choice of a team leader.

Indeed, as the record shows, individuals with all the required capabilities to create and sustain high-performing organizations are as rare as they are admired. The odds of finding good team leaders, by contrast, are substantially better. Most people can be effective team leaders. Certainly, in our research, we found good team leaders in frontline jobs, supervisor and foreman positions, middle management spots, and within the ranks of top executives. Accordingly, we think managers and others ought to worry much less about picking the ideal team leaders than about helping them to succeed afterwards—which means paying lots of attention to whether *specific* team leaders are in fact doing and not doing whatever *their* teams need in order to perform. This should begin with an understanding of team leadership practices, most of which we think are well illustrated by the following story of David Rockefeller and the team who created the New York City Partnership.

## THE NEW YORK CITY PARTNERSHIP

At the end of the 1970s, New York City took its first steps back from the brink of economic chaos when, thanks to the Municipal Assistance Corporation, the city avoided financial bankruptcy. Guided by Mayor Ed Koch's sharp tongue and humorous touch, some of the confidence returned to New York's historically brash but recently battered spirit. The city, however, still faced a long economic recovery. Major businesses, for example, continued to flee, taking both employment and a chunk of the tax base with them. Plenty of skeptics predicted the city's demise as the nation's financial and business capital.

In this uncertain, fast-changing environment, many business leaders, including the CEOs of some of the nation's largest enterprises, worried that the Chamber of Commerce and the Economic Development Council—the two primary organizations representing their interests in city affairs—were not as effective as required. So when George Champion, who had chaired both the chamber and the council for several years, decided to retire, a number of business and city leaders asked David Rockefeller to succeed Champion and to merge and renew the two institutions. Because of Rockefeller's stature and respect, his long history of philanthropic activities, and his chairmanship of Chase Manhattan Bank, the executives thought that he was the only person who could forge the "common voice" for business they believed necessary to protect both the reputation and the reality of the city's economic strength.

Luckily for New York and the business community, Rockefeller said yes to the job; just as luckily, he said no to the mission. Under his guidance, the Chamber of Commerce and the Economic Development Council did combine to support what became known as the New York City Partnership. But Rockefeller and the team of chief executives he shaped to lead this merger transformed their purpose from fostering a common business lobbying voice to creating a new organization "to help make New York City a better place to live, work, and do business."

From the spring of 1979 through early 1981, Rockefeller's team worked as hard at shaping their purpose and goals as they did at overcoming the resistance throughout the city, including at the chamber and council themselves, to assembling the considerable resources of the business community under a single banner. In addition to Rockefeller, the initial core team included Arthur Taylor, former president of CBS and "interim" president of the newly formed Partnership, as well as four CEOs: Richard Shinn (Metropolitan Life), Paul Lyet (Sperry-Rand), Ed Pratt (Pfizer), and Virgil Conway (Seaman's Savings Bank). Before the team finished, however, others joined its ranks, including John Whitehead (Co-chairman of Goldman, Sachs) and Ellen Strauss (president of WMCA, and future president of the Partnership). Other civic-minded business executives, of course, played very important roles in both the formation and conduct of the Partnership. But their contributions came in the form of the money, resources, influence, and judgment that usually get associated with steering committees, boards of advisors, and advisory councils. By contrast, everyone on the core team, including Rockefeller himself, put themselves at risk and did the kind of hard work characteristic of real teams.

The core team traveled all over the city for meetings with civic and community leaders in order to test the Partnership's mission against the most pressing needs and interests of the day. They also attended an endless series of breakfasts sponsored by Rockefeller to solicit comments and criticism from executives of large and small businesses alike. They lobbied city, state, and federal officials. They explored the experiences of business groups in other cities. And they continually tested, shaped, and argued among themselves over their purpose ("help solve some of the city's key problems") and approach ("prioritize problems for attack and then focus on a few").

It was a classic team effort with the performance results to show for it. The team founded and institutionalized an entirely new concept for New York's business leadership, pulling together more than a hundred CEOs and other major executives from big business, small business, community, and other social service groups. In addition, they sparked a number of initiatives aimed at alleviating serious concerns, including the creation of tens of thousands of summer jobs for young people, raising millions of dollars from private and government sources to fund thousands of units of affordable housing, establishing practical and effective neighborhood crime prevention networks, and executing a strategy for bringing jobs to the outer New York boroughs. While they did not solve all of the city's critical problems, they made an important dent in some.

In all this, David Rockefeller was critical. He had been initially approached because of his stature, or what one team member called his "convening power." And there is no question he did command attention and generate lots of money and general support for the Partnership. But getting his core team and dozens of other CEOs and well-known leaders to check their corporate egos at the door to work on urban problems did not happen simply because of Rockefeller's raw power or prestige. It happened because he was a good team leader.

## WHAT TEAM LEADERS DO AND DO NOT DO

Those who lead small groups must look to the specifics of the performance challenge to help them choose how best to lead. If the group can deliver performance as an effective working group through maximizing each individual's contribution, then the leader can rely on the normal decision-making and delegation approaches often associated with good management. If, on the other hand, performance requires a team approach, then the leader cannot assume that good management will be enough. Neither the leader nor those he or she leads should expect the leader to make all the decisions about directions taken, how resources get deployed, and how individuals are performing. Instead, the leader must show—in everything he or she does and does not do—a belief in the team's purpose and in the people who, individually and together, make up the team.

Moreover, the strength of a leader's belief in what the team is all about can be incredibly powerful. During our research, we came across a compelling example of this in a report by Roger Mudd in the television series "Learning in America." The program, "Schools at Work," described four schools from different sections of the country, each of which was in a disadvantaged community, and each of which had achieved remarkable results:

> "For so many years the achievement had been so-so, it had been accepted as the norm. . . . The first challenge was attendance—just getting these kids to school. Today, attendance is close to perfect—98 percent."
>
> "My first year, I think our scores at the sixth grade were at the forty-fourth percentile, which is totally unacceptable. . . . This last year we were at the ninety-seventh percentile—in *all* areas."
>
> "Math scores show the biggest turnaround. Seven years ago only half the students were achieving at or above grade level. Now more than 90 percent do!"

Behind these kinds of results, which were accomplished through the efforts of both principal/faculty and faculty/student teams, were deep-seated beliefs of the principal and faculty team leaders:

> " . . . an embedded belief, an almost wordless devotion to the cause of public education and its worth to a democracy."
>
> "I don't believe that any youngster should fail in public education in America. I don't think that children fail, I believe that schools fail children. . . ."
>
> "And we have a belief that unites us that all children can learn, (a belief that together) we can get the job done."

It is easy to see how powerful beliefs like these motivate and energize potential team leaders to instinctively act in ways that create real teams. Similar beliefs, although sometimes less evangelical, characterize the best team leaders. As a result, they do not need remarkable leadership qualities, or even extensive training. They simply need to *believe in their purpose and their people.*

The power of such attitudes gets demonstrated time and time again in teams. Randy Geyer of the U. S. Army log cell had such beliefs. So did Mack Canfield of the Dallas Mafia, Doris Dunlap of the *Tallahassee Democrat* ELITE Team, William Janacek of the Deal-to-Steel Team, and Bill Greenwood of the Burlington Northern Intermodal Team. And so did David Rockefeller. From the outset, Rockefeller strongly believed in both the purpose and capabilities of his team. As with other effective team leaders, the stronger this belief was, the more it enabled him to instinctively strike the right balance between action and patience as he worked to do the six things necessary to good team leadership.

**1. Keep the purpose, goals, and approach relevant and meaningful.** All teams must shape their own common purpose, performance goals, and approach. While a leader must be a full working member of the team who can and should contribute to these, he or she also stands apart from the team by virtue of his or her selection as leader. Teams expect their leaders to use that perspective and distance to help the teams clarify and commit to their mission, goals, and approach.

Teams usually do not want leaders to go beyond this. As one of the regular members of the team, of course, a leader can make any and all specific suggestions. But when he or she wears the "leader's" mantle, comments intended as suggestions may be interpreted as mandates. This is especially likely to happen in business contexts where most people are conditioned to hear "orders" when their managers speak. But if leaders specify too much about purpose, goals, and approach, they will, in effect, have used their distance from the team in a normal hierarchical as opposed to team fashion. By doing so, they may gain compliance to "their" purpose. But they are likely to lose commitment to a team purpose. This is especially true at the beginning of a potential team's efforts when all eyes and ears are so keenly tuned to how the leader will use authority to build a team.

Rockefeller, for example, soon became unshakeable in his belief that the Partnership should solve problems and sponsor projects as well as lobby, and most of the core team agreed. Ed Pratt, however, did not. He caused the team to debate this issue for several months.

In this, Pratt had Rockefeller's open blessing. Why? Because Rockefeller also had an unshakeable belief in an approach based on candor and facts—not unlike how Bill Janacek anchored the Deal-to-Steel Team with his credo of "focus on the process, not the people." Rockefeller instinctively knew that unless the team openly struggled with the issue, they would never develop the commitment required to make it happen. He also knew the team would not risk sharing their conflicting views unless he gave them the space and encouragement to do so. This paid off; Ed Pratt, for example, became one of the most committed members of the team.

While Rockefeller's commitment to a problem-solving purpose for the Partnership was steadfast, he did not dictate or order the team to adopt it. Moreover, like all well-balanced team leaders, Rockefeller demonstrated both patience and silence when the team discussed the specifics of its purpose, goals, and approach beyond the overarching problem-solving theme itself. "All he did was sit there and wait until the problem homogenized," recalls one observer. "He didn't feel any great compulsion to force a solution before its time." Agrees another, "It was almost like a shared leadership. David would just sit there and watch."

**2. Build commitment and confidence.** Team leaders should work to build the commitment and confidence of each individual as well as the team as a whole. As we discussed earlier, there is an important difference between individual commitment and accountability versus mutual accountability. Both are needed for any group to become a real team. Thus, the leader must keep both the individual and the team in mind as he or she tries to provide positive, constructive reinforcement while avoiding intimidation.

Unfortunately, it is all too easy to coerce people in organizational settings, including small groups. Given his stature, for example, Rockefeller could have intimidated other CEOs. In that case, we suspect, things would have fallen apart fairly quickly because his team was entirely voluntary. Inside businesses, leaders of small groups who intimidate also come up short. The people involved may not have the exit options available to volunteers, but over time they will lose their enthusiasm and initiative when dealing with an intimidating leader. Certainly, they do not coalesce into a team. Either they never take the risks needed to build mutual trust and interdependence, or, if they do, they are not rewarded for it. Executives who rely on intimidation can get things done better in a hierarchy than in teams.

Positive and constructive reinforcement fuels the mutual accountability and confidence so critical to team performance. In fact, more than anything else, Rockefeller's leadership of the Partnership is remembered for his remarkable habit of providing meaningful positive feedback. Another team leader who did this well was Steve Frangos of the Kodak Zebra Team mentioned in Chapter 3. When he assumed control of the black and white film manufacturing activities at Kodak, they were considered unexciting. Color was the place to be, and many people in black and white felt like second-class citizens. Frangos worked hard to transform this perception both among his core leadership team and the rest of the 1,500 people working in black and white. Using examples ranging from the Gulf War to life-saving surgeries, Frangos built a noble sense among his team that black and white products "were more important to society" than many other Kodak offerings.

Indeed, the Zebra theme itself created a fun yet performance-oriented team environment. Frango's team created Zebra costumes, cheers, slogans, and songs to constantly reinforce their commitment to black and white products. This may seem hokey, but it worked for Frangos and the Zebra Team. According to one observer, "Frangos and the Zebra stuff eliminated the fear of failure and created a team where everybody stands on the shoulders of everybody else."

**3. Strengthen the mix and level of skills.** Effective team leaders are vigilant about skills. Their goal is clear: ultimately, the most flexible and top-performing teams consist of people with all the technical, functional, problem-solving, decision-making, interpersonal, and teamwork skills the team needs to perform. To get there, team leaders encourage people to take the risks needed for growth and development. They also continually challenge team members by shifting assignment and role patterns.

This effort can involve tough choices. No team reaches its goal with a chronic skill gap relative to its performance objective. Rockefeller, for example, guided the core team to practice an unwritten but powerful rule that made membership, whether continuing or new, depend on tangible contributions to specific city problems. John Whitehead, for example, earned his membership in the core team by leading the economic development project that increased affordable back-office space in the city. Conversely, membership was denied (and in some cases taken away) from people who contributed little. Obviously, the rule tested commitment. But, it also tested and developed the skills needed to make something specific and meaningful happen in New York City's difficult urban environment.

**4. Manage relationships with outsiders, including removing obstacles.** Team leaders are expected, by people outside as well as inside the team, to manage much of the team's contacts and relationships with the rest of the organization. This calls on team leaders to communicate effectively the team's purpose, goals, and approach to anyone who might help or hinder it. They also must have the courage to intercede on the team's behalf when obstacles that might cripple or demoralize the team get placed in their way.

Almost always the mutual trust so critical to a team begins with the leader who must show that the team can depend on him or her to promote team performance. Greenwood of the Intermodal Team did this with the hub proposals, as did Janacek of Deal-to-Steel with the request for budget authority. So did Rockefeller. Early on, for example, Mayor Koch posed an obstacle to the Partnership because he may have felt threatened by them; he certainly felt strongly that they occasionally stepped out of bounds. "In the early days," Koch recalls, "they were too full of themselves. They didn't understand that they were not the answer to New York's prayers. I was offended by their tone. So they changed."

In fact what happened was that Rockefeller was savvy enough about government and urban affairs, and about Koch's ego, to encourage the Partnership to strike the most constructive tone possible in their communications while simultaneously making sure the mayor appeared at key functions and was recognized for his mayoral leadership. It did not have to happen this way; Rockefeller could have taken on the mayor. By not doing so, he demonstrated again how patience can be the best guide for a team leader trying to further the team's cause.

5. **Create opportunities for others.** Team performance is not possible if the leader grabs all the best opportunities, assignments, and credit for himself or herself. Indeed, the crux of the leader's challenge is to provide performance opportunities to the team and the people on it. When the Dallas Mafia team leader Canfield made room for a more junior investment banker to lead a prestigious account, he did just that. So did Frangos at Kodak, when he encouraged a chemical engineer who "could not balance his checkbook at home" to take responsibility for preparing the Zebra Team's $200 million budget. Stepping out of the way to provide opportunities to others, however, does not mean abdicating responsibility for guidance, monitoring, and control. Colonel Geyer, for example, regularly let members of the log cell brief the top brass, but always attended the meetings himself just in case they needed his help or support.

Rockefeller also emphasized opportunities for others. The active leadership role in the core group often shifted back and forth among the members, depending on the situation. Certainly Rockefeller was always the official leader, but he often displayed the wisdom to step back when others were in a position to lead key discussions or spearhead critical initiatives. For example, when some key CEOs began to waver in their support of the Partnership, Dick Shinn emerged as the team's leader in bringing them back into the fold. When the specifics of formal organization structure were at issue, Arthur Taylor was usually the de facto leader. When critical priorities needed to be established, John Whitehead took the helm.

Rockefeller also created opportunities for members of the "extended team." Arthur Barnes, president of the New York Urban Coalition, remembers advocating that the Partnership should address educational issues if it was to have credibility within working class communities. Several business executives opposed this, believing education was too controversial and should be excluded from the Partnership's activities. Yet, to his surprise, Barnes prevailed—a fact he attributes to Rockefeller's insistence, and the core team's agreement, that everyone have an opportunity to speak out, and that the best arguments eventually succeed. "That was one of the proofs that this thing was real," says Barnes. "You could persuade these guys if you had the facts."

**6. Do real work.** Everyone on a real team, including the leader, does real work in roughly equivalent amounts. Team leaders do have a certain distance from the team by virtue of their position, but they do not use that distance "just to sit back and make decisions." Team leaders must contribute in whatever way the team needs, just like any other member. Moreover, team leaders do not delegate the nasty jobs to others. Where personal risks are high or "dirty work" is required, the team leader should step forward.

Like all good team leaders, Rockefeller quickly made it clear that no task was too humble or insignificant for him to do just because of his rank as leader, not to mention his stature in the city and the world. He attended the vision-shaping breakfasts, community outreach meetings, lobbying efforts, and fundraising dinners that provided context and direction to the Partnership. He even spent hours personally making sure that seating arrangements at large events did not juxtapose two clashing personalities. Most of all, he made it evident that his most precious resource—his own time—was available to anyone with Partnership business.

Throughout the preceding paragraphs we have highlighted what leaders do and have drawn comparisons and contrasts with what they do not do. There are, however, two critical things real team leaders *never* do: *they do not blame or allow specific individuals to fail, and they never excuse away shortfalls in team performance.* This, again, is behavior that most of us admire and can practice. But organizations built on individual instead of mutual accountability often foster the reverse. Too often, when expected results do not materialize, individuals get singled out for blame, or outside forces like the economy, the government, or the weather get identified as the cause. By contrast, real team leaders honestly believe that success or failure is a team event. No outside obstacle is an excuse for team failure, and no individuals fail. Only the team can fail. The leader assumes that the team's task includes overcoming whatever obstacles get in its way. The best illustration of the power of this attitude is in the following quote from the Roger Mudd PBS series described earlier:

> Here's a school where 90 percent of the youngsters have some form of public assistance . . . many of the youngsters come from single-parent families, teenage mothers, *all the factors that educators have used to explain away failure* exist in this school today. And these youngsters can outperform the best and brightest in any school in America. (Emphasis added.)

# CONCLUSION

Obviously, a team leader critically influences whether a potential team will mature into a real team or even a high-performance team. It is common sense, then, that picking people with the proven or potential capacity to lead a team will enhance the chances of team performance. In particular, it is important to avoid individuals who, for whatever reasons, have unbending attitudes contrary to the team approach. Such people are a distinct minority, but appointing them as team leaders is a mistake. Unless a leader believes in a team's purpose and the people on the team, he or she cannot be effective.

Too many managers, however, behave as though the selection of a team leader is the *only* thing that matters. In doing so, they ignore critical aspects of team leadership we have observed. First, over-worrying the selection unduly constrains the choice. Lots of different kinds of people can be effective team leaders; unlike corporate leadership, guiding a team is not the special reserve of a select few. A Randy Geyer can do it as well as a David Rockefeller.

Second, focusing on selection alone abdicates the responsibility to help the leader after he or she has started. Most people, whether from the assembly line or the board room, must develop as team leaders on the job. Their habitual response when tapped as leaders of small groups, at least in business contexts, is to try to be a good manager by making all the decisions and delegating and evaluating all individual responsibilities. This can be effective in working groups, but team leadership demands a different set of attitudes and behaviors. Most people can learn them—indeed, most of us have practiced them at least occasionally by the time we are adults. But the attitudes and behaviors of a team leader are unlikely to be our first instinctive response when we are selected; we usually will have to relearn and reapply them.

Moreover, and perhaps more subtly, each team requires a different balance between action and patience. Keeping each element of the team's basics relevant is a moving target. It requires the leader's constant attention if he or she is to build commitment and confidence, strengthen the mix and level of skills, manage relationships with outsiders, remove obstacles, and still do real work within the team. Because each team differs in its performance challenge, composition, and approach, the job of the leader needs to change over time. Hence, team leaders always need to grow after they are selected.

Accordingly, managers and others often should pay more attention to helping team leaders perform than selecting them. They can do this by conscientiously monitoring the performance of the team, the elements that indicate where the team is on the performance curve, and the team leader's attitude and behavior toward the team's purpose and the team itself. Periodically assessing the team against the criteria listed at the end of Chapter 3 will help anyone, whether part of the team or not, evaluate team performance and effectiveness. Asking the following questions can help evaluate the team leader's attitude, behavior, and effectiveness:

1. Has the leader adopted a team or a working group approach?
   Does the leader:
   a. make all important decisions?
   b. make all work assignments?
   c. make all evaluations of individuals?
   d. ensure work is conducted primarily on the basis of individual accountability?
   e. do any "real work" beyond decision making, delegating, and agenda setting?

2. Is the leader striving for the right balance between action and patience within the team? Does the leader:
   a. promote constructive conflict and resolution?
   b. use distance and perspective to keep the team's actions and directions relevant? Intimidate anyone on the team?
   c. constantly challenge the team to sharpen its common purpose, goals, and approach?
   d. inspire trust in people by acting in concert with the team's purpose and the team?
   e. create opportunities for others, sometimes at his or her own expense?

3. Does the leader articulate a team purpose and act to promote and share responsibility for it? Does the leader:
   a. think about and describe his or her assignment in individual or hierarchical versus team terms?
   b. identify and act to remove barriers to team performance?
   c. blame individuals for failure to perform, either within or beyond the team?
   d. excuse away performance shortfalls by pointing to "uncontrollable" outside forces?

That team leaders can and do learn on the job is illustrated well by Steve Frangos of the Kodak Zebra Team. Throughout his career, Frangos was known as someone with good interpersonal skills. Yet, by Frangos's own admission, when he took on the manufacturing job he still believed in the command-and-control approach to management. "I was taught," he says, "that you couldn't be a good manager unless you control everything and everyone." In this, he was not unlike Janacek of Deal-to-Steel, Mott of the *Tallahassee Democrat,* and many other ultimately effective team leaders who started off by asserting too much control over their potential teams.

Luckily, says Frangos, he learned the value of giving up control—albeit in a rather unexpected way involving room assignments at an off-site. Frangos believed he needed to make the assignments in order to satisfy everyone, but his attempted solutions failed miserably. Late the first night, his group was unhappy, and Frangos was pacing the halls in his pajamas. Two people finally told him to go to bed, and that they would take over the job—which they did and did better than Frangos. It was a trivial incident, but played a big part in turning around Frangos's attitude and behavior.

Frangos started to move to one side while still exerting a guiding hand over the group. This took many forms, from literally sitting at the side instead of the head of a table to formally reorganizing the manufacturing unit to delegate more control and initiative to the team. Over time, Frangos became as conscious of what he did *not* do or say as a team leader as what he did. For example, in one meeting we observed, he leaned over to us and mentioned, "I have opinions on all this, but I'm not saying anything."

All this involved risk to Frangos. He had to consciously modify his long-standing managerial approach. Moreover, he had to do so in a job some people were surprised he was given. Frangos had come through the ranks on the less technical finishing side of the film business versus the more complex sensitizing side. Accordingly, it was unusual for him to be named chief of manufacturing—sensitizing people typically called the shots, not the "whack it, hack it, pack it" guys from finishing.

Team members, however, including those in the technically difficult sensitizing area, did not mistake Frangos's silence for weakness or indecision. They knew he had an unshakeable commitment to the team's purpose of putting black and white film back on the Kodak map and to the team's specific performance goals regarding cycle time, inventory, customer satisfaction, on-time delivery, and productivity. But they also knew—and appreciated deeply—that Frangos wanted the team, not himself, to lead black and white's resurgence.

In the ultimate accolade to the team leader who has struck the right balance between action and patience, one of the Zebras says of Frangos, "So much of what we have been able to do comes from the fact that Steve has let us be what we want to be." Frangos himself favors a quote from the Chinese philosopher, Lao-Tzu to describe his view of team leadership: *"As for the best leaders, the people do not notice their existence. The next best, the people honor and praise. The next, the people fear; and the next, the people hate. When the best leader's work is done, the people say, 'We did it ourselves.'"*

# CHAPTER EIGHT

# Teams, Obstacles, and Endings: Getting Unstuck

Obstacles are a continual fact of life for teams. They occur from the moment a potential team gathers until the team comes to an end. Obstacles also differ as much as the teams, performance challenges, organizational settings, and business contexts that produce them. The Burlington Northern Intermodal Team, for example, encountered weak support from management, policies against advertising, distrust of truckers, and mediocre talent in the intermodal department. It also faced bad weather, intense competition, and a poor economy when it had to prove its strategy with the two new hubs. Any of these obstacles could have derailed the team's progress and performance. None of them did. Indeed, working through the obstacles made the team stronger.

Endings are also a fact of life for teams. They are one of the most critical obstacles that teams must face in achieving their performance potential. Moreover, specific ending situations can be as different as teams and obstacles. Some endings are planned, others spontaneous; some are abrupt, others drawn out; some are traumatic, others a relief; some perpetuate performance, others erode it. Despite these differences, however, most endings come down to one or two basic kinds of transitions that matter in terms of performance. Either the team must convey a continuing purpose and set of ongoing tasks to another group or team (as is the case with most teams that run, make, or do things), or the team must ensure that its final recommendations are carried out by others who will implement them. In either case, unless the ending is a well-handled transition, valuable performance can be lost.

Most of this chapter addresses what "stuck" teams can do about getting unstuck. The chapter concludes by discussing the specific obstacles of team endings, and how to handle the transition without losing performance momentum.

## DEALING WITH OBSTACLES

The threat posed by any particular obstacle depends as much on the team's readiness and capability as the obstacle itself. The test posed by the first two hubs, for example, might have undone a less resilient team than Intermodal. Yet, while some teams are stronger than others, we believe teams—as a unit of performance—surpass individuals as well as larger organizational groupings in the resourcefulness and flexibility with which they overcome barriers to performance. The ELITE Task Force described in Chapter 4 provides an excellent illustration. Even the most persistent and talented individuals at the *Tallahassee Democrat* could not have consistently outlasted the time pressure, bad communication, and cross-functional mistrust that prevented better advertising customer service. And the more conventional or organizational solution, the creation of the Advertising Customer Service department, actually exacerbated these problems. ELITE, on the other hand, not only dealt with the barriers blocking performance, but thrived on them.

Real teams adapt to challenges remarkably well. Nevertheless, nearly all of us have been on potential teams or pseudo-teams that became stuck instead of energized by obstacles. Sometimes, potential teams never get off to a good start. That might have happened to the Enron Deal-to-Steel Team if Janacek had not brought the two subgroups back together. Other groups, like the Cosmo Products executives, see the value in the team approach, work on establishing a sense of purpose and teamwork, and then stall. And still other times, a team gets through many problems and is performing well when some unexpected event like the reassignment of the leader sends the team on a downward spiral.

We are all familiar with the frustrations associated with stuck teams. They include:

- A loss of energy or enthusiasm ("What a waste of time.")

- A sense of helplessness ("There's nothing anyone can do.")

- A lack of purpose or identity ("We have no clue as to what this is all about.")

- Listless, unconstructive, and one-sided discussions without candor ("Nobody wants to talk about what's really going on.")

- Meetings in which the agenda is more important than the outcome ("It's all show-and-tell for the boss.")

- Cynicism and mistrust ("I knew this teamwork stuff was a load of crap.")

- Interpersonal attacks made behind people's backs and to outsiders ("Dave has never pulled his own weight and never will.")

- Lots of finger pointing at top management and the rest of the organization ("If this effort's so important, why don't they give us more resources?")

In the worst cases, stuck groups stop trying for team performance altogether and become pseudo-teams. The costs are high. Not only is the specific team performance opportunity lost, but such episodes demoralize people, resulting in much of the reluctance people have regarding the team approach in general.

There is no way to completely avoid stuck teams—obstacles really are a fact of life for teams and sometimes they will be insurmountable. Indeed, unless a team's own purpose and performance goals present a significant challenge, there may not be a foundation for a real team effort. Even team-friendly environments include barriers that can, at times, cause teams to get stuck and self-destruct. Finally, all potential teams have hierarchical, functional, and individual differences that are at once a source of strength and a source of problems.

The good news is that potential and even pseudo-teams can get unstuck as long as they address barriers that relate to their specific performance challenge. In fact, teams can make no greater mistake than to try to solve problems without relating them to performance. Broken interpersonal dynamics, for example, often trouble stuck teams. Clearly, it is a mistake to ignore such issues altogether. But it is also a mistake to try to get people to "work together better" as an end in itself. Instead, the parties involved must identify specific actions they can take together that will require them to "get along" in order to advance performance. Otherwise, the values associated with teamwork or getting along just will not stick for very long.

By now the critical link to performance may seem obvious, but many business managers behave otherwise. For example, typical responses to stuck teams include replacing the leader, changing one or more team members, disbanding the team altogether, or helping clear the air with team building, training exercises, or a facilitator. More often than not, how any of these steps relate to team performance is left unstated. Management assumes, for example, that a new leader or new member—by reason of individual perseverance or skill alone—will make the critical difference to performance and get the team back on the right track. And they treat team building, training, and facilitation the same way. No one helps the team focus on the real performance results of getting unstalled. Even worse, no one asks the new leader, new member, facilitator, or trainer how he or she plans to help the team refocus on the team basics.

More disciplined attention to performance makes these typical approaches more effective. It also makes people within the team as well as management beyond the team try some things they might otherwise overlook. Consider, for example, the apocryphal story of a sailboat adrift at sea. An unexpected squall has damaged the rudder, compass, and mainsail. The crew members have not seen land since leaving port several days earlier and are running low on food and fresh water. Tensions are high; everyone has grown acutely aware and resentful of the weaknesses of the other people on the boat.

At their darkest moment, someone suggests switching their attention away from reaching land, which appears beyond the realm of possibility, to the more realistic goal of trying to fix one or more of the broken parts of the boat. One crew member asks another to help him try an old trick from his youth that he thinks might put the rudder back in service. Working together, the two of them succeed. Encouraged, two other crew members decide to use material from the jib to repair the mainsail, while a third tackles the broken compass and comes up with a juryrigged solution. These small victories do not get the boat any closer to land. But they do make the boat *and the crew* more seaworthy than before. Within half a day, the crew sets off in what they think is the direction of a nearby island. Sure enough, they make it, and from there are eventually rescued by a passing boat.

None of the traditional methods for helping a stuck team was available to this crew. They could not change their membership or seek outside facilitation or training. The story is fictional. Nonetheless, it characterizes the real situation of many stuck teams in business situations. Eventually a new leader or member might get inserted. But in most companies most of the time, stuck teams are left alone, adrift in the organization. They have to figure out how to help themselves. Even when a new leader or member does get added, the team still must figure out how to help itself. Such changes only delay questions of why and how the newly configured team is going to succeed. And that can only be answered when the team turns its attention to the basic elements of team performance—purpose, working approach, and, especially, immediate performance goals.

## A TALE OF TWO TEAMS

To illustrate the dynamics of stuck teams, we will contrast the progress of two different new-product development efforts at a company we call "Metronome Inc.," a semiconductor manufacturer in the United States. The company has a strong performance orientation and is led by a chairman who outspokenly advocates new organizational approaches and thinking. By most standards, Metronome has a team-friendly environment.

Metronome routinely uses teams to develop new products, that is, finding new applications for microchips. Of the two teams we describe, one wanted to develop a microchip for computer disk drive technology and the other a chip for fiber optic cable connections.

Like all potential teams, these two faced the usual task of getting the team basics in place. In addition, Metronome's unique culture, organization, and business posed significant obstacles for these teams to deal with:

- **The culture tolerates failures.** Like many other technology companies, product failures are treated as learning opportunities at Metronome. This approach, however, has a double edge. By reducing the fear that failure will have adverse career consequences, the company encourages risk taking. On the other hand, it also potentially sacrifices the healthy fear of failure that can motivate teams to higher levels of performance. Both the disk drive and the fiber optics teams could have fallen in the trap of acting as if their success or failure would have no meaningful consequences, either for themselves as individuals, together as a team, or for Metronome itself.

- **Metronome depends both on design engineers and product engineers.** Design engineers create the designs on which new products depend. Product engineers determine how to convert those designs into products that work. Most design engineers differ in skills, attitude, and ambition from most product engineers. To overstate the distinction, design engineers thrive on coming up with new ideas while product engineers get excited about wrestling with theoretical ideas and making them work within the constraints imposed by production technology and economics. Sometimes design engineers and product engineers treat each other with respect; other times, they show a real lack of appreciation for each other's problems and skills. Both the disk drive and the fiber optics teams required the contribution of design and product engineers; both could easily have become stuck by a lack of cooperation between them.

- **Marketplace requirements for microchips are very demanding.** It is challenging to create new chips that are both workable enough to meet existing customer needs while advanced enough to meet anticipated customer needs and competitor challenges. Each Metronome team faced the difficult choice between entering the market earlier with less-advanced functionality or postponing market entry in favor of more sophisticated development. Each team depended heavily on the joint contributions of design engineers, product engineers, marketers, and general management to resolve this dilemma.

How did the disk drive and fiber optics teams handle these and other obstacles? In the words of Mark Voorhees, who helped us research this book, the two teams are "in the same company, but seem like they're on different planets."

The disk drive group is a real team. It shares a common purpose of using its first generation "new chip" to secure a position in the disk drive market and then developing a subsequent generation to achieve profitability. The team believes its success is essential to Metronome's success. So does Metronome's chairman, who closely monitors the team's progress. The disk drive team's first chip release failed, and it badly wants to learn from the failure in order to avoid another one. The team's focus, said the team leader, is not on "Who screwed up?" but on "Where did we go wrong?"

The team has confidence in its skills and approach. "We just happen to have the best design people and the best marketing people right here," claims one engineer. Design and product engineers work closely to make sure no one drops the ball. "In every interface and every boundary," says one, "there is a gray zone and a potential crack. We're trying to make sure we overlap and not have any cracks." Finally, the team has a clear performance focus: it must deliver the new chips to customers by a certain date or lose an entire year before it gets another chance.

All this contributes to the focus, enthusiasm, energy, and commitment of the team. "We are either going to whiff in three, or it is going to be well over the wall," exclaims one team member. "There are not that many products at this company you can have that much excitement with."

In marked contrast, the group working on the fiber optics chip is clearly stuck. It lacks both enthusiasm and energy as well as any clear theme or identity. When asked for the team's purpose, one member replied glibly, "Fiber optics for profit." Nor is there any confidence or sense of fun and reward. When asked how the team was approaching its effort, someone piped up, "We'll drive off any bridge we get to." These cutting one-liners are telling; cynicism has a hold on this team.

Many of the nine members of the fiber optics team are unsure about their roles and contribution. Over the course of their effort, at least four different people have tried to take charge without success. "We still have no leader," said one of the four. Furthermore, Metronome's "failures are okay" culture has stymied the fiber optics team. No sense of urgency, for example, exists either within the team or in the manager overseeing the team. "Our job," said one member, "is to put a sample out in the marketplace and see if anybody bites." Echoed the manager from outside the team, "They're just seeding the market."

Design and product engineers on the fiber optics project routinely bicker, producing tension that is decidedly not constructive. For example, when discussing a proposed variation to an existing chip design, the chief design engineer commented too quickly, "Since it involves almost no new design work, the production challenge is exactly the same as before, only easier." To which one of the product engineers fired back, "Maybe you think it's easier, but the new variation requires a whole new subset of production activities." The happy collaboration of design and product engineers that helps the disk drive team is on the rocks here.

An analysis of the team's troubles reveals they suffer all the major dilemmas of being stuck:

- **A weak sense of direction.** Teams like the fiber optics group lose their way when they pursue inappropriate or ill-defined goals. They also get lost when they assume that everyone on the team understands and agrees on why and how they are working together. It is not that different interpretations by themselves are bad for teams; indeed, when discussed openly, varying perspectives can enrich a team's sense of purpose and approach. But when those differences remain unexpressed and unresolved, they generate confusion about the team's fundamental reason for being and undercut the incentive to work together to achieve common goals.

The fiber optics team's goal could range from a long-term, noble purpose of changing the face of an entire industry to a commitment to meet the narrowly defined needs of specific customers in the near term. Either could sustain team performance; but, the team must choose one, or else individuals will continue pursuing separate objectives. The chief design engineer, for example, holds fast to the longer-term vision while the lead product engineer worries more about nearer-term goals and, even then, has a confusing set of three different product releases to handle at the same time. All of this confusion and ambiguity about the basic purpose of the team pulls it apart.

- **Insufficient or unequal commitment to team performance.** On stuck teams, interpersonal conflicts and entrenched positions often get interpreted as a lack of commitment on the part of one or more individuals to work as a team. The team gets diverted from its performance goals and falls into endless side-bar conversations, out of earshot of the full team, about personal styles and biases. This, in turn, further weakens the trust and respect so critical to the mutual accountability and commitment required for team performance.

On one hand, each person in the fiber optics team wants the new chip to succeed and is committed to doing his own part to make it happen. But the quality of their commitments are at once too weak and too individual; there is only a superficial commitment, at best, to the team and team performance. Moreover, the perennial conflict between the design and product engineers causes other members to despair. They seem resigned to accepting that "these two guys just won't ever see eye to eye." Consequently, several people feel—and act—like they are just putting in time until their next job. Unless some mutual sense of commitment to team performance develops, individuals will opt for other, more positive experiences.

- **Critical skill gaps.** Skill gaps are an inevitable part of teams. There are few teams we know who have started with every skill completely developed and in place. Yet we also know of no team that succeeds with a significant, unresolved skill deficiency relative to its objectives. Often the most troublesome gaps have to do with technical or functional competencies. But teams also get stuck when they lack the necessary team skills of problem solving, decision making, and interpersonal relations needed for performance.

In terms of technical and functional skills, the fiber optics team includes competent design and product engineers, but has a marketing person who, because he is new to Metronome, has not yet filled the role he needs to play on the team. In addition, the team has clear gaps in the decision-making skills needed to define a team purpose and set of performance goals. Finally, a lack of interpersonal skills exacerbates the barriers that separate the design and product engineers.

- **External confusion, hostility, or indifference.** All organizations, whether friendly or hostile to teams, inevitably create some obstacles for them. Some might confuse the team with contradictory or overly ambitious sets of demands. Others might overtly or covertly fight the team. Still others might seemingly care less about what the team does or whether or not it succeeds. Sometimes, of course, a we/they atmosphere can energize a team. But it can also prevent a potential team from ever getting off the ground, or wear out the team once it does.

  Unlike the disk drive team that knows Metronome's chairman monitors its progress, the fiber optics team has yet to see any signal from more senior management that its performance matters. In particular, senior management has provided little guidance on how to balance the long-term versus short-term opportunities in fiber optics. The key manager overlooking it, in fact, does understand the team is stuck. But he feels no urgency to do anything about it. Moreover, he thinks the team's difficulties stem from career indecision on the part of the design engineer who is the product inventor and the natural team leader. Yet, this manager seems content to let the team flounder while the design engineer figures out his career path.

- **Leadership in need of help.** This is perhaps just a special category of skill gap. Most people can learn to be effective team leaders.

But, like teams themselves, team leaders most often begin their roles without all the needed skills in place. When team leaders themselves need help, it falls to other members to fill the gap until the leader's skills develop.

At various times, the fiber optics team had possible leader candidates, for example, the design engineer who invented the product, the production engineer who oversaw the first release, the marketing manager, and another, more seasoned product engineering supervisor. Each could have asserted leadership over the fiber optics team. But none of them fully succeeded, and no single or cohesive collective leadership has emerged. As a result, the efforts of the team remain largely uncoordinated. It is no wonder, therefore, that the team cannot figure out how to deal with the many obstacles in its path. It is clearly a stuck team.

## APPROACHES TO GETTING UNSTUCK

What can stuck teams like Metronome's fiber optics group do to get unstuck? And how can higher management help the team? Once again, there is no magic formula to fit all occasions. Sometimes, in fact, the best thing to do is abandon the team approach. The ComTech Cellular executives we described in Chapter 5, for example, probably will experience continued frustration in pursuing a team approach; they may be much better off following a working group approach.

Assuming, however, that the team approach really is the best option, the key to getting unstuck lies in addressing the particular obstacles confronting the team with a strong performance focus. We have seen five approaches work well, often in some combination. The first two, revisiting team basics and going for small wins, address performance directly. The other three— exposing the team to new information and different approaches, seeking outside counsel or training, and reforming the team— provide indirect spurs that, when successful, trigger a renewed team focus on performance. Each of these lies within the team's own grasp to try; or, each can also be introduced by higher management.

**1. Revisit the basics.** One of the primary messages of our book is that no team can rethink its purpose, approach, and performance goals too many times. All teams—and certainly, stuck teams—benefit from going back to ground zero and spending the time to uncover all hidden assumptions and differences of opinion that, when assessed by the full team, might provide the foundation for clarifying the team's mission and how to accomplish it.

For example, the team of executives charged in the mid-70s with turning the wreckage of seven bankrupt East Coast railroads into a profitable enterprise called Conrail remained stymied until it reshaped its purpose from developing a strategy for profitability to working aggressively to deregulate the entire railroad industry. Similarly, a Motorola team we describe later in Chapter 9 had trouble getting beyond a focus on teamwork until, after revisiting its approach, it decided to modify the roles of key players in the team.

Metronome's fiber optics team simply has no clear purpose or common goals. It needs a zero-based discussion of purpose, goals and approach—something it might do by evaluating itself, or with help from management or facilitation from beyond the team.

**2. Go for small wins.** Nothing galvanizes a stuck team as well as performance itself. Even the act of setting a clear and specific goal can lift a team out of the morass of interpersonal conflict and despair. Achieving specific goals is even better. Cynics within a stuck group, for example, might find fault with revisiting team purpose and approach as an insincere and fruitless effort to discuss again what has already been discussed too many times before. Specific performance results, however, carry no such handicaps.

But identifying and achieving attainable goals requires a lot of hard work, especially for stuck teams who too often assume they cannot alter their existing list of goals. The fiber optics team, for example, pursues a mix of short- and long-term performance objectives that no two people, let alone all nine, understand and agree with in exactly the same way. Put differently, there are no specific performance goals they "own" as a team. To address that deficiency, they need to challenge their respective performance assumptions, agree on at least one doable goal, and then go after it.

The effect of redefining goals can be remarkable. For example, another team at Metronome, concerned with on-time deliveries, found itself stuck in a way similar to the fiber optics team. It had originally adopted the inspiring goal of achieving "zero missed deliveries," a great-sounding objective but one that proved too elusive. A year into the project, the on-time group found itself stuck and frustrated. But in its case, the leader suggested that the team alter the goal to "cutting missed deliveries by half" every twelve months. Within a brief period, the team was making measurable—and positively reinforcing—progress toward better performance.

**3. Inject new information and approaches.** Fresh facts, different perspectives, and new information play a major role in the development of teams. The twelve-wall-long paper trail of the fouled-up Table Top project sparked performance in the Enron Deal-to-Steel Team, just as the highly symbolic "rat tracks fax" did for ELITE. One of the things that helped the New York City Partnership shape its purpose was learning about business groups in ten other cities.

Competitive benchmarks, internal case histories, best practices, front-line work measures, customer interviews—these and other sources of insight can provide stuck teams with the fresh perspective needed to reshape their purpose, approach, and performance goals. The fiber optics team, for example, could seek out other teams inside Metronome who have become stuck and find out what they did to get mobilized. This might lead it to learn from the on-time delivery team just described. To do so, however, any frustrated team has to muster the will to seek out such information as opposed to continuing to stall in relative inactivity. And the team must also have the discipline to put whatever information and fresh facts it discovers to good use by asking the all-important question: "So what does this mean for our team's purpose and performance challenge and how we need to tackle it?" Management, of course, can help provide this kind of input.

**4. Take advantage of facilitators or training.** Whether they are complete outsiders or company employees outside the team itself, facilitators can get stuck teams moving in a constructive direction. Usually, successful facilitators bring problem-solving, communication, interpersonal, and teamwork skills to teams who lack them. The ultimate key, however, to whether a facilitator provides enduring help depends entirely on how effectively the facilitator's efforts help the team turn its collective attention back to its purpose and performance challenge. Facilitators who only address personal feelings and interpersonal conflicts, for example, often divert the team's attention from more basic needs.

The same lesson applies to training. Stuck teams, like any potential team, can benefit from any good training program that highlights the importance of key skills, common team purposes, good teamwork, clear goals, and the role of the leader. But unless the team immediately translates this new awareness into "trial" actions, it will return to its real task with nothing to show other than, probably, an increase in cynicism and despair. To avoid this pattern of awareness without trial, some companies like Motorola have instituted a just-in-time training curriculum and resources upon which both groups and individuals can call to help them solve issues exactly when those issues arise.

**5. Change the team's membership, including the leader.** Many teams avoid getting or staying stuck by changing their own membership. Sometimes this occurs when teams literally separate or add members, as happened when the Rapid Response Team separated Paul David and added Nancy Taubenslag. In other cases, like Enron's Deal-to-Steel effort, teams just circumvent stragglers without actually excluding them formally. Some teams actually set rules of membership that require periodic rotation of members to insure fresh input and vitality over time.

Teams, left to themselves, do not change their leaders as often as they change their membership. Rather, new leaders usually get inserted by higher management. The key to whether a new leader, like a new member, will help the team get unstuck lies in whether such moves enable the team to circumvent the obstacles blocking team performance. In other words, new leaders are not panaceas—they only raise the question of what the new leader and the rest of the stuck team are going to do differently now to get themselves moving again. Metronome's fiber optics team actually experienced the "new leader who made no difference" phenomenon when a seasoned product engineer was added to the team and turned out to be no more successful leading it than the design engineer, other product engineer, and marketing professional had been earlier.

Each of the five approaches to unfreezing a team can either spring from the team's own efforts or happen as a result of management intervention. For example, anyone with authority beyond the fiber optics team—from the manager overseeing it all the way to Metronome's chairman—might mandate a clearer charter, specify particular performance goals, expose the fiber optics team to other approaches or fresh facts, provide facilitation or training, or change the leader or otherwise modify the team's membership.

If done well, such intervention can be a boon to a stuck team. For example, when the Garden State Brickface Team held the crew draft (Chapter 3), it effectively intervened to help previously stuck groups of foremen and workers rethink their basic membership and approach in ways that caused many of them to become real teams who cared about job-by-job performance. When the Lake Geneva Team (described in Chapter 11) regularly rotates three of its members each year, it revitalizes the team and injects new information and perspectives.

If done poorly, however, such actions can get interpreted as management intrusions that pose yet one more burden on the team. When management interventions fail, it is often because the managers go for a "quick fix" without thinking carefully enough about the specifics of the stuck team's problems. Management hears that the team has interpersonal conflicts and sends the members to sensitivity training. It assumes the current team leader is at fault and replaces him or her. Or it gets frustrated by poor results and makes additional demands that only cloud, instead of clarify, the group's confusion.

Management must also have a sense of when to intervene. Julie Sackett of Motorola's Government Electronics Group (Chapter 9) argues correctly that it is good for teams to "stay stuck for awhile" because of what they learn through overcoming obstacles on their own, without help from outside. In effect, her comment echoes our own belief that real teams thrive on obstacles. The trick, however, is to distinguish between those teams that are constructively and energetically trying to figure out how to get beyond some barrier to performance and those that either have given up or are in danger of doing so. If a team is really stuck beyond its collective capability, management must intervene.

## HANDLING TRANSITIONS AND ENDINGS

All real teams and high-performance teams inevitably end. It is an obstacle that cannot be avoided, and it does affect the team's performance results. Yet, we met few people who thought carefully about how team endings or transition points relate to performance. Three such points in particular warrant scrutiny: 1) when a task force or special project completes its official charter; 2) when a key person leaves or joins a team; and 3) when a new team leader is appointed. While these are similar in some ways to stuck team situations, we want to address more specifically the effect of such transitions and endings on real teams and high-performance teams. As a result, the question shifts from "How do we get unstuck?" to "How do we maintain performance momentum, either by transitioning our purpose and task to another group or by ensuring implementation of our final recommendations?"

Most teams who recommend things, like task forces and special project teams, are supposed to end. Time extensions may be granted to sharpen or complete recommendations or follow through on implementation, but the normal assumption is that the team will disband once its conclusions are in. This assumption, however, can unnecessarily sacrifice a performance opportunity if, in the course of its project, the task force or special group has become a real team. A comparison of the endings of Deal-to-Steel (Chapter 6) and ELITE (Chapter 4) illustrates this point. By the time their official duties concluded, both were real teams and both wanted badly to play a role in implementation. Fred Mott of the *Tallahassee Democrat* took full advantage of this; Ron Burns of Enron did not. Burns strongly favored giving implementation responsibility to the marketing company presidents, which, by itself, made a lot of sense. Nevertheless, we argue that he unnecessarily overlooked a chance to further exploit a real team whose purpose and performance goals matched his own. Certainly, keeping a task force going beyond its charter requires trade-offs; the individuals involved, after all, do have other jobs and people who depend on them. But more often than not, once a real team exists, disbanding it sacrifices performance potential.

Theoretically, any time the membership of a team changes, the team itself has ended. In fact, this is not always the case; some real teams absorb new members and move on without a hitch. Many teams, however, fail to think carefully about the transition caused by a change in membership—an interesting oversight given how regularly such changes occur in teams who run things and teams who make or do things. The challenge is to initiate the new member into the team without, on the one hand, sacrificing the pace and focus of team performance and, on the other, losing the chance to learn from the new member's fresh perspective. New members pose a two-sided challenge: the team must welcome the fresh perspective, and the entrant must earn his or her position on the team. When successful, the team's purpose, goals, and approach might change, but the new member will come to understand and own them regardless. When unsuccessful, the team's direction *never* changes, and the new person remains an unintegrated outsider.

The dilemma of a new person is a curious one. He or she faces all the risks involving conflict, trust, and hard work necessary to shape a common purpose, goals, and approach to which he or she, like the others, is mutually accountable. The rest of the team, on the other hand, has already taken the risks and, consequently, may question the need for doing so again. "Why reinvent the wheel?" and "Why do we have to go through this again?" are natural questions on the minds of team members who admit new people into their ranks. Yet, if the team does not allow the new person the solution space to challenge and to share risks, it is, in effect, excluding the person from the team and losing a performance opportunity as well. Avoiding such outcomes depends on paying careful attention to balancing the needs of the new person, the needs of the team, and the demands of performance.

The most critical transition for a real team or a high-performance team is when a new leader, especially one from outside the team, gets appointed. Though not previously noted, the Burlington Northern Intermodal Team actually survived the departure of two of its members as well as the addition of one member. But the team reverted to a normal working group when, following Bill Greenwood's promotion, a new leader not previously part of the team was appointed. As one of the original members put it, "It's hard to stay focused as a team when the new guy has completely different ideas about what he wants to do."

Here again we see the impact on team performance of assumptions and practices emphasizing individual contribution and accountability. Almost always, new leaders want to put their personal stamp on the team. Since they have the formal authority, and are expected to do so, they pose an inevitable threat to the team's purpose, goals, approach, and sense of mutual accountability. There is no easy way to deal with this except to reform the team around a new set of team basics. As we pointed out in Chapter 7, the leader's role—especially how he or she balances action and patience—shifts as the team progresses up the performance curve. Expecting a new leader who is unfamiliar with the team to accept and slide into such arrangements is like expecting a historical event to occur without the preceding history. We suppose it can and does happen, but we found no examples in our research.

Thus, it is more useful to think about the arrival of a new team leader—from beyond the team—as an ending of the team. By doing this, the people involved are far more likely to return to team basics, including the performance-driven choice between team and working group. To people on the team, this may feel like starting over. Unless they do so, however, the odds of continued team performance seem low.

Given the realities associated with new leadership, it seems to us that managers should think far more cautiously than they often do when considering the appointment of a complete outsider. Sometimes, of course, it is inevitable because of other priority needs. Certainly, if the team in question has lost its performance zeal and impact, such appointments are worthwhile. But we are not discussing that case. Rather, we are suggesting that, when a real team or high-performance team is in full gear, a change in formal leadership ought to favor insiders. Furthermore, if there is no other choice than to appoint an outsider, then management beyond the team, the departing leader, the new leader, and the full team ought to discuss—as explicitly as possible—the implications of that move for performance.

## CONCLUSION

Teams must deal effectively with both obstacles and endings to realize their full performance potential. Each time a potential team overcomes an obstacle, it strengthens itself as a team. It develops confidence in itself as a team, learns how to work more effectively together, and builds individual and collective skills in the process. Unfortunately, almost every potential team encounters one or more obstacles that appear to be insurmountable. The result can be what we have called a stuck team. And while it is constructive for any potential team to struggle with being stuck, it can also be discouraging and, in time, demoralizing to the point of destroying the team. In this chapter we have tried to point out what teams can do to get themselves unstuck, and what higher management can do to help stuck teams.

Real teams always outperform similar groups of individuals acting alone or even as an effective working group. But it is also true that an effective working group always outperforms a pseudo-team. Thus, the risk that potential teams take in pursuing real team performance lies in getting so stuck that they become permanent pseudo-teams. To a large degree, that risk depends on how well the potential team handles the inevitable obstacles found in its path.

When teams do get stuck, the perils they face deepen and become increasingly troubling. At the beginning of a potential team effort, the people involved must find a way through conflict, hard work, and action to build a common direction and approach built on mutual trust and accountability. By comparison, once a potential or pseudo-team is really stuck, and especially when negative interpersonal tensions have crept in, people look more warily on moving forward as a team. Revisiting team basics and building trust get more difficult because many individuals believe they have already tried to do those things and have come up short.

In addition, by the time a team gets stuck, it usually faces many obstacles at once, such as a lost sense of direction, critical skill gaps, and insufficient commitment, as well as external confusion, hostility, or indifference. To figure out what needs to happen, it needs to disaggregate these issues. But to move forward toward performance, it probably cannot deal with the issues one at a time. Instead, it must *simultaneously* strengthen its sense of direction and commitment, fill skill gaps, and respond to external pressures. The best way we know for doing that is through concentrating—as a team—on performance.

Real and high-performance teams usually deal with obstacles well enough to avoid demoralizing stuck situations. Such teams, however, cannot avoid the inevitable obstacle of the team ending. Nevertheless, too many teams take such endings, whether planned or not, for granted. As a result, significant performance potential gets lost, either because a successor group loses momentum or fails to really accept the final recommendations of the team with enough enthusiasm and understanding to implement them. More often than not, such transitions could benefit greatly from a conscious assist from higher-level management. Again, such efforts must focus on performance.

If the most practical thing a stuck or ending team can do is acknowledge the reality of using a hierarchical working group, its members ought to do so. That way they will at least improve their individual performances because they will not waste valuable time on counterproductive team efforts. If, on the other hand, they aspire to, or require, team performance, then notwithstanding all the tough obstacles and resistance, they must find a way to move forward as a team. The choice here can be rough. Listen, for example, to one person we met who found himself in the middle of an interpersonal dilemma hindering a very stuck team:

> If you're not getting along with someone, it's a lot easier just to not do anything else about it as far as the next day is concerned. If you don't do anything about it, it doesn't hurt so bad today. But two months down the road you're going to be much worse off than if you just suck it up and deal with it right up front. It's more painful right then, but it's a lot less painful in the long run.

The good news is that being stuck—and even team endings—can serve invaluable purposes for teams. Being stuck forces the members to rethink team basics, build confidence in and commitment to one another, and develop a renewed source of energy by "overcoming" and moving on. Team endings can lead to purposes being reshaped, performance goals being extended, and new skills and perspectives being introduced. While valuable momentum and continuity can be lost, the long-term benefits will outweigh the short-term losses so long as the focus on performance prevails.

# PART THREE

# Exploiting
# the Potential

Figure III-1

# THE HIGH-PERFORMING ORGANIZATION

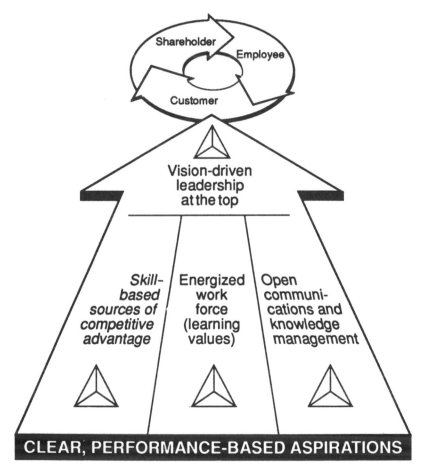

## PERFORMANCE RESULTS

TEAMS will be the primary building blocks of company performance in the organization of the future (see Figure III-1). Such organizations will not promote teams for their own sake. Rather, the performance ethic of the company—that is, the focus on balanced results that benefit customers, employees, shareholders, and other key constituencies—will generate the challenges that give rise to teams. Teams, in turn, will deliver performance that enriches and sustains the company's overall performance ethic. This reinforcing cycle of performance and teams, teams and performance, will characterize tomorrow's winners.

To build such strengths, many companies must manage themselves through a period of major change that depends on people throughout the company becoming very good at things they are not good at today. Teams will help direct, energize, and integrate such broad-based changes in behavior. They will set performance aspirations, intensify focus and commitment, energize work forces, build core skills, and spread knowledge to those who need it the most to perform.

Often, though not always, such transformations will be led by a team at the top. Building team performance at the top, however, is more difficult than anywhere else. Senior management groups find it hard to establish a *team* purpose, goals, and work-products for which they can hold themselves accountable as a team. Absent these, such groups ought to exploit the working group option. Nothing is more corrosive to a company's performance ethic than a pseudo-team at the top.

The primary role of top management is to focus on performance and the teams that will deliver it. Top leaders increasingly recognize that teams improve individual performance, energize hierarchy and structure, and enhance basic management processes. By finding the teams that matter, and then supporting them as they reach for performance, top managements can help spawn the teams that will help lead their companies to high performance. The wisdom of teams lies *not* in encouraging teams for their own sake, but rather in helping those on potential teams have the chance to pursue their own performance challenges.

# CHAPTER NINE

# Teams and Performance: The Reinforcing Cycle

$S$IGNIFICANT performance challenges do more than anything else to foster teams. The issue is not whether such challenges exist; every organization faces them. Indeed, as phenomena like customer service, total quality, and continuous improvement and innovation become more important in sustaining competitive advantage, the kind of performance challenges that produce teams multiply. From a total-organization perspective, the more critical question is whether established managerial values and behaviors—or what we call the company's "performance ethic"—helps or harms the team-inducing effect of performance challenges.

We have observed a mutually reinforcing relationship between the strength of a company's performance ethic and the number and performance of teams. Companies that have powerful performance ethics create and pursue the performance challenges that favor teams. Those teams, in turn, deliver results that help sustain the overall performance ethic.

The converse of this cycle also happens. Companies with weak performance ethics obscure or even destroy team performance opportunities. Significant performance challenges get lost in the managerial shuffle of turf, politics, the not invented here syndrome, and business as usual. Potential teams are less likely to move up the team performance curve and more likely to become pseudo-teams. The lost team performance opportunities, in turn, further weaken the overall performance ethic of the company. The more visible such team performance failures, the more cynical people become. This is what happened at Cosmo Products after the group at the top tried to become a team and failed.

What do we mean by strong performance ethic? Simply stated, we mean that everyone in the company relentlessly pursues common performance results. It also means they seek results that benefit at least three groups: customers, employees, and shareholders. When this happens, there is an organizationwide commitment to performance that inspires meaning well beyond economics. People—not everyone, but certainly a critical mass—are proud to be a part of such companies. Hewlett-Packard employees, for example, are strongly performance-oriented. They also take more pride in "earning the loyalty and respect of our customers" than they do in the financial earnings of the company, but both matter to them. In their book *Corporate Culture and Performance,* John Kotter and James Heskett also emphasize how the culture of the best companies, including Hewlett-Packard's, relates performance to all three constituencies. Our balanced performance ethic is a similar idea.

To sustain this kind of balanced performance, such organizations 1) deliver superior value to their customers, which in turn generates both 2) attractive returns for the company's owners and 3) personal growth opportunities and attractive earnings for employees who, of course, are responsible for delivering superior value to customers. Figure 9-1 is a simple conceptual illustration of how the three basic elements of performance interact for every company. When other stakeholders exist (suppliers, regulators, communities, and so forth), they too get blended into this balanced approach to performance. For example, companies like Motorola that depend upon critical suppliers to help them deliver value to customers provide those suppliers opportunities for growth and earnings based on the quality of their contributions. It is actually viewed as an honor to be an approved Motorola supplier.

Striking the right balance among these constituencies differs both from company to company as well as over time in any single company. The performance balance for an investment bank like J.P. Morgan would differ from that for Disney or Chrysler or Exxon.

Figure 9-1

# DIMENSIONS OF A BALANCED
# PERFORMANCE ETHIC

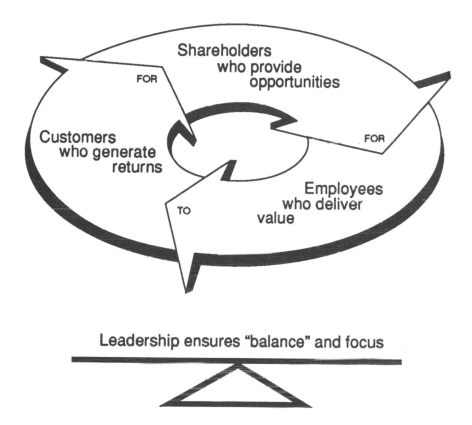

Moreover, the right balance for Exxon following its Alaskan oil spill probably would differ from the appropriate balance five or ten years later. The critical point, however, is that balanced performance results require specific attention to each of the key stakeholder constituencies that determine an organization's success over time.

Companies often place disproportionate emphasis on one element of the three. We believe such an imbalance over time will ultimately distort the basic performance ethic of the company. In the 1970s and 1980s, for example, many companies overlooked a concern for other stakeholders in favor of concentrating on shareholder value and strictly financial measures of return and performance. In theory, of course, shareholder value and financial results can reflect a concern for customers and contributions from employees, suppliers, and others. In practice, however, the narrow focus on financial performance too often sacrificed or squeezed out an accompanying and badly needed orientation toward customers and employees, with unfortunate results.

In recent years, companies have begun to swing away from shareholder value toward a concern for the customer. While this may ultimately create a sounder performance orientation than focusing on financial measures alone, we still believe that overemphasizing any single constituency will throw a company's performance ethic and long-term results out of balance. Over time, managerial choices that are based *only* on shareholder value or employee morale or even customer service will become unsound. Eventually, the ignored constituencies will notice and speak out. When they do, managers obsessed with a single constituency (e.g., shareholder value) find it difficult to understand the concerns raised. When this happens, managers tend to revert to behaviors based on the divine right of their positions. This, in turn, creates distortions. Turf and politics take over.

Potential teams suffer in such an environment for several reasons. To begin with, a fewer number of specific performance challenges are created. Second, when important performance opportunities do arise, they are assigned to existing organizational units that reflect the roles of individuals and larger organizational groupings rather than teams. Third, the challenges themselves—purpose, goals, expectations—suffer from a lack of clarity. Fourth, the necessary team-performance risks associated with conflict, trust, interdependence, and hard work are less likely to be taken. Finally, people are more inclined to avoid being personally disappointed by "giving it their best" only to see managerial actions beyond their control distort the outcomes of their efforts.

Of course, it is possible for potential teams in such companies to overcome these obstacles. The Burlington Northern Intermodal Team was an excellent example of a team that emerged within an organization that, at the time, had a modest performance ethic. Conversely, it is also true that potential teams in companies with a strong performance ethic can fail to move up the curve if they do not pay attention to team basics in a disciplined way. Ultimately, regardless of the strength of a company's performance ethic, the people on the team are responsible for their team's results. But the clarity of the performance challenge, the number and difficulty of the obstacles, and the confidence, readiness, and skills of the people involved will more likely favor real team performance inside companies with strong performance ethics versus those with weak ones.

The examples in this chapter illustrate the relationship between a company's performance ethic and team performance. The first illustration from Hewlett-Packard is a classic example of a company with an ingrained performance ethic that stimulates real team formation without extensive team-building efforts, or even a management that thinks about teams per se. The second story, about the Motorola Connectors Team, shows how the decisions, actions, and events that mark any group's evolution from potential team to team will more likely occur inside a strong performance-oriented company. Finally, the third example, from a disguised company we will call "Brandywine," describes the corrosive effect on individuals and teams of a weak performance ethic.

# HEWLETT-PACKARD

Most of us know the history of Hewlett-Packard, one of the unique entrepreneurial accomplishments of our time. Moreover, HP was created by one of the most famous "teams at the top" in U. S. corporate history. Indeed, David Packard and William Hewlett created more than a series of electronic instruments. They also built a performance culture devoted to delivering quality service to customers, attractive returns to investors, and unique job satisfaction to employees. HP's culture is an often-cited model of customer service and employee values that extends well beyond the electronics industry. It also spawns lots of teams. Paradoxically, HP is now run by a very effective working group at the top that is not a team by our definition. Thus it provides not only a compelling illustration of how a strong focus on performance results and teams go together, but also how effective top leadership groups who are *not* teams can still sustain an environment that generates and is enhanced by real teams.

Packard and Hewlett did not set out to become a team; they wanted to build a business. Yet in order to achieve their purpose, they certainly became a team and also fostered an extended team all around them. Dick Alberting, recently retired executive vice president of marketing and international fondly remembers the formative years in the 1950s when the entire organization "worked as a team with a spirit of teamwork and collaboration" that infected everyone. Obviously, HP was driven at the time by David Packard and Bill Hewlett's unique vision, strong performance values, and their team approach at the top.

Dick realizes that the current size and diversity of today's organization cannot be expected to operate in the same unified way it did in "those days." Yet, the company's balanced performance ethic continues to foster teams. Moreover, it does so despite the fact that the heritage, policies, and managing process at HP do not emphasize teams per se. The company, for example, stresses the importance of individual opportunity and accountability. In fact, when we first spoke with Dean Morton, executive vice president and chief operating officer of Hewlett-Packard, about our interest in teams he looked puzzled: "We don't really think that much about teams here—I'm not sure we have that many that would be of interest to you."

As we explored further, it became clear that HP has dozens of teams, but they do not often think about themselves as teams. In Dean's mind, initially at least, the term implied either a special project task force, or a cross-functional staff team. He was not thinking about teams that run things. The more we talked, however, the more apparent it became that teams were actually an integral part of the normal managing process at HP.

Over the years, for example, many of the small groups of people charged with exploiting business opportunities have become teams that run things. As we talked with Dean Morton and others about these, we saw a pattern that revealed the team-inducing impact of their balanced performance ethic. When the company identifies new opportunities, it emphasizes the performance challenge as potentially beneficial to customers, employees, and shareholders—or what one executive called "an almost religious interest in achieving legitimate operating earnings."

HP's approach is to clearly identify an important business opportunity and the performance challenge it represents, and assign the best possible mix of people to exploit it. *Competence, experience, and potential are the primary group membership criteria. Commitment to fully exploiting the opportunity is expected, not merely hoped for.* Team leadership and team-building skills are assumed, and the group is expected to figure out how to get the job done. So, as a result of "working it out," real teams often appear. In fact, Dean often prefaced a team description with a comment like:

> This was in fact a rather unlikely team, because the characteristics of the leader and many of the other members would lead you to believe they would never form into a team—yet somehow it all came together.

Invariably, the groups Dean described had become so focused on their purpose and business challenge, and so committed to their ambitious performance goals, that they would fall into real or high-performance team behavior patterns without really thinking about it. As Lew Platt, current CEO, later observed, "Crappy performance is one of those things that can help you build a team pretty fast." A couple of specific examples illustrate this pattern.

In 1969, Dean Morton was named general manager of HP's then Medical Equipment Division. HP's top management believed that the burgeoning medical products market was an ideal growth opportunity for HP, and they challenged Dean to exploit it. He selected a group of able up-and-comers with the right mix of skills to pursue the opportunity. This core team eventually came to include Morton, Lew Platt, Burt Dole, Stan McCarthy, Bob Hungate, and Ben Holmes. Morton actually thinks of the team as also including many others. As we probed further, however, it became clear that a smaller group was the real core team, with others contributing significantly but in an extended team mode.

Early on, Morton proposed a different and risky new vision that his team adopted: to concentrate solely on exploiting the medical instruments opportunity in the emerging patient-monitoring business, and to get out of the one business that was profitable at the time. This was not an easy decision, but top management was completely supportive of the team's new focus, although not without subtly re-emphasizing the basics of performance on which HP was built. As Dean recalls, even in the early years: "We had a lot of pressure from Palo Alto. The pressure was never direct—I didn't get memos saying you'd better straighten up. But the pressure was clearly felt." In other words, top management was supportive of the team's new purpose and goals, but never let up on their performance ethic.

Like most real teams, this one took shape over time and had to overcome numerous obstacles in the process. One of the most significant in Dean's mind is captured in a description that appeared in an HP publication excerpted below:

> The pace was hectic and it seemed like everybody was stretched beyond his limit. It was then that we encountered the famous "dry film" problem. A vendor had delivered defective P.C. board coating material . . . that found its way into most of our current production and . . . shipments. After assessing the potential impact on safety, we decided we should recall all the defective products from the field and rework everything currently in production. We estimated it would take several months to recover from this disaster. . . . A team of engineers, manufacturing, and product assurance professionals . . . was assembled under the able leadership of Joe Simone . . . in three weeks we accomplished what should have taken as much as three months. The dedication and teamwork of people from all areas of the Division, working side by side, bailed us out of a problem *which would have destroyed many organizations.* This was perhaps our finest hour during my five years as . . . general manager.

This is also typical of HP's team experiences over the years; they are all driven by performance challenges. It is important to note, however, that it was not just the financial performance standards that motivated this team. It also found real meaning in the medical products business. "It's really a neat business," Lew Platt says. "You get involved in electronics, and do good at the same time."

It is neither surprising nor coincidental that Platt went on to form a team of his own at the analytical products group. In his view, this team was "even more of a high-performing team." Morton had been promoted to running several business units, one of them the analytical products group. Unhappy with the unit's performance, Morton moved Platt in as leader. Platt claims he knew little or nothing about the business (which makes highly specialized measuring devices for chemical research laboratories), and neither did a couple of his top lieutenants. What was even more troubling, in Lew's mind, was the fact that the chemical industry was about to plunge into a depression.

In typical HP fashion, however, Platt formed a team that included division managers who did know the business and had the complementary skills necessary to make a real team work. Despite very different personalities and styles, there was a strong sense of dedication that permeated the group, which, judged by its results as well as Platt's belief, soon became a high-performance team. It converted analytical products into HP's highest-margin business. In the process it also spawned several other teams within the division that achieved minor miracles. One team, for example, took a design for a tabletop spectrometer that was written on a napkin and created a marketable unit within the remarkably short time of six months. The unit was much smaller and less expensive than anything "the world had ever seen," says Platt.

But this is all business as usual at Hewlett-Packard. Nobody thinks of such episodes as primarily team efforts until confronted with our definition. They each came about because of HP's performance ethic, management philosophy, and a significant performance challenge. Of course, there are also examples in the company where performance teams did not happen, or where they were unnecessarily delayed. Nevertheless, HP provides an excellent picture of the natural team-inducing effect that specific performance challenges can have on the groups that pursue them within a company whose performance ethic is both balanced and strong.

In our next example, the Connectors Team at Motorola, we explore the nature of this relationship more closely. Again, the point we wish to emphasize is why teams are more likely to form in companies with strong performance ethics. Certainly, no performance ethic or culture, no matter how strong or well-balanced, will guarantee team formation; that responsibility belongs to the group members themselves. But when performance clearly outweighs anything else in importance, obstacles that in some companies might cripple potential teams actually stimulate them.

## MOTOROLA'S CONNECTORS TEAM

The Connectors Team is part of the basic parts supply activity within Motorola's Government Electronics Group (GEG). Motorola's performance focus is captured on a wallet-sized card carried by its employees that reads:

> "Our Fundamental Objective
> (Everyone's Overriding Responsibility)
> Total Customer Satisfaction."

To achieve "total customer satisfaction," Motorola pays attention to several key constituencies including customers, employees, shareholders, and suppliers. For example, the company's key goals include increased market share, superior financial results, and best in class in people. To most people at Motorola, the company's mission—"to be the premier corporation in the world"—is as emotionally appealing as it is rational.

Suppliers are also a critical constituency at Motorola. At GEG, for example, materials and supplies account for more than half of the cost of doing business and cut to the heart of its ability to produce hundreds of different kinds of electronic systems and equipment for NASA, the U. S. Department of Defense, and other governmental and commercial customers. In fact, the Connectors Team actually grew out of GEG's effort to partner more effectively with suppliers. In 1989, GEG's leadership team decided to shift supply management from a decentralized, functional organization that depended on the expertise and performance of individuals to a centralized, process-oriented organization that depended primarily on teams.

This vision began with a view of supply management as a cross-organizational process that transforms the contributions of suppliers into the satisfaction of customers. The performance goal was to get both external and internal customers the supplies and materials they needed when they needed them at the lowest total cost. To do this,

GEG's leadership team knew it had to move away from an organization emphasizing individual and functional accountability to one that focused on developing teams that began with suppliers and finished with customers.

GEG's formal designation of teams in late 1989 was just that, namely, the creation of organization units that were called "teams" but actually represented only potential teams. According to Susan Harwood, one of the architects of GEG's move to teams, many of these potential teams had become real teams two years after the reorganization. Of these, we think the evolution and performance of the Connectors Team illustrates how a strong performance culture promotes teams.

Like the other potential teams, the Connectors Team was charged with doing the activities necessary to get customers what they needed when they needed it at the lowest total cost. It was also expected to measure itself against five specific criteria: reject rate, number of corrective actions, cycle time, late deliveries, and number of suppliers. When members of the group first got together in January 1990, they agreed on a number of specific performance goals, for example, reducing the percentage of defective components from 3.5 percent to 1 percent by the end of the year.

They also discussed a broad array of subjects, including how to overcome the conflict between the two sets of experts involved in purchasing: engineers and purchasers. Several of the engineers, who were responsible for specifying and inspecting products, believed the purchasers did little more than read catalogues and call suppliers. The purchasers, on the other hand, who ordered and paid for products, thought engineers had tunnel vision and routinely created unnecessary obstacles that prevented efficient purchasing. Not surprisingly, purchasers and engineers differed in their respective views of how best to pursue performance.

This conflict dominated the Connectors Team as it struggled to figure out priorities, how to work together, and how to build confidence as a team. Throughout this period, the team's leader, Sandy Hopkins, kept it focused on improving quality, cycle time, and cost. Significantly, she refused to make all decisions herself, and actively involved others in attacking and resolving problems. She also regularly held team meetings and tried to build camaraderie through pizza lunches, cocktail hours, and parties that included families. She did not, however, focus on team-building exercises per se.

By October, engineers and purchasers were at least working together, and overall performance had improved. Yet, the Connectors Team was still not a real team. It had clear performance goals and had begun to develop common aspirations, particularly around its own empowerment and skill development. But it still had not developed a common team approach or full sense of mutual accountability. Furthermore, discontent was growing due to a gap between talk about empowerment versus the actual nonempowering roles of two key managerial positions: the engineering manager and the purchasing manager. In effect, the members were still feeling each other out to discover how serious everyone was about achieving their joint goals.

To break this logjam, Sandy asked the team to reassess its goals and objectives, decide how the work effort should be organized, and figure out a fair and effective approach to evaluate both team and individual performance. This turned out to be a key event in the group's emergence as a real team. As a result of these discussions and analysis, the team members rededicated themselves to specific performance goals in improving quality, cycle time, and cost. For example, they committed themselves to halving the defective component rate to 0.5 percent by the end of 1991. In addition, however, they also began to articulate among themselves a broader, more meaningful purpose to what they were doing. Said one team member:

> We were the pilot for the team concept in the new supply management organization, and we wanted to achieve results. Other teams at Motorola were production teams and there was a feeling going around that teams wouldn't work in a service area like supply. We had something to prove.

The team made several decisions that solidified its common team approach and sense of mutual accountability. First, it set some rules. Everyone on the team had to identify two others who could serve as backups during vacation periods and sick days. To eradicate the attitude of "it's not my job" from the team, it was agreed that whenever anyone needed help, the person asked had to respond even if the activity was not in his or her area of expertise. And the team also agreed on a peer appraisal system that gave everyone the opportunity to evaluate everyone else and, through Sandy, feed it back to the person being evaluated. Clear-cut rules of behavior like these are an important element of all successful teams.

Second, the team eliminated the two managerial positions that had retarded empowerment. This effectively modified the membership of the team because only one of the two managers whose jobs were eliminated chose to stay. The other believed he could not take a perceived demotion and left. By January 1991, however, the Connectors Team was a dramatically more effective group of people than it had been at its formation a year earlier.

Energy and enthusiasm reached higher levels as the team started pushing itself harder and in more innovative ways. One of the engineers, for example, decided to become completely qualified as a purchaser as well. Instead of being threatened, the purchasers on the team worked hard to teach her the basics of the job. The peer review approach worked so well that the team agreed on the additional—and, for many teams, difficult—step of directly providing each other feedback instead of relying on the team leader for this task.

In a major move, the team challenged a long-standing GEG policy by recommending that suppliers be trusted to do their own inspections. The team argued that both quality and cycle-time would improve dramatically by making suppliers fuller partners in meeting the team's specific performance goals. Management was asked to allow the Connectors Team to qualify certain suppliers for self-inspection. Management said no, that it was too risky. But the team did not give up. It worked hard to address management's concerns, brought the recommendation back for a second hearing, and was rewarded with approval. The fact that the team was able to regroup and overcome the initial defeat added to its growth and level of commitment.

By mid-1991, the Connectors Team had all the earmarks of team performance—tangible results, increasing personal commitment to one another, multiple skill development, dedication to purpose and goals, and shared leadership roles. This outcome, however, was not inevitable; some other GEG potential teams, for example, had not advanced as far as the Connectors Team. Nevertheless, we think the strong performance culture of both Motorola and GEG helped the Connectors Team in a number of specific ways:

**1. Performance comes first at both Motorola and GEG, so the team instinctively set clear performance goals at the beginning and never lost sight of them.** In many organizations, when potential teams first gather, they lack a clear idea about which performance objectives matter the most. This was not so in the Connectors Team. In reorganizing the supply management activity, the GEG leadership team had explicitly specified reject rates, on-time deliveries, number of corrections, cycle-time reduction, and number of suppliers as critical. Each of these, in turn, were reinforced by the overall corporatewide initiatives like "Six Sigma Quality" and "Total Cycle Time Reduction." Accordingly, the Connectors Team was able to quickly move beyond agreeing on common goals to tackling *how* the members would work together to do it.

**2. Motorola and GEG practice values of cooperation and involvement, so the team leader instinctively involved all members in establishing the team's purpose, performance goals, and approach.** Motorola's values reflect a dedication to "constant respect for people," "becoming best in class in people," and "participative management." Moreover, several GEG leaders personified these values through their own actions. The head of GEG, for example, made it clear that he wanted, needed, and expected people throughout the group to help the division become "the best." As a result, Sandy Hopkins had many reassuring role models for sharing solution space with the people who reported to her. She could, with confidence, involve people in decision making.

**3. GEG's own management team had taken a bold step in streamlining the supply management structure, so the team had a precedent when it decided to rid itself of the two managerial positions.** When the GEG leadership team reorganized the supply management function, it reduced the number of levels in the hierarchy from seven to four in order to improve both the speed and effectiveness of decision making. In doing so, it demonstrated that performance, and contribution to performance, were the critical yardsticks by which any managerial position should be evaluated. It also demonstrated a belief that teams were to be *the* basic unit of performance. Accordingly, the Connectors Team had a strong example in its own division when it acted to eliminate managerial positions it believed were retarding team performance.

**4. Motorola encourages open challenges of established policy to achieve performance, so the team was not out of line in questioning GEG's long-standing policy against supplier self-inspections.** GEG's reorganization of the supply management activity explicitly addressed the link between the division's performance and the performance of its suppliers. Indeed, the supply management vision of "transforming the contributions of suppliers into the satisfaction of customers" grew out of a desire to replace adversarial relations between GEG and its suppliers with partner-like relations. Thus, notwithstanding the radicalness of the Connectors Team's recommendation to let suppliers inspect themselves as well as the initial reluctance of GEG leadership, it would have been far more surprising had the leadership rejected this performance-focused initiative rather than accept it as they did.

Of course, each of these separate decisions, approaches, and events that helped to move the Connectors Team from a potential team to a real team could happen in a company with a less robust performance ethic. But they are less likely to happen. Groups are less likely to establish clear performance goals, managers appointed as team leaders are less likely to share decision-making control, teams are less likely to restructure themselves by removing jobs, and established policies on "the way we do things around here" are less likely to get challenged.

In companies where mediocre performance is accepted as reality, potential team opportunities are more likely to generate personal disappointments than performance results, as the following story illustrates. It takes place in a large company that we call "Brandywine," and is recreated through the disguised but very real eyes and experience of "Bill Perkins," one of the highly talented young executives in the company.

# BRANDYWINE

Brandywine Corporation is a basic industrial company with plants, distribution and sales units, and raw material holdings throughout North America. It is in a traditional commodity business in which results depend heavily on plant size, market position, resourcing locations, and operating efficiency. By any measure, it is a tough business.

Like many large companies, Brandywine has a corporate center that oversees its far-flung operations. And, like many others, the "sense and feel" at corporate differs from that of the field. In fact, in Brandywine's case, corporate not only seems like a different company, but has a weak performance ethic that profoundly influences the rest of the organization.

When Bill Perkins, a former plant-level executive, took a job at corporate, he noticed this difference at once. But he only absorbed its full impact over time. Eventually, he became almost totally dispirited. According to Bill:

> Nothing ever changes. I know this group means well, but they always get caught up in the administrative minutia. They are so accustomed to mediocre achievement that company performance doesn't constitute a real issue for them. Every major shortfall gets blamed on "external forces": prices are down—the industry is at overcapacity again—exchange rates are unfavorable—the union is impossible—and on and on.
>
> Charlie (the president) promised me a real job up here. I know he meant it, but every time I try to get onto a critical issue, he tells me to back off. I honestly think he's afraid to try to address these things directly for fear that it won't work out. I guess he's been burned too many times in the past.
>
> I really wish I'd stayed in my old job at the plant. At least that was a real job—and I could make a difference, even if it was only in the results of my little unit. Now it's so frustrating to see us walk away time and time again from our obvious shortfalls. We have become past masters at explaining away performance gaps—as opposed to facing up to what is needed to deliver results that will fill the gaps.

Looked at through Bill's eyes today, Brandywine's leadership group seems resigned to a fate of perpetual mediocrity—a victim of its environment, powerless to do much about it. For the past ten years the company's financial and market results have languished in the bottom quartile of its industry. And that mind-set has poisoned the spirit of people like Bill Perkins.

Before Bill took the corporate job, a series of events presented at least the possibility of a more promising picture. At the time, top management seemed eager to attack the performance problem. It believed the key to Brandywine's performance was in emphasizing the involvement of employees. It created "The Brandywine Code" of how to treat people, which became fundamental scripture for all managers and employees. This led at first to hundreds of "involvement groups" across the company, and later to the development of self-managing worker teams at the plant level. People really felt good about the company; they took real pride in being part of an organization that cared.

In addition to building employee satisfaction, the president and other top executives seemed determined to upgrade the company's financial results and customer position. They declared a renewed dedication to customer service and shareholder returns. Full of confidence, the president asked fifty or so of the company's best managers—not just from corporate, but from all over—to figure out how to restructure Brandywine into the lowest-cost producer in its industry.

This group split into several task forces. They set high goals for themselves, worked long hours, and committed themselves to results. Inspired by the president's visible determination, most of the task forces became real teams dedicated to dramatically improving the company's capabilities. Bill Perkins had been a member of one of the more successful of those efforts, and had been invigorated by the experience. Six months after starting, the task forces produced a series of exciting recommendations that the president accepted and turned over to line management for implementation. But, unfortunately, the handoff was badly fumbled.

For the most part, the line managers did not share the task forces' commitment to performance. Many of them were from the old school, which at Brandywine meant a much weaker performance orientation. They resisted. And while some cost reductions occurred, nearly all other major recommendations were effectively stymied. The president and other top executives certainly were not pleased with the results; but, instead of insisting on implementation, they got distracted by a series of events like industry price reductions and union activities.

When a year passed without further action, people in the company began to wonder whether the president had been serious about cost restructuring and performance. Then, in an unexpected flurry of activity, the president commissioned a new committee to "redesign" the top of the company. In addition to getting the earlier recommendations moving again, the new committee was supposed to figure out how to build teams above the plant level that would complement and enhance the team efforts of the workers themselves. At this same time, the president also asked Bill Perkins to join corporate in a key advisory role reporting directly to him and charged with monitoring the progress of the new committee. Perkins believed that this was an important chance to make a difference.

But the redesign committee accomplished little. Its effort never got beyond informal discussions that, in the private opinions of those on the committee, only endorsed preordained conclusions based more on political than performance rationales. Its failure reinforced skepticism throughout the company. Senior executives continued to act within safe boundaries that would not disturb their individual positions. For line and middle managers, it was business as usual. And, in the worst impact, many of the frontline worker teams fell prey to the performance indifference at the top. Increasingly, many of these teams turned from achieving performance gains to "improving morale and openness."

Many individuals who participated in these efforts were disappointed, but not particularly surprised. They had seen such efforts fail in the past. Bill Perkins, however, and a few of his counterparts across the company were more than disappointed—they felt disenfranchised and abandoned at the height of their commitment to change Brandywine from a mediocre company to a leading competitor.

In summary, the president's attempts to strengthen Brandywine's performance results and capability had the reverse effect. The company remained in the bottom quartile. And, sadly, complacency and cynicism returned with renewed force. Brandywine's weak performance ethic actually destroyed teams. Many potential worker teams became pseudo-teams, no real teams arose above the frontline level, and a weakened achievement ethic ate away at the vitality of the entire organization. The valiant efforts of Bill Perkins and a few others like him meant little other than a reproach to their own personal careers and development goals. In short, those who took the risk suffered—but for reasons not related to performance.

## CONCLUSION

Performance results—that's what teams are all about. When the goals of the team do not define specific results that are important to the overall company's goals, team accomplishments are unlikely to be very powerful. Similarly, performance challenges create real teams. Hence, if a potential team exists in a corporate environment where company goals are unclear or confused, both its challenge and its accomplishments are likely to be severely constrained.

In organizations like Hewlett-Packard and Motorola, a strong performance ethic gives people both the confidence and capability to figure out for themselves the best way to go after specific performance opportunities. Not surprisingly, when those opportunities call for multiple skills and perspectives, people often become real teams. The rigor with which such organizations set and pursue their goals provides fertile ground for the growth of teams, not only by highlighting performance challenges but also by making clear what kind of results teams are expected to produce and by persuading the people on teams that results matter more than politics.

By contrast, potential teams in companies like Brandywine are less certain about, or even indifferent to, performance. They have far more difficulty agreeing on team basics. Even worse, they are far less likely to pursue their tasks with confidence. Instead of looking squarely ahead at a job to get done, potential teams in weak performance cultures tend to look over their shoulders at changes in directions from above, at cynical, uncooperative behavior from other departments or divisions, and at unenthusiastic "it's not my job" attitudes among themselves.

Nonetheless, when teams do emerge in such environments, they have often had to overcome strong obstacles, as in the case of the Burlington Northern Intermodal Team. This tends to make them more resilient, more conspicuous, and even more heroic. As a result, they can have a disproportionately positive influence on the performance ethic and environment for teams that follow them. As a result, teams are among the brightest hopes those organizations have for pulling themselves out of their stagnation. As we will explore more fully in the next chapter, teams play a significant role in bringing about "major change," that is, significant improvements in performance capability that depend on broad-based behavioral change. And since a company's performance ethic is really the summation of its collective managerial values and behaviors, any strengthening of that ethic ultimately depends on behavioral change.

As a result, leaders in companies like Brandywine can often make a major difference in their situation by simply identifying a few key performance challenges and getting potential teams to pursue them. Moreover, in our experience, despite the impact of a weak performance ethic, there always are enough Bill Perkinses around who, if asked, will suspend their disbelief and try again. The opportunity to make a difference does that to people; it keeps them coming back even when experience cautions them to do otherwise. But if the sponsoring leaders do not demand and then relentlessly support a fearless pursuit of performance by the teams involved, the efforts will produce nothing except more cynicism, more frustration, more risk aversion, and more playing it safe. If, on the other hand, even one of these teams succeeds, especially if it is a team that runs something, it can help an indifferent or confused company begin to clarify direction and recover an overall sense of performance.

# CHAPTER TEN

# Teams and Major Change: An Inevitable Combination

NO serious business leader, adviser, or scholar disputes the vital characteristics necessary for high performance in the 1990s and beyond: visionary leadership, empowered work forces, dedication to customers, total quality, continuous improvement and innovation, supplier partnering, strategic alliances, skill- and time-based competition. Each is considered critical. Yet for many companies, building and sustaining these capabilities will require a period of major change unlike any that most of them have ever experienced.

Major change is a relative notion pertaining to degree of difficulty. Whether an organization faces major change depends on the magnitude of 1) the behavioral changes required for company performance, that is, how many people have to change their behaviors, skills, or values, and 2) the degree of readiness or resistance inherent in what is often described as "the way we do things around here." What is major change for the United States Postal Service may be normal change for Federal Express. This can also vary inside a company; for example, what is major change for Motorola's Government Electronics Group may not be major change for another group.

Opportunities as well as threats can pose the need for major change. Sometimes the threats or opportunities are external (e.g.,

Motorola's self-declared "war" against its Japanese competitors, or the huge real estate losses that hit the banking industry in the late 1980s and early 1990s). Sometimes the stimulus for change is internal, for example, the arrival of a new CEO or the discovery of a new technology. Sometimes they occur simultaneously. In the 1970s, for example, Xerox faced a Japanese invasion in the copier business at the same time their scientists developed the first personal computer and related technology. Both the threat and the opportunity required major change.

Like most people, companies recognize and respond more readily to threat-based major change. Signals, such as poor performance, disappearing competitive advantages, confused or panicky top management, and morale problems, help create the sense of urgency needed for change. In the Xerox example just mentioned, the company eventually responded to the Japanese threat but never developed any sense of urgency about the computer opportunity.

On the other hand, the behavioral changes at the *Tallahassee Democrat* (Chapter 4) came from an opportunity, not a threat. There was nothing seriously wrong or broken about the paper's financial or operating performance. Rather, Fred Mott, his leadership team, and the frontline ELITE Team all realized that the opportunity to strengthen the *Democrat*'s performance required a new set of values and behaviors with respect to customer service.

We believe that four fairly straightforward questions—two about magnitude and two about readiness—can help companies determine the degree to which they face major change:

1. Does the organization have to get very good at one or more basic things it is not very good at now (e.g., new skills and values)?

2. Do large numbers of people throughout the entire organization have to change specific behaviors (i.e., do things differently)?

3. Does the organization have a track record of success in changes of this type?

4. Do people throughout the organization understand the implications of the change for their own behaviors and urgently believe that the time to act is now?

A "yes" answer to questions 1 and 2 and a "no" to 3 and 4 indicate a major change situation. As our colleague Julien Phillips has noted, managing major change requires a set of actions diametrically opposed to those of normal managerial approaches. For example, normal change involves managing exceptions and outlying events while allowing the "system" to take care of the bulk of the work. Managing major change, by contrast, requires working directly on what most people do day to day because that is the only way to foster new behaviors, routines, and capabilities. Normal change involves monitoring established routines and processes to ensure that they achieve the purpose for which they were designed. Managing major change requires intentionally derailing and finding replacements for such activities. Finally, normal management involves relatively limited risk taking at the point where the cost and value of products and services are determined, especially at the customer interface. But managing major change demands risking new approaches and experimentation aimed directly at the most critical activities of the company itself.

Through our client work as well as research, we have become familiar with dozens of major change efforts. Interestingly, none of the companies we know believes it is finished yet, including those like General Electric and Motorola that seem to be succeeding. Thus, we think it is premature to advocate any single, best path to managing major change. But we do see a useful pattern emerging that distinguishes the leaders. First, as one leading change expert Steve Dichter suggests, nearly every promising major change effort appears to attack change along three critical dimensions: top-down culture-shaping initiatives, bottom-up goal achievement and problem-solving initiatives, and cross-functional redesign and integration initiatives. Second, the leading change efforts have moved along all three dimensions simultaneously and iteratively instead of sequentially. Third, and most important for this book, teams have played a critical role in all three dimensions.

General Electric provides a good illustration of all three dimensions of major change. Jack Welch and his top management have initiated a number of top-down culture-shaping changes, including:

- Establishing a clear, performance-driven vision that commits GE to become either number one or number two in each of its chosen industries by building a culture based on "speed, simplicity, self-confidence, and boundarylessness."

- Emphasizing organizational simplification through delayering, a process called "Work-Out" aimed at eliminating unnecessary work, and another process called "Best Practices" that seeks to spread success stories.

- Providing corporate resources and attention to support people at all levels—especially, the front lines—with essential problem-solving, decision-making, and interactive skills.

In addition to these top-down initiatives, General Electric has made great strides both in bottom-up activities and cross-functional redesign and integration. A good example of both can be seen in the redesign of GE's Salisbury, North Carolina, plant, which makes lighting panels and other switching gear.

Prior to the mid-1980s, Salisbury employees approached their jobs like workers in most large, traditional hierarchies. They worked nine to five, did what they were told, avoided anything that was not their job, and otherwise generally played by traditional command-and-control rules. Salisbury had five levels, from plant manager to front-line worker; managed through orders, rules, and procedures; measured quality in terms of compliance; compensated based on narrowly defined job classifications; and focused accountability on the individual.

That Salisbury no longer exists. As a result of an effort led by GE's Phil Jarrosiak, the plant now has three levels, is organized around self-managing teams of multiskilled individuals, compensates and rewards the teams for the performance of the entire redesigned process through which the plant makes and delivers more than 70,000 product variations, and measures quality in terms of customer expectations. *The plant now runs without supervisors and has reduced costs by more than 30 percent, shortened delivery cycles from three weeks to three days, and reduced customer complaints by a factor of ten.*

Successes like Salisbury help explain GE's progress. Nevertheless, few people at GE believe they are "out of the woods" of major change. Still, their progress is impressive. They have reported significant performance gains since 1986. In 1991, these included a fifth consecutive annual improvement in working capital turnover, an all-time high in operating margins, and a fourth consecutive year of more than 4 percent gain in productivity. In the view of GE's leaders, none of these performance results was possible without broad-based behavioral changes among people throughout the company. As top management concluded in its 1990 letter to shareholders:

> These are numbers that couldn't be improved as significantly as they have been by the actions of the top one hundred, or one thousand, or even five thousand people in a company our size. *They can only be moved by the contributions of tens of thousands of people who are coming to work every day looking for a better way.* (Emphasis added.)

As companies like GE grapple with major change, they inevitably discover the unique role teams play in energizing top-down, bottom-up, and cross-functional initiatives. Team dynamics relating to focus, direction, size, skill, and mutual accountability promote both performance and behavioral change. As we illustrate with the examples in this chapter, such characteristics are essential to each of the three dimensions of major change.

## TEAMS AND TOP-DOWN CULTURE SHAPING

To illustrate the impact of teams on top-down culture-shaping initiatives, we will compare the change efforts at two leading professional service firms: the well-known accounting firm of Deloitte, Haskins & Sells ("DH&S," now merged into Deloitte and Touche) and a disguised firm we will call the advertising agency of "Scintil & Cleve" (S&C). In both cases, a concern about who would succeed the managing partner initiated a series of events that ultimately opened up much more profound opportunities for change. In DH&S's case, guided by a steering committee and task force that each became real teams, the firm shifted its basic identity, including the strategy it followed, the services it offered, and the professional skills it emphasized. It also significantly upgraded performance by improving its market position, taking millions of dollars out of over-head, and reversing years of declining profitability. By contrast, S&C attempted to stimulate the skill and behavioral changes it needed with structural modifications, individual assignments, and new management processes. Teams played no role. Several years later, S&C had yet to demonstrate any marked change in the behaviors critical to its ongoing performance—nor had its performance results improved.

## DH&S

By the early 1980s, the accounting profession was under increasing profit pressure because clients no longer valued the annual audit as highly as they once had. This particularly affected DH&S, which was known throughout the industry as the "auditor's auditor," a high-quality, premier position that increasingly failed to translate into premium billings or profits. Responding to the pressures on audit and to the growing demand for services in tax, consulting, and information technology, all eight major accounting firms, including DH&S, accelerated their pursuit of service diversification and industry marketing strategies. However, the DH&S Management Committee (which ran the firm) believed the problem was endemic to the industry and that DH&S was doing as well as anybody at making the necessary adjustments. The most significant action it took was to modify the management-by-objectives program to set individual goals in nonaudit services for every partner.

A few years after this decision, the issue of management succession arose in the normal course of events. By then, however, DH&S's market position had fallen to dead last among the profession's Big Eight. When three senior partners were asked by the Management Committee to address the succession issue, they quickly discovered widespread dissatisfaction in the firm. Partners complained that DH&S lacked a clear and compelling diversification strategy, that the management-by-objectives program had failed, and that they really disliked being at the bottom of their field.

Confronted by all this, the three senior partners decided to take the unusual step of asking for a broader charter. They wanted the opportunity to convince the Management Committee and the firm at large that DH&S faced a significant performance challenge, one that might demand a fundamentally different strategic and organizational approach. In particular, they requested that the Management Committee name them as a Steering Committee and allow them to assemble four other task forces to look at client needs, competitive position, economics, and organizational effectiveness.

With the Management Committee's approval, the Steering Committee tapped fifteen of the firm's most highly regarded partners for the task forces and also brought in outside advisers. The effort began raggedly. The four task forces were confused about how their respective initiatives were supposed to join together; the fifteen DH&S partners were unsure what value the outsiders would add; and none of the fifteen believed he had much time to commit to do the work. Many were unenthusiastic about the assignment. For example, Bill Stevens, who later became a key leader of the change, recalls, "It felt a lot like when I was a senior accountant on prestigious audits and I was pulled off to help with some small assignment. I remember driving home thinking, 'Why me? I'd rather keep working on major accounts.' "

A few key early events reversed this inauspicious beginning. The first happened a month later when the four groups came together for a joint working session. The meeting began after lunch, stretched through dinner, and went on to midnight. Few of the partners involved, many of whom were senior and well established, had ever worked so late on nonclient business. As one person later recalled, "The effect of looking out over the New York harbor at midnight and realizing we were the only ones in the building somehow infused us with a sense of purpose that had been missing up until then."

The second galvanizing event was far less atmospheric. The economics task force came up with an analysis that showed real earnings per partner at DH&S had declined steadily by about 2 percent per year for at least the previous decade. Up until now, the fifteen partners on the task force, like partners throughout the firm, had a general sense of stagnating performance. But now they had hardnosed, bottom-line proof of an unhealthy firm.

The more the four task forces worked, the more the fifteen partners realized that reversing the persistent decline in real profits per partner was not only urgent, but would require significant behavioral changes throughout DH&S. Hundreds of partners and associates would have to learn a variety of new skills concerning client development and nonaudit-related services. The task forces recognized they would have to undertake a massive communications and support effort aimed at helping all DH&S professionals get involved in understanding the need for and direction of change. There was simply no other way to "make this a firm we can all be proud of again"—words the team used to capture its broadening sense of purpose.

With their common sense of purpose, the task forces also developed a common approach with three key aspects. First, they agreed to work as a single team as well as four separate subteams. Therefore, they gathered periodically as a full team to synthesize findings. These meetings were open-ended and hard work. They tended to last all day and ultimately yielded full consensus and strong commitment. Second, they insisted on full ownership of the work. For example, they decided DH&S people, not outside experts, had to do as much real analytic work as possible so that their analyses would be more credible to themselves and their colleagues. Third, they decided to reach out to the rest of the firm through workshops designed to engage as much of the partnership as early and often as possible in the cause for change.

After four months of intensive effort, they went before the Management Committee. By then, the specific recommendations provided a powerful top-down picture of what and how DH&S would have to change. For example, in articulating and syndicating the vision of changing DH&S from an "auditor's auditor" to "true business advisers," the task forces established a new basic direction. In focusing on client service quality as well as profits per partner, they provided the balanced central performance measures by which to gauge progress. In holding workshops among small groups of partners throughout the firm, they fueled the intensive communications, involvement, and support necessary to build a sense of urgency for major change.

In addition, both the fifteen-partner task forces and the three-man Steering Committee had become teams that were determined to lead the change. In the words of one task force member, "we were fifteen zealots" who would not be denied. Their initial hesitations about how much time to commit to the effort had faded; many now routinely used nights, weekends, and holidays to do their tasks. All were determined to continue in whatever role would promote and expedite the needed changes. Their commitment and accountability spread to the Steering Committee team as well, one of whom said, "If we fail to make these recommendations happen for the task force, I will feel worse than if I were letting down my own children."

The Management Committee could feel this strong sense of shared purpose and mutual accountability. They approved the recommendations, and as the change got under way, several members of both teams took on new roles. Michael Cook, who was the most junior member of the Steering Committee, for example, became managing partner of the firm and made the change effort his number one priority. Indeed, Cook's selection by his predecessor, Charles Steele, symbolized how the commitment to change started at the very top of the firm. Bill Stevens, who had headed up the task force on competition, worked throughout most of the 1980s as the chief implementor of the overall change program that grew out of the task force efforts.

When asked today about the role of teams in the change, both Cook and Stevens agree that teams were the determining factors. According to Cook, without the team approach the firm could never have generated the widespread involvement, buy-in, and commitment necessary for such broad-based behavioral changes. Cook also notes that the firm continued to use the team approach for a number of subsequent initiatives critical to the overall change, including reducing overhead costs, revamping the firm's compensation systems, and dealing with the merger with Touche & Ross. Moreover, Cook says that the experience on the teams allowed high-potential partners like Stevens to develop faster and more broadly than they might have otherwise. Stevens agrees with Cook's assessment, and adds one more critical contribution of the teams, namely a deep sense of personal camaraderie and satisfaction that lasts to this day. "We're not unlike World War II veterans I've heard about," he says. "We still get together every chance we get to relive the experiences we had."

## S&C

On the surface, there are similarities between DH&S and the change efforts of the advertising firm of Scintil & Cleve. Both were triggered by concerns over top management succession, both recognized that performance ultimately depended on successfully inculcating behavioral changes throughout the partnership group, and both emphasized lots of discussion and participation by people throughout the firm. Unlike at DH&S, however, the managing partner of S&C chose to try to bring about the change with a series of structural modifications, new individual responsibilities, and different management processes. Teams played no role either in shaping the recommendations or in implementing them.

By the mid-1980s, S&C faced the same dismal trends that afflicted other advertising agencies. For most of the previous decade, large clients such as packaged goods companies, had hired their own MBAs to work on many of the tasks that once were the province of the agencies. As a consequence, the agencies saw their job content shrink to producing "words and pictures" and buying media space and time. With the diminished role came diminished revenues.

In response, the agencies fashioned a strategy that asked clients to have their brands "speak with one voice to the market." For example, this strategy would encourage a company like Procter & Gamble to engage the same agency for media, public relations, direct mail, promotion, and all other advertising for a product like Pampers. This, in turn, required the agencies to become full service houses, which set off a wave of mergers and acquisitions throughout the industry.

Thus, when S&C's top three officers began to think about succession, they recognized that many broader issues were in play in addition to naming a new leader. They commissioned an effort to examine a reorganization of the agency, and involved many people from throughout the firm in developing recommendations. The effort lasted nearly a year, during which the top three executives became even more convinced that S&C's future success would depend on broad-based behavioral changes.

In shaping organizational responses to their challenge, however, the top three leaders chose to use approaches more typical of normal change than major change. They restructured the top management committee of the agency, assigned a handful of individuals to critical new roles, and called for some new management processes aimed at encouraging joint account planning. No team-based contributions emerged during the year-long period prior to the reorganization, and no teams were asked to have any role following it. *The change focused strictly on individual accountability.*

The impact of S&C's reorganization, though positive, paled in comparison to the changes at DH&S. Several years later, S&C continued to face the need for major change. Not surprisingly, its performance also continued to drift, buffeted by continuing storms in the advertising industry. The lack of teams does not explain this entirely, but it certainly marks a critical difference between these two major change initiatives.

## BOTTOM-UP GOAL ACHIEVEMENT

In major change situations, bottom-up efforts must focus on shaping new values and changing behaviors at the front lines where the value and the cost of a company's products and services are determined, including the customer interface. Of the literally dozens of major change efforts we know well, we do not know a single successful example that did not include using teams in bottom-up initiatives. Where teams fail to flourish, frontline behavioral changes either never start or falter once underway; where teams are successful, the needed skills and values—plus the desired performance—happen.

The frontline change effort at Sealed Air Corporation illustrates this critical insight into the role of teams. Sealed Air is a medium-sized company that, among other things, makes the sheets of plastic bubbles that little kids—and grown-up "kids"—like to pop. In 35 plants worldwide, the company also manufactures polyethylene foam packaging material, Dri-Loc absorbent pads that supermarkets use for meat and poultry, Jiffy protective mailers, and foam-packaging systems.

But that is not all this company "makes." In a more fundamental sense, it makes its customers happy with unique products and services; it makes lots of money for its investors; and it makes employees both productive in and satisfied with their jobs. In other words, Sealed Air has a well-balanced performance ethic.

Throughout the 1970s and early 1980s, Sealed Air's sales and earnings each grew at just under 30 percent a year by bringing technology and innovation to bear on the packaging needs of a number of different markets that the company entered through acquisitions. By the middle to late 1980s, however, Sealed Air's chief executive Dermot Dunphy recognized this strategy was not going to work as well as it had in the past. Patents, for example, were beginning to run out, and fewer acquisition candidates were available.

Dunphy believed performance now depended as much on productivity as on innovation. In order to build this new productivity capability, he intentionally painted Sealed Air into a corner that posed both a significant performance challenge and a real sense of urgency. He did this by recapitalizing the company, paying a huge dividend to shareholders, and then challenging himself and all other Sealed Air employees to work themselves out from under the resulting mountain of debt. He also shaped an exciting new strategy based on becoming a world-class manufacturer that emphasized customer service, quality control, just-in-time manufacturing, and employee involvement. Clearly, Dunphy set up a major change challenge at Sealed Air.

Not surprisingly, teams have become a vital part of making Dunphy's strategy work. Interestingly, there was never a concerted effort to form teams per se. As Dale Wormwood (senior vice president) said, "If there was a conscious change in that direction, it was not 'Let's have teams. . . .' Teams have been a natural progression caused by our need to increase productivity and achieve WCM [world-class manufacturing]."

In other words, as management challenged people to meet specific performance goals, teams just turned out to be one of the most practical ways to make that happen. More specifically, potential teams have sprung up all over Sealed Air—on the shop floor and throughout management levels. Some include hourly workers only, some combine both hourly workers and managers, some have members from several plants for issues like safety, and some include customers as members. Not all of these groups have been equally effective, nor are all real teams yet.

After visiting several Sealed Air plants, we are convinced that each location's relative progress toward the world-class manufacturing goal in large part reflected the number of potential teams who had become real teams. For example, at the company's Ft. Worth, Texas, plant, several real teams have emerged since the plant was built in the late 1980s. After losing money the first year, the plant turned a profit in the second year and has not turned back. It now has the highest operating margin in the whole company. Among other contributions to this performance, teams have set cycle-time records, come up with dramatically innovative ways to use recycled materials, moved toward self-management, and begun cross-training many workers. Lots of real teams are evident.

By contrast, Sealed Air's Totowa, New Jersey, plant has been more successful at stimulating employee involvement than forming real teams. Performance in the plant is up because of numerous helpful employee suggestions. But Totowa has yet to make the kind of quantum leap in performance seen at Ft. Worth. Nor does it have many real teams yet. Meanwhile, a third Sealed Air plant, in Rockingham, North Carolina, lies somewhere in between Totowa and Ft. Worth. It has made more dramatic performance advances than Totowa, though it still trails Ft. Worth. Also, fewer of its potential teams have become real teams than at Ft. Worth, but it has more real teams than Totowa.

Like performance, the frontline skills and behavioral changes Sealed Air needs to become a world-class manufacturer reflect the number of teams at each plant that have moved up the team performance curve. These skills include technical and functional mastery over multiple tasks and manufacturing processes. They also include problem-solving, decision-making, interpersonal, teamwork, and leadership skills. In each case, more employees have developed such skills at Ft. Worth than at Rockingham, and more at Rockingham than at Totowa.

Teams certainly are not the only explanatory variable at work. For example, unlike Ft. Worth, both Totowa and Rockingham have been troubled in the past by drug and alcohol problems, low literacy rates, and employees with minimal educational backgrounds. To-towa also has a significant language burden; a fourth of the workers speak Spanish and little English, while most of the native English speakers know little Spanish. Moreover, the plant leaders at Ft. Worth and Rockingham are more confident than their Totowa counterparts in their knowledge of what it takes to become a world-class manufacturer and more comfortable in empowering their workers to make it happen. Still, the comparative relationship among teams, performance, and broad-based behavior change in the plants is unmistakable. And it is a relationship we have observed in every bottom-up major change effort we know, including those at GE, Motorola, and the *Tallahasee Democrat* described in this book.

## CROSS-FUNCTIONAL REDESIGN AND INTEGRATION

Major change, by its nature, is intentionally disruptive and largely unprogrammable. In comparing the management of major versus normal change, one top executive said, "It used to be like I-75. You'd lay it out from Toledo to Tampa. Now it's more like a white-water raft ride. You try to get the right people in the raft and do the best you can to steer it. But you never know what's just around the bend." This description captures the heart of the change challenge, namely, to "unfreeze" an organization and then guide it through the multiyear period usually necessary to learn the new behaviors, skills, and values required for performance.

During this "raft ride," integration and coordination across the functions and activities of a company are critical. Part of this coordination comes from the top-down vision and direction. Effective change managers and champions pay maniacal attention to focusing on a few, well-chosen themes of change: "Six Sigma" at Motorola, "speed, simplicity, and self-confidence" at GE, "world-class manufacturing" at Sealed Air, "innovation" at 3M, "superior client service" at DH&S, "quality" at Ford—all are examples of enduring change themes that have been thoroughly communicated for years.

In addition to such top-down focus and communication, much of the required integration comes in how well companies redesign the cross-functional and cross-cutting processes necessary to their change efforts. Broadly speaking, two categories of such processes exist. The first includes standard processes like compensation, training, and planning that support everyone in an organization. The second includes cross-organizational work flows like new product development, integrated logistics, brand management, and order generation through fulfillment that, taken together, provide a "customer-back" picture of what the organization does.

Each of these standard processes and broader cross-functional work processes must reinforce the broad-based behavioral changes on which performance depends. Or, as Geary Rummler and Alan Brache have said, management must use the support processes and redesigned work flows to bind together and manage the "white spaces" that inevitably appear on a company's organization chart. As with the other dimensions of major change, teams play a critical role. Thus, DH&S used a team-based approach to redesign its compensation approach, GE and Motorola emphasize teams and team skills in their training, and the *Tallahassee Democrat* used a team approach to planning, budgeting, and review.

We have also seen a number of examples of how teams have redesigned work flows to make them more performance-driven and effective. The ELITE Team basically reengineered the entire workflow by which the *Democrat* sold, produced, and serviced advertisers. Motorola's Government Electronics Group redesigned its supply management approach and then built the new organization around teams. Similarly, helped by the Zebra Team, Kodak has organized its black and white manufacturing activities around what it calls a "flow" that cuts across formerly isolated functions and departments.

# CONCLUSION

During periods of major change, the performance aspirations of a company depend on many people throughout the organization learning new, specific values and behaviors. The most effective efforts simultaneously provide top-down direction, bottom-up goal achievement and problem-solving actions, and cross-functional systems and process redesign. In addition, two other patterns distinguish the best major change programs. First, all initiatives taken are driven by performance results. A new organization structure, a new management information or compensation system, or even a new strategy do not become ends in themselves, but rather are means to the end of balanced performance. Second, the underlying performance goals of the change programs or processes themselves practice the behavioral changes they are trying to bring about. If new levels of customer service are critical to performance, for example, then the change programs emphasize the identification, practice, and measurement of specific customer service behaviors from the outset. They do not just train people in preparation for better customer service and then sit back and wait for good things to happen.

This all-important link between performance and behavior change explains why teams contribute so much to major organizational transformations. Real teams powerfully join specific determinants of behaviors—commitment, skills, and accountability—to specific performance purposes and goals. Accordingly, teams can help identify and build the particular behavioral changes demanded by performance for any specific company. Teams were as effective helping DH&S shape new, nonauditing skills as they were promoting world class manufacturing at Sealed Air, customer service at the *Tallahassee Democrat,* and supplier partnerships and total quality at Motorola's Government Electronics Group.

Naturally, management should use organizational approaches in addition to teams to stimulate change. But no approach matches the flexibility, unique performance, and behavioral characteristics of teams. To understand why, we suggest looking at the common pattern of behavioral changes often predicted as necessary to meet the performance challenges of the future for many companies (see Table 10-1).

Real teams reflect these "to" behaviors. Conversely, teams cannot exist if their members are stuck in the "from" patterns. Such, however, is not the case with other approaches to bringing about change in getting work done. New divisional, SBU, or functional arrangements, for example, may stimulate needed performance in important ways. But none of these arrangements requires the "to" behaviors; each can continue to operate effectively with the "from" behaviors. Similarly, individual assignments and responsibility patterns—while always critical to new levels of performance—do not require the

Table 10-1
Behavioral Changes Demanded by Performance in the 1990s and Beyond

| FROM | TO |
| --- | --- |
| Individual accountability | Mutual support, joint accountability, and trust-based relationships *in addition to* individual accountability |
| Dividing those who think and decide from those who work and do | Expecting everyone to think, work, and do |
| Building functional excellence through each person executing a narrow set of tasks ever more efficiently | Encouraging people to play multiple roles and work together interchangeably on continuous improvement |
| Relying on managerial control | Getting people to buy into meaningful purpose, to help shape direction, and to learn |
| A fair day's pay for a fair day's work | Aspiring to personal growth that expands as well as exploits each person's capabilities |

"to" behaviors for success. As a result, neither structural design modifications nor individual reassignments will, by themselves, necessarily require people to understand or practice the new behaviors demanded by performance. And because practicing new behaviors is how adults best learn to modify their behaviors, these more traditional approaches to organization change can come up short. It is no accident, then, that every single major change effort we know about has depended on teams.

# CHAPTER ELEVEN

# Teams at the Top:
# A Difficult Choice

"I know teams work. But I still am not convinced it is worth the time and effort to push further in the direction of making our Executive Office into a team. After all, we are pretty effective now, and it is not clear to me what or how much we gain by trying to develop more of the characteristics of 'real teams.' The essence of the issue is defining a set of team goals for ourselves as a group beyond dealing with the broad strategic and leadership issues of the corporation. And so far, it is not evident to me what those would be. I must admit, however, I am intrigued by the possibility."—Robert Winters, CEO, The Prudential Insurance Company of America

"In my mind, there is a definite parallel between the self-managing worker teams we are trying to develop across the baseline of the organization and our top management group. We are really trying to create the same behaviors of openness, collective problem solving, multiple leadership, and mutual trust and respect in both situations. So there are important parallels. But somehow it is still different and more difficult at the top."—George Fisher, CEO, Motorola

WE have spoken with many executives like Robert Winters and George Fisher about whether leadership groups should aspire to team performance or are better off following the working group approach. For a variety of reasons they have persuaded us that this is a more important and difficult choice than either of us expected when we began this book. First, with the exception of major change as described in Chapter 10, the performance demands on groups that run things do not necessarily require the significant incremental contributions of teams. In many cases, the individual bests produced by effective working groups add up to the total performance required. Second, there are deeper sources of resistance, more misconceptions, and tougher obstacles to forming real teams at the top than at anywhere else in the organization. Third, the discipline required to shape a team—and, in particular, the mutual accountability characteristic of teams—depends on identifying collective work products and approaches that, at first blush, often seem elusive to executives. In this chapter, we will explore each of these aspects and then, in the conclusion, return to the choice of team versus working group to offer our own perspective on how to address it.

## WORKING GROUP PERFORMANCE MAY BE ENOUGH

As we indicated in Chapter 5, working groups are neither good nor bad. As Table 11-1 shows, they are simply an approach that differs from that of a team. While we believe the performance results of a real team will almost always outstrip that of a working group, working groups can and do help their members perform well in their individual roles. Often this is all that total performance at the top requires. Hewlett-Packard, for example, is run today by an effective working group at the top. HP has performed well for decades, has one of the world's strongest performance ethics, and regularly generates real teams without actually promoting them. All of this, of course, could also happen with a team at the top; indeed, all of it did when the team of Packard and Hewlett ran the company.

Many successful large corporations today are run by effective working groups, an option that makes good business sense and often represents the most realistic approach given the people involved. Senior executives are more comfortable operating in working

Table 11-1
Differences between Working Group and Team

| Working Group | Team |
|---|---|
| Strong, clearly focused leader | Shared leadership roles |
| Individual accountability | Individual and mutual accountability |
| The group's purpose is the same as the broader organization mission | Specific team purpose that the team itself delivers |
| Individual work-products | Collective work-products |
| Runs efficient meetings | Encourages open-ended discussion and active problem-solving meetings |
| Measures its effectiveness indirectly by its influence on others (e.g., financial performance of the business) | Measures performance directly by assessing collective work-products |
| Discusses, decides, and delegates | Discusses, decides, and does real work together |

groups. In the typical senior working group, individual roles and responsibilities are the primary focal points for performance results. There is no incremental performance expectation beyond that provided by individual executives working within their formal areas of responsibility. The performance contract is between each executive and the leader as opposed to mutual accountability among all members of the group. The dominant group activities are sharing information, reinforcing performance standards and expectations, strengthening basic values, and making critical decisions. Most of each executive's time and attention is spent outside the working group with people in his or her part of the organization. Finally, the group performance ethic revolves around total company and individual (as opposed to team) success and failure.

The more open, constructive, and supportive the members of these groups are, the more effectively they share useful information and insights as well as help motivate one another. They can also be extremely effective in collectively reinforcing standards or values across the group and in bringing multiple judgments to bear on critical decisions. Certainly, they can and do practice teamwork as defined earlier. These attributes are not trivial benefits, and for large, multibusiness enterprises like Prudential, they are the most common performance benefits for groups at the top to obtain.

Robert Winters and the other top officers of Prudential's Executive Office have worked hard at becoming an effective working group since he became CEO in 1987. Over that period, the performance of the company has improved significantly. It has grown in overall size and diversity, improved its profitability, developed a number of strong business units, and increased the quality of management across the company.

The individuals in the Executive Office are responsible for directing the affairs of a wide variety of enterprises including, among others, commercial, group, and individual insurance, institutional asset management, corporate and real estate finance, venture capital, stock brokerage, and investment banking. As a group, their central purpose is to provide leadership and guidance to the entire corporation. In the past several years, they have sought to do so through a variety of activities typical of top management groups. For example, they have developed and disseminated a corporate vision and values statement, launched a new strategic planning and review process, discussed a variety of strategic and operating challenges at length, and made a number of critical decisions together. They also have spent a lot of time reviewing and managing the careers of key people, and have paid considerable attention to how they and others could better reinforce their vision and values.

The Executive Office meets twice a month for two and one-half hours and also has quarterly two-day off-site sessions. The agenda for the biweekly meetings is fairly standard, focusing on operating matters and communications updates and needs. The two-day away sessions revolve around longer-term challenges. The topics are selected by Winters and his staff, who carefully prepare the background and positioning materials needed for rich and worthwhile discussions. Thus, the Executive Office benefits from a well-planned, carefully thought out management process.

In the opinion of many people in the company, however, this group has the potential to become more of a real team. The members possess an extremely rich set of skills and experience; their discussions are open, constructive, and effective; they are clear on their vision for the corporation; and their aspirations are high. On the surface at least, it would not take much to make them a real team.

On the other hand, Prudential does not face performance problems that the members of the Executive Office feel would require them to shift away from the current working group mode. Hence, they see no real urgency for making the leap from working group to potential team. And as Winters indicates in the opening quote of this chapter, he questions whether the potential benefits of becoming a real team are worth the extra effort required or the risks entailed. Moreover, he realizes that simply trying to become a team for its own sake makes no sense. Indeed, for Winters and the Executive Office, the working group option works. A reason for Winters' Executive Office to consider a team approach, just like for any other group that runs things, would have to stem from a set of performance aspirations that demanded significant and incremental contributions beyond the reach of individual performance.

## WHY TEAMS ARE TOUGHER TO FORM AT THE TOP

When we began our exploration of teams, we expected to find a different set of elements and risks involved in teams at the top. We were wrong. Teams that run things—at whatever level in the company—must meet the same criteria and take the same risks as teams that make, do, or recommend things. We did find, however, that there are far fewer examples of real teams at the top than elsewhere, and those tend to have a smaller number of team members. We also found that when such teams exist, they strongly influence the performance of their enterprises.

Many of us, for example, know about the performance legacies of such well-known teams as John Whitehead and John Weinberg of Goldman, Sachs; Walter and Peter Haas of Levi Strauss; and David Packard and William Hewlett of Hewlett-Packard. There also are a number of less familiar team examples at the top of companies of various sizes, including the Burlington Northern Intermodal, Garden State Brickface, Motorola's Government Electronics Group, and *Tallahassee Democrat* teams. Still, team performance at the top of any organization is more the exception than the rule. Based on empirical evidence alone, teams at the top are tougher to form.

We cannot explain all of the reasons for this. But we do believe there are five popular yet misguided beliefs about how executives are expected to act at the top that bedevil the formation of real teams. Some of these are more subtle in operation than others; each tends to make a self-fulfilling prophecy out of the working group approach—*all warrant careful questioning by those at the top considering the team approach.*

1. **"The purpose of the team at the top is identical to the purpose of the company."** Potential teams at the top, just like potential teams anywhere else, must identify a common team purpose and set of performance goals that require them to do real work together as a team. Groups at the top, however, tend to see their team purpose as synonymous with the overall company purpose.

At one level, of course, the executives at the top are responsible for the company's purpose. But the same thing is also true of potential teams elsewhere, although to a lesser degree. All employees in a company are responsible, in some way, for the purpose of the company. Unlike at the top, however, potential teams elsewhere—for example, those responsible for making task force recommendations or reducing machine set-up time or bringing a new product out in record time—can more easily distinguish between their *team* purposes and their generic purpose of supporting the company.

By contrast, "leading a corporation" represents a relatively abstract challenge that takes a long time to realize, is often difficult to assess, and is rarely suggestive of a clear set of team purposes, team goals, and team work-products. For example, most groups at the top only measure themselves by how well the company does along various economic criteria. Certainly, this approach will assess the top group's influence on the work of others. But it fails to measure what they do as a team against performance goals and work-products they set for themselves.

Consider, for example, the Enron Corporation vision described in Chapter 6. The senior Enron executive group articulated an aspiration to make Enron "the first natural gas major and the most innovative and reliable provider of clean energy worldwide for a better environment." This vision provides Enron's *entire organization* with an all-important rational and emotional reason for pursuing the major changes required for industry leadership, customer service, innovation, and environmental responsibility. Moreover, it helps shape what each Enron senior executive needs to do—as an *individual leader*—with his or her part of the organization. Based on this vision, Ron Burns, the head of the pipeline group, initiated "Project 1990s" and the Deal-to-Steel Team. It is not apparent, however, what *team* performance goals the Enron executive group should pursue in support of their vision. It is even less clear what set of discrete work-products they should hold themselves mutually accountable for.

2. **"Membership in the team is automatic."** It is counterintuitive at best, and unimaginable at worst, that someone who reports directly to the head of a company or a division, let alone the head himself or herself, would not be a member of the team. On the other hand, as the stories in this book relate, real teams ultimately only include members with the complementary skills, common commitment, and mutual accountability to get the team's job done. When "official" team members fail to meet those standards, the rest of the team operates without them, whether formally or informally.

This, however, is far easier to do down the line than at the top. Strong individual performers with advanced functional skills who lack teamwork or interpersonal skills are more difficult to exclude from the team, if only out of fear of losing their individual contributions. And ego, visibility, and even personal commitments and compassion can make it hard to exclude weaker performers. As a result, many potential teams at the top that face seemingly insurmountable skill problems feel like they are in a "damned if you do, damned if you don't" situation.

Notwithstanding the difficulties, however, team membership at the top does *not* have to be hierarchically dependent. One of Bill Greenwood's direct reports in Burlington Northern intermodal, for example, was not a member of the team. This individual contributed to intermodal's overall purpose and was valued by Greenwood and others for doing so, but never made the personal commitment to the team's purpose, goals, and working approach. The team at the top of Motorola's Government Electronics Group also did not include all direct reports to the head of that group. And the members of the Lake Geneva Executive Team described later in this chapter do not include all executives in that company's top management group. In each case, an intense focus on a specific performance challenge and set of joint work-products plus the "everyone does real work" standard of team membership permitted real teams to form that excluded some individuals without ostracizing them. Our point here is not to argue that teams at the top must exclude individuals, but rather that the assumption that they cannot do so is invalid.

3. "The role and contribution of team members, including the leader, are defined by their hierarchical and functional position." In the vast majority of groups that run things, the expected contribution from each person coincides with that individual's formal job description. The head of marketing, for example, worries mainly about marketing, operations about operations, finance about finance, and so on. Each individual might constructively counsel his or her peers and otherwise practice teamwork values. Or, at the other end of the spectrum, executives might harshly criticize one another or fume in accusative silence. But in either case, their individual spheres of influence define their solution space for performance. Like Knights of the Round Table, they recognize and respect that each has his or her own individual quest to pursue. Put less metaphorically, at the top of companies, *"my job" is far more clear-cut and easier to commit to than "our job."*

Deeply ingrained biases toward individual accountability and achievement reinforce the executive behavior patterns that run counter to team requirements. Teams at the top, like teams elsewhere, must develop a sense of mutual trust and interdependence. Yet by the time most executives get to the top, they find it hard to allow their performance to depend on people who are neither their boss nor their subordinates. And the risks of personal failure are much greater because many top executives view themselves as candidates for the top job at their or other companies. Thus, while they have confidence pursuing accomplishments in their individual roles, they are uncomfortable with the idea of gambling on a switch to team behavior patterns. Even Ron Burns, for example, who provided effective leadership to Enron's Deal-to-Steel Team (Chapter 6), eventually rejected the task force's bid to follow through on implementation. Instead, he chose to hold the pipeline company presidents individually responsible for carrying out the task force's recommendations by tracking their progress against quarterly scorecards. "Those who don't buy in will be flushed out by the scorecard," he said.

All of this puts even more pressure on the leader. Because of the leader's unique role and influence, it is commonly assumed that he or she alone will either make or break the group's performance. A corollary of this dictates that the leader alone must prescribe the group's purpose, goals, and approach. Such assumptions reach beyond the executive suite. When big trouble threatens or occurs, boards of directors replace individual CEOs, not teams at the top. Consequently, everybody—the leader and the leader's direct reports—knows that the leader's job, not theirs, is most squarely on the line.

As a result, many leaders are cautious about giving up "solution space," even to individual executives, let alone to a team; and they instinctively rely on their own wisdom and control rather than on team approaches to management. They are not expected to express uncertainty, depend on others for help, and display attitudes of not knowing the answers. Hence, it is difficult for them to be team leaders, which in turn discourages the shared "purposing" required to develop common directions and mutual accountability. Meanwhile, the leader's colleagues find it more comfortable to hang back a little and play it safe rather than aggressively challenge the leader and themselves to establish a common purpose, set of performance goals, and approach built upon the ethic of "only the team can fail."

**4. "Spending extra team time is inefficient."** Executives rarely have much discretionary time. Moreover, they must spend most of their time leading the people in their separate parts of the organization. When they gather as a top management group, their goal is to minimize the time spent together without, of course, sacrificing the effectiveness of the discussions and decisions they make. They stick to well-prioritized agendas.

Unlike other teams, executive groups are not likely to "roll up their sleeves" and do real work together such as interviewing customers, digging into analyses, and experimenting with new approaches. In fact, executives expect themselves, and are expected by others, to delegate such efforts to down-the-line people, then review the outcomes in meetings. Consequently, each executive's contribution often reflects two aspects: 1) work done by other people; and, 2) the executive's own judgment and experience. Each of these is essential to a well-functioning working group; neither equates with the "real work" of teams.

5. **"Team effectiveness depends only on communications and openness."** This all-too-common misconception equates teamwork with teams. The Cosmo Products executives fell into this trap (Chapter 5). So did the ComTech Cellular general managers (Chapter 5). Certainly, the discussions and decisions of top management groups benefit from shared practices emphasizing active listening, cooperation, sharing, giving the benefit of the doubt, and recognizing the interest and achievements of others. But once again, the purpose of such behaviors is primarily to enhance the quality of decisions that, in and of themselves, do not necessarily reflect joint team work-products or a sense of mutual accountability.

*In combination, these five assumptions drive executive groups to the working group approach without any consciousness that a choice is being made.* The essential work-product of such groups becomes decisions based on effective management discussions and other processes; these decisions then get assigned to individual members who are held accountable for carrying them out. Unless the group takes joint responsibility for the outcome of such decisions, however, such activity does not constitute the kind of real work required for team levels of performance.

The work-products of a team reflect an incremental performance value that exceeds the sum of each member's individual effort. They also require the joint, real work of people on the team themselves, and they build a sense of mutual accountability for results. Of course, real teams at the top do not operate without effective "discuss and decide" meetings. But when real teams make such decisions, accountability for carrying them out is mutual, not only individual.

We will illustrate the difference between the individual accountability for decisions of working groups versus the mutual accountability for team decisions with two examples. The first example, a disguised two-billion-dollar company we call "Slader Field Corporation," concerns the classic top management decision—reorganizing the company. In it, we will see an effective working group that, nonetheless, does not have a shared sense of accountability for the decision made. The second example, from a disguised company called "Lake Geneva Multinational Corporation," comes in the form of a dialogue we observed and have paraphrased here. The quality of the discussion itself conveys a picture of a real team at work, the members of which hold themselves mutually accountable for the decisions they make.

## SLADER FIELD

The idea to reorganize emerged mid-autumn in the mind of Slader Field's CEO, Jeff Selkirk. He believed the company would perform better if it were structured differently. He shared his thoughts with his two closest advisers, asking them to help him think through how to reorganize and who to put in which jobs. It was winter before Jeff was confident enough in his basic direction to take the next step. Jeff then spent several weeks holding one-on-one discussions with the key players in his senior management group. These men and women had a range of reactions from excitement to disappointment, depending largely on the nature of the new assignments Jeff asked them to consider. Of the few executives who were less than thrilled, none rejected Jeff's proposal out of hand; each supported him.

Jeff then asked the group to go away for a three-day off-site meeting to agree on the implications of the reorganization, flesh out how it would work in detail, and develop a plan for announcing it. Jeff wanted to use the off-site to get his group to buy in to the decision. Accordingly, he asked for and sincerely sought a full airing of the planned actions and how to make them work best. Nevertheless, in a clear distinction understood by everyone, Jeff did not expect or want anyone to seriously challenge and rework the fundamental direction of the decision he had already made.

The off-site met all of Jeff's expectations. The executives had honest and candid discussions about many of their concerns, and they put together a thorough communications plan for letting key people hear personally about what was happening and then announcing the reorganization broadly. Every one of the executives bought into the decision in the sense that, as individuals, they committed themselves to do their best to carry out their new assignments.

The Slader Field executives, however, did not emerge from the meeting with a sense of mutual accountability for making the decision work. Notwithstanding the time and effort, there was little doubt that the decision belonged to Jeff. Most of the executives were enthusiastic. A few, though mollified by the discussions of their concerns, remained quietly apprehensive or skeptical, though willing to move forward. Every one of them, however, including the skeptics, was committed to doing his individual best. After all, Jeff was the CEO and a reorganization decision like this was his to make. Like the others, Jeff understood this. Accordingly, all parties believed they had conducted themselves responsibly and effectively. And for a working group they had. But they were not a team. Consequently, while the new organization made progress, much potential performance went untapped.

## LAKE GENEVA EXECUTIVE TEAM

When real teams meet to discuss and make decisions, they tend to focus entirely on performance, particularly on those issues that cut to the heart of the team's basic purpose and goals. They almost automatically avoid the administrative and bureaucratic issues that bog down other groups. In addition, the decisions that emerge are team decisions, for which everyone feels a strong sense of mutual accountability.

To illustrate this, we asked a top management team from the Lake Geneva Multinational Corporation to let us observe one of their confidential discuss and decide sessions. This team of six Americans and six Europeans sets the compensation for the top 150 executives in the company. None of them are personnel officers. Instead, each of the twelve holds a senior position in one of Lake Geneva's major geographic, product, or staff groups. Several, though not all, are also members of Lake Geneva's Executive Office, which is not a team.

Significantly, this team has evolved a much broader purpose and set of performance goals than simply determining pay. All of the members believe Lake Geneva's performance depends heavily on continually maintaining and upgrading a superior pool of executive leaders throughout the company. To achieve that purpose, the team developed criteria against which to evaluate each senior executive. Furthermore, it measures itself as a team against specific goals of improving the profile of Lake Geneva's top 150 people. It also rigorously measures and tracks the overall quality of the pool. Each member is assigned particular executives to monitor. Each personally spends several weeks every year interviewing colleagues of those executives, talking with the executives themselves, and preparing required documentation for the committee. In more difficult cases, like that of "Marion Meyer" in the following discussion, the committee assigns two or three members to prepare the case. *None of this work is done by staff; the team does not allow it.*

As we look in on this meeting, Frank Andrews, an American, is just concluding a long discussion he has led on the performance and potential of Ursula Mandreik.

> FRANK: . . . so I'm still recommending that we leave Ursula in Category 3 another year.
>
> WILL: (the group's official chairman, a fact not discernible from either his position at the table or his behavior):
>
> Any more questions or discussion on Ursula's case before we vote again?
>
> KRUGER: Just one last comment. I understand why Frank recommends leaving her in Category 3, but her overall business performance results—particularly compared to some of our European colleagues—simply do not warrant that evaluation level, despite

her new product introduction results. If we don't drop her a category this year, we should certainly flag her case for special attention next year. I think we are temporizing here on a rigorous application of our criteria. Remember our rule: any exceptions to criteria are automatically flagged for special review next time.

WILL: We've already agreed on that, Kruger. Now let's vote, and then take a ten-minute break. (At which point everyone marks something on a small blank slip, folds it, and passes it to Will. He and Roberto, who is sitting next to him, tabulate the results while others leave the room to make their inevitable late morning phone calls.)

ROBERTO: Well, at least the vote is not as close as last time. Frank did his homework very well, don't you think? I was particularly influenced by that new information about how effectively Ursula has led the creation of that new product group. Three new products up and running in 18 months is impressive.

WILL: Yes, but I'm also glad that Kruger made his final point about next year. Unless her annual business results pick up significantly, we will not be treating her fairly relative to others around the world.

(Roberto goes to the blackboard, which has lots of dots with names plotted on a two-axis grid with one labeled "business performance" and the other "institution building." He places Ursula's name on the grid. In most groups like this, Roberto's tasks would be performed by a staff person, but no staff people are allowed in this meeting. By this time, the members have returned to their seats.)

ROGER: So who's up next? We'd better jolly well get moving, or we'll have to start changing our flights. Given the six man-weeks we each spend on this task, you'd think we would be further along by now.

WILL: Marion Meyer is next. You will all recall that when we looked through Marion's case last month, the financial aspects of his division's business results were extremely impressive, both relative to last year and relative to other units around the company. This makes the third year in a row that Marion's division has shown that kind of improvement, and Martin's recommendation was that we move him up a full category. The problem that some of you had with that recommendation was that neither the division's market position nor people development performance has kept pace with the financial results. For some reason, Marion has not been able to build the kind of potential leadership group under him that we expect of people in the next category. Since the first vote was inconclusive, we asked Martin and Roberto to get us more information.

MARTIN: We talked with Marion's boss again and with three of the executives who have worked most closely with him over the past two years. We were also able to get helpful inputs from people who have worked for him, two of whom have left the company. We also asked Andre to check into the evaluation files of those under Marion to get a factual indication of their progress and potential. All this took us three extra days, but I think you will agree that it was well worth it.

The good news is that he is improving a lot. Most people believe that he is giving much more attention to the development of his people than before, and the actual results as summarized in that sheet I passed out earlier seem to confirm that. The bad news is that he still has a way to go. While he is no longer regarded as a "people eater," he still hasn't yet attracted or nourished the high-potential talent we are looking for. Compared to other units around the world, Marion's leadership group is still weak.

However, given the marked improvement in this area, and in light of his persistently strong financial results, we are still strongly recommending a full category change.

(At this point, the door flies open, and Glen, the CEO of the company, bursts in and rushes to his seat.)

GLEN: Sorry, guys, but it was Charlie Jones [chairman of the finance committee] and I couldn't get off the phone.

MIGUEL: Too bad, Glen. That will cost you fifty pesos—put it in the kitty for the New York homeless at the end of the table.

GLEN: Fifty? Don't you think that's a little steep, given that Charlie's such an important board member?

MIGUEL: Rules is rules, Glen. The fine for late return is $10 per minute. How about it, guys?

EVERYBODY: (in virtual unison) Fifty bucks! Right on! (Glen grins sheepishly as he pulls the fifty out of his wallet.)

WES: (Resuming the prior discussion) Marion works for you, Mark, what do you think?

MARK: As Martin indicated, Wes, I've already given my comments to him. I don't feel right about circumventing our process to answer your question just because I happen to be a member of this committee.

KEN: He's absolutely right, Wes. Remember our rule that committee membership should not provide an opportunity for special pleading, positive or negative; let's stick with our process. If you have a question, and in fact, even if the question is "What does Mark think?," it should be directed through Martin.

MARTIN: Mark's view has not changed since our last session. He believes that Marion has improved more than enough on both scales to warrant the category change. He also believes that our view of the potential of Marion's management group has been unduly harsh because the members are young and developing well under Marion's leadership. Moreover, when he took over the job, he had a pretty sorry group to work with. He may not have developed them to their full potential as executives yet, but they are improving. In case you've all forgotten, five years ago this committee viewed Marion as a marginal executive, and was considering termination. Now he's in the top third of our executive group and still climbing. If ever there was a case for betting a little on the future, this is it.

KEN: That's not the issue, Martin. Marion's been in that role for more than five years now. That's more than enough time to correct any people gaps he might have inherited. If he's really a Category 2 executive, he should have a top-notch pool of talent under him by now. Moreover, he should probably be developing enough excess to transfer people to other units in short supply. If we allow ourselves to overlook this gap just because of his annual business performance, we are allowing him to sacrifice the long term for the short term.

ROGER: That's expecting too much. Not too many executives have been saddled with the dearth of talent that Marion inherited. Besides, it has taken a tremendous effort on his part just to get the business turned around financially, much less be ready to give away some of his talent pool to others.

WILL: Okay, guys, let's get back to the facts at hand. I don't mind our giving attention to the difficulty of the situation, but we've already discussed that at length. Let's also stay with the new facts Martin, Roberto, and Andre have developed about Marion's performance, both short and long term.

WES: I agree. And as I see it the facts are these: Marion's business performance has improved financially by over 20 percent for three years in a row, but his market share continues to slip, as Martin's latest report clearly shows. That gives me almost as much concern as the fact that his executive talent pool has remained roughly constant. Granted they are each improving as individuals, but how come Marion hasn't been able to attract some higher-caliber people into the group? This guy is neglecting the building blocks so essential for our future position in Prague.

GLEN: I'd like to inject a strategic consideration at this point. You all know how critical Marion's area is to our growth strategy. I'm worried that if we don't give him a clear, positive signal this year, we could lose him. Given the relative weakness of those under him, I don't think we should take that chance.

KRUGER: I take your point, Glen, but I think it is largely irrelevant, and dead wrong. Our basic purpose here is to evaluate our colleagues' performance, not to shore up shaky strategies. Besides, it seems to me your comment further enforces the point that Marion has not done the people development job we needed. If we do have to replace him, it could be very good for the company overall. It would force us to bring in a young, high-potential person from another unit. And almost every time we do that, we win. Let's not forget that the fundamental mission of this group is to upgrade the quality and productivity of our total executive pool, not just to distribute bonus money. If anyone is not delivering balanced performance results, we should both pay accordingly and be prepared for replacements accordingly.

WILL: Time out, guys. It's getting a little hot and heavy here. Besides, it's nearly lunch time. Luckily, we've scheduled a little boat ride across the lake in the hope that the fresh air will clear our heads. I'd also like to use that time to discuss how to implement the four termination decisions we reached at our last session. We will continue the discussion of Marion after lunch.

GIORGIO: Hold it, everybody. Before lunch, I have a special award to present. As you all know, Ken here has been a member of this committee for a long time—which is okay. The only problem is that he always wears the same stupid sweater. Not only does the sweater have holes in the sleeves, but it's actually beginning to smell. We had hoped that Ken would have done something by now to give us an excuse for giving him a present, but he hasn't. And we can't wait any longer. Ken, here's a new sweater we all chipped in and bought for you—provided you promise never to wear the old one again.

KEN: Well, I don't know, guys, this old sweater means a lot to me . . . (at which point Roger and Wes both grab Ken, and force him to take off his sweater, to the obvious delight of all. The group then broke for lunch, after which they decided to hold Marion Meyer's performance rating constant.)

It should be clear by now that we are watching a real team in action, where mutual accountability is the norm. It has open conflict and debate that are supportive and constructive. Neither the hierarchy of the company nor the formal positions of any of their members bears on its decisions. The CEO has no more influence than any other team member; in fact he is treated by and treats others as any normal member would. It tracks its progress against the team's purpose. It obviously is committed to the process and approach that it has developed.

The members all work incredibly hard at their task, often double- and triple-covering difficult cases like Marion Meyer's. Each member plays different team roles in the meetings depending on the situation. All keep each other honest and accountable with regard to the quality of work, wisdom of decisions, and the achievement of their agreed-upon team goals.

The official leader plays whatever role is appropriate for the team, sometimes being a tough mechanical disciplinarian to get through the agenda, and sometimes staying completely out of the discussion to let others do the job. The leader is more evident for what he does not do than for what he does. Certainly, he has no more influence on the team's decisions than any other member.

The group also enjoys itself. Meetings are invigorating as well as productive. The members have time for a little hi-jinks designed both to poke fun at one another and to display the strong mutual respect they have. They regularly rotate people off and on the committee, and without exception, former members we talked with openly miss the experience. They are not all close friends, but they have a strong regard for one another as people as well as executives. They are also a high-performing leadership team at the top of their company. This makes them doubly unusual.

# BREAKING THROUGH TO TEAM PERFORMANCE AT THE TOP

Some people suggest that only groups blessed with "good personal chemistry" can perform like the Lake Geneva Team. This perspective, however, is too narrow and even self-defeating. Good personal chemistry is an exceptional phenomenon among any group of people, whether senior executives or not. Moreover, it is far more likely to characterize smaller numbers of individuals, even two or three people, than all those involved at the top of most companies. Naturally, if certain executives have good personal chemistry, they should, as a group, take advantage of it. But the kind of mutual accountability that characterizes the Lake Geneva Team, like that present in the Burlington Northern Intermodal Team and the Dallas Mafia, developed first out of delivering specific team work-products against a team purpose and only later, if at all, out of a growing sense of personal compatibility.

The most practical path to building a team at the top, then, lies not in wishing for good personal chemistry, but in finding ways for executives to do real work together. When they succeed, a discernible pattern emerges with respect to their assignments, approach, and contributions, including:

**1. Carving out team assignments that tackle specific issues.** These are narrower and more concrete than leading the organization as a whole toward the realization of a vision, mission, or strategy. And while the development of visions and strategies themselves can represent joint work-products of senior managers, it requires more than review and approval efforts. Moreover, the exhilaration of having jointly created a meaningful vision or strategy fades rather quickly if senior managers do not use the vision or strategy as a guide to identifying and pursuing a continuing stream of narrower, more concrete team tasks, like designing a new program to upgrade management marketing skills or carrying out a merger integration effort.

The Dallas Mafia, for example, committed itself to specific team goals regarding business mix and staff quality, then realized those objectives by negotiating with key accounts, recruiting high-talent candidates for the office, training new professional hires, and exposing younger people to greater responsibilities. The Burlington Northern Intermodal Team worked directly on a variety of team work-products including hub construction plans, advertising campaigns, capital budget proposals, and the purchase and installation of interoffice communication software and equipment. As we suggested in Chapter 5, the Cosmo Products executives might have, but did not, set themselves the team task of improving the quality of the new-product development process. These are the kinds of top management work-products that require and enable real teams.

**2. Assigning work to subsets of the team.** Most teams we have observed do not create their work-products as an entire team. Task forces, project teams, and worker teams almost always assign individuals and subgroups within the team to do the preparatory work that can support a rich and meaningful full-team working session. Senior management groups, by contrast, spend nearly all of their joint time as a full team reviewing the work of others, discussing issues, and making decisions.

The successful teams at the top we know have broken out of this pattern by assigning specific tasks to one or more individuals and by expecting them to deliver essential work-products for integration by the entire team in subsequent working sessions. This causes members to do real work together beyond full-team meetings, allowing *team* involvement and accountability to grow outside the context of discuss and decide sessions.

**3. Determining team membership based on skill, not position.** Skill-based membership relieves the difficult constraint of hierarchically imposed membership. Not everyone who reports to the CEO has to be on a single team. It is important to be tough-minded about the skill requirements and not simply assume that the formal position of the member defines his or her skills for team purposes. Otherwise, the team will suffer the fatal flaw of skill deficiency relative to its goals.

A skill-specific approach allows the option of multiple smaller teams, constituted to address particular issues and match up different skill profiles. The smaller groupings and the focus on single issues give top executives the chance to experience teams which, especially if membership in these subgroups overlap and interlock, offers the potential for a larger team at the top.

**4. Requiring all members to do equivalent amounts of real work.** The assignments call upon each team member (including the leader) to do real work, as opposed to delegating and reviewing the work of others. In real teams, when tasks are assigned to team members, they are expected to do the work themselves. To be sure, task force or worker team members might ask for help, and staff support may be required. But each team member's sweat equity in the work-product is always evident. So is their firsthand knowledge of the output. By contrast, senior managers normally follow a pattern of real work delegation that has an insidious effect of precluding a team contribution. Staff work has the stamp, but none of the sweat, of the delegating senior executive. This, in turn, subtly but tangibly limits the commitment and appreciation by everyone in the group for the work-product itself. It also limits the insights and, hence, the innovative potential of the group.

By contrast, members of the Intermodal Team operated equipment, negotiated with suppliers, wrote advertising copy, constructed pricing models, and set up communications networks. As a result, the members of the team doing any particular piece of real work had personally invested in its lessons and outcomes, earning a higher regard and deeper trust from their teammates. To be sure, the Intermodal Team also delegated work to others. The members did enough real work themselves, however, to engender the mutual respect and mutual accountability characteristic of team performance.

**5. Breaking down the hierarchical pattern of interaction.** The work assignments and the contributions to be made often should be unrelated to hierarchical position. When Fred Mott and the other senior managers at the *Tallahassee Democrat* agreed to jointly prepare each other's budgets, they broke down one of the most critical barriers to team performance: the assumption that each person's real work contribution to the team must only reflect his or her formal position and role in the hierarchy. Almost by definition, that path leads to working groups and not teams because it precludes personal, value-added contributions that go beyond the important but already assumed contribution each person makes from his or her hierarchical role.

At the *Democrat,* for example, like most other companies, each division head is expected to put together a budget. Typically, however, division heads are not expected to roll up their sleeves, dig in, and help resolve the thousand and one trade-offs that go into preparing the budgets of *other* division heads. Nor would most executives have the time to do this for every separate division. But most executives, like those at the *Democrat,* do have time to get deeply involved in at least one other division's budget. When the team running the *Democrat* took this approach, it had the effect of developing mutual appreciation and mutual accountability for "making the whole paper work, not just our part of it."

Such nonhierarchically oriented assignments provide fundamental building blocks for team work-products and team performance. When an executive *not* responsible for human resources, for example, interviews a candidate for a job *not* in that executive's division, other team members appreciate both the time and effort as a contribution *to the team.* The same effect occurred when Dallas Mafia chief Canfield agreed to report to a more junior colleague on a critical account, and when Garden State division head Charlie Baum took on the role of helping the head of sales with customer follow-up. Naturally, many of the contributions of executives must relate to their respective hierarchical roles and experiences. Without a consistent flow of contributions that go beyond those given roles, however, each person is deprived of the opportunity to do real work on behalf of the team.

**6. Setting and following rules of behavior similar to those used by other teams.** Top managers, of course, must spend time together reviewing the work of others and making decisions. As we have suggested, the most critical distinction between the discuss and decide activities of teams versus working groups lies in the degree of mutual accountability for the results of decisions made. Senior management teams can facilitate a greater degree of mutual accountability by setting and following the same rules of conduct we outlined in Chapter 6 that help all teams provide focus, avoid hierarchical constraints, and promote openness, commitment, and trust.

The patterns of assignments and team work-products we have just reviewed should also be treated as clear rules of conduct. By identifying specific team tasks, assigning them to individuals or subgroups to do themselves, and making sure that many of them call for nonhierarchical and nonformal contributions, top managers can and do deliver team work-products in support of team performance goals that have a major incremental impact on company results.

## CONCLUSION

The critical issue posed by this chapter is how to determine when corporate performance aspirations warrant team levels of contribution at the top. The subtle and difficult choice between working group and team is not a one-time event. Top groups need to periodically re-examine whether their chosen mode of operation best fits the changing performance challenges they face. By choosing a working group mode, groups at the top avoid the risks of making the leap and failing. Team performance requires an investment of time that must come out of already tight executive schedules; thus, team efforts can lead to neglect of individual responsibilities. A failed team attempt at the top breeds skepticism about teams generally, and can even cause the group to fall into pseudo-team attitudes and behaviors that are debilitating and difficult to break. These downsides pose a high price, especially if the group at the top remains uncertain about the benefits of a team.

On the other hand, choosing the team approach promises significant performance potential and offers important benefits over a working group, some of which cannot be measured—for example, the higher degree of commitment in a team. In addition, of course, there is the tangible benefit of incremental gain that comes when team performance goals and work-products are achieved. Team performance possibilities at the top are not trivial, nor can the choice be dismissed lightly.

Ultimately, the difficulties inherent in the choice depend on three subtle judgments: 1) whether the collective aspirations of the group are attainable through the sum of individual performance; 2) the intrinsic quality, skills, and attitudes of the individual executives; and 3) the decisions and attitude of the leader. In our experience, these considerations seldom receive the careful deliberation they deserve.

Whether a gap exists between the group's collective aspiration for the company and their potential individual contributions depends on some tough judgments. For example, we have observed that if the organization faces major change of the kind we described in Chapter 10, some kind of team performance at the top is necessary. Short of that, however, it is inherently hard to estimate the potential "individual bests" of key executives. Talented and committed executives who share insights and best practices and are mutually supportive can accomplish a lot, even when they are not a team. What they do not do, however, is roll up their sleeves and deliver the kind of collective work-products and incremental performance of teams.

The quality, capability, and attitude of each individual in the executive group also must be considered. A group of "all star" caliber executives can achieve more as a working group than lesser-talented people. Indeed, if there are skill deficiencies at the top, a team approach may make sense because real teams will find ways to make up for individual shortfalls as well as provide a more supportive, performance-focused context for skill development. On the other hand, if the executives are all stars, the performance potential of a team would be even higher, and may even include a better chance of becoming a high-performance team.

The capabilities and attitudes of the executives also influence the extent of the risks involved in moving from a working group to team approach. The constructive conflict and hard work necessary to build trust, interdependence, and mutual accountability will not occur without openness and candor. And since the personal stakes are so high for executives at the top of their companies and careers, such candor risks more than hurt feelings and bruised egos. Strong individualists may refuse to subordinate their personal ambitions to the team. And, if pushed, such people can and do leave.

Finally, there is the leader. Leaders at the top of most organizations are expected to take the working group approach. Indeed, even for groups at the top to openly discuss working group versus team choice requires the leader's support and encouragement. Unless leaders go out of their way to make the team option clear and compelling, and unless they persist in driving a potential team, including themselves, down that path, the working group is so automatic and so reflexive that it will almost always take over. We believe more top leaders should introduce the team choice to their colleagues and discuss it openly and continually.

Without being overly prescriptive, such discussions will be enhanced by considering carefully the answers to a few key questions that help determine whether the group can establish a practical team purpose and goals, pull together the needed skills, and shape a realistic team working approach. To that end, the following may be useful.

## Team Purpose and Goals

**1.** Can we convert the company mission into a more *team* specific performance purpose for our group, including incremental performance goals that we can achieve together working as a team? If so, what are they?

**2.** What specific issues, opportunities, or problems would lend themselves to a team effort and a set of collective work-products? Can we test the water by trying a team effort on one or two of them?

**3.** How can we ensure that we each subordinate our individual priorities to the group's purpose and goals?

**4.** How can we measure our mutual progress toward our goals as well as monitor our effectiveness in becoming a team?

## Complementary Skills

**1.** Do we have important skills that are *not* best captured by our formal roles and responsibilities?

**2.** Can we better utilize the basic skills and experience of our group by working together beyond as well as within our formal, functional responsibilities?

**3.** Could some of us build skills in other areas, and thereby help strengthen the overall capabilities of the group?

**4.** Can we modify our membership to include others down the line to enhance our collective ability to achieve particular goals?

## Working Approach

**1.** Can we break up hierarchical patterns by assigning work tasks based on skills rather than position? Can we assign leadership roles to someone other than the CEO?

**2.** What specific rules would help us work better together, and "equalize" our individual, real work contributions to group goals?

**3.** Can we reconfigure our group into subteams more appropriate to the specific issues, opportunities, or problems identified?

**4.** How can we most effectively foster teams down the line?

There is no guarantee that answers to these questions will result in team levels of performance at the top, but they will help establish the conditions that increase the awareness of the group as to when team opportunities might be created, and thereby increase the likelihood of team performance.

"Team at the top" is a misunderstood concept. Unless an organization faces major change, it is probably not required. But neither is it ever a "foolish" option. It depends entirely on the performance situation and the individuals involved. We believe that many top management groups function best as working groups; we also believe that many can become teams, particularly as they recognize the flexibility of the concept and avoid the misconceptions of how executive teams should behave. We also believe that it is both possible and useful to try the team approach on selected issues before moving completely away from the working group approach. Becoming a team at the top is difficult, but it is not as hard as many would make it. It is a powerful option that deserves more disciplined attention than it is receiving.

# CHAPTER TWELVE

# Top Management's Role: Leading to the High-Performance Organization

TOP management's role regarding teams is changing. In the past, it largely has left the nourishment of teams to others. In seeking to improve performance, it has put its time and attention into changing strategies, individual assignments, larger organizational forms, management processes, and important leadership initiatives. If companies already had a strong performance ethic, many real teams formed nonetheless. But in companies with weaker performance orientations, like Burlington Northern in the early 1980s, benign neglect at the top has contributed to team performance being the exception rather than the rule.

The primary role of top management, of course, is to lead the organization toward performance, not to create teams. Moreover, when considering the best means to tackle any specific performance challenge, teams do not offer an all-purpose panacea. Top managers must consider teams in balance with strategy, individual assignments, hierarchy and structure, and basic management support and cross-cutting work-flow processes. But for reasons we have outlined throughout this book, we believe teams are becoming a much higher priority than ever before. Simply put, teams will be the primary building block of performance in the high-performance organization of the future. As a result, effective top managers will increasingly *worry about both performance and the teams that will help deliver it.*

Perhaps it is presumptuous to suggest that something as simple and time-tested as teams could unlock the performance potential of the organization of tomorrow. Yet teams seem to keep doing just that—especially in companies that excel. Teams at the top increasingly create powerful new visions and make them happen; truly empowered work forces invariably include teams; and successful quality and business re-engineering efforts are team-based. This is neither episodic nor accidental. Top managers who aspire to high performance, therefore, must increasingly understand and emphasize teams. And they must do so themselves. They cannot afford to delegate this job to others.

The key to top management's evolving role regarding teams lies in focusing its attention as well as company policies and resources on the teams that matter most to performance. By policies, we mean the actual practices that people throughout the company look at to judge how important teams really are to top management and why. Only if certain key policies favor team formation and performance will the organization at large consider team opportunities positively. In particular, who gets assigned to team opportunities and the promotion and compensation decisions those opportunities open up signal whether teams and team performance really matter to top management.

If team assignments are not, as a matter of policy, an integral part of normal, successful careers, they will not attract the best people, generate enthusiasm, and produce team performance results. So long as individual accomplishments overshadow team accomplishments, people will remain cautious about joining teams. By contrast, policies that ensure that people routinely have team experiences and get rewarded for their team contributions as handsomely as for their individual contributions will encourage team formation and team performance. Moreover, among the most important rewards is making available a new team or individual performance opportunity. If teams and team members do not get a fair share of the new opportunities, then once again, team approaches will remain secondary to values of individual accountability and achievement.

Even more critical than policies, however, is how management uses company resources plus its own time and attention to foster team performance. Here, top management's role is threefold. First, it needs to identify which teams will most affect performance. Second, it needs to know how to help teams move up the performance curve. And third, top managers need to know what to do about the issues unique to teams that run things versus teams that recommend things versus teams that make or do things.

Top managers who are familiar enough with the common challenges faced by all teams can make high-value contributions to enhance those specific ones that matter most. Such familiarity includes understanding the issues in making the choice between team and working group, and knowing whether, when, and how to help teams with the disciplined application of team basics. Moreover, top managers can make a big difference by closely monitoring where specific teams are on the performance curve and, if they are pseudo-teams or high-performance teams, what to do about it.

To identify where teams matter most as well as the issues unique to different kinds of teams, it is useful for management to distinguish among teams that run things, teams that make or do things, and teams that recommend things. By now, this point may seem obvious. Yet most top executives we met thought more narrowly about teams. Intellectually, of course, they understood the distinctions among the various kinds of teams we describe. But at work, faced with their company's own performance challenges, they tended to overlook the full breadth of team opportunities. The following sections help address these issues.

## TEAMS THAT RUN THINGS

These include groups from the top of the enterprise down through the SBU, divisional, or functional level. A team that runs things could be in charge of tens of thousands of people or only a handful; but so long as the group oversees some business, ongoing program, or significant functional activity, it is a team that runs things. Unlike teams that recommend things (e.g., task forces), these groups typically have no clear end dates. In a sense, their work is never done.

As a general rule, top managers usually should pay attention to all groups that run things. Often the scope of top management responsibility makes that impractical. For example, Prudential's Robert Winters and his Executive Office described in Chapter 11 cannot concentrate equally on every group that runs things. Instead, like their counterparts elsewhere, they focus on the groups that will make the biggest difference to overall corporate performance.

Today, most top management attention to groups that run things takes the form of monitoring individual responsibility and performance. Increasingly, that focus must shift to team performance. The relevant challenges most unique to teams that run things include: 1) the choice between team and working group, 2) the role of the team leader, and 3) the problem of transitions. As we noted in our discussion on teams at the top in Chapter 11, the choice between team and working group is as subtle as it is important. Many groups that run things can be effective as working groups. The key judgment—for the groups themselves and for top management—is whether the particular performance challenge at hand requires a team approach with all its attendant risks. If the sum of individual bests will suffice, pursuing team performance becomes an option but not a necessity. If, on the other hand, the group must deliver substantial incremental performance requiring real, joint work-products, the managers involved should take the risks to move from working group to potential team to real team.

How top management can best help potential teams that run things to make the leap depends in part on the strength of the company's performance ethic. Companies like Hewlett-Packard and Motorola tend to generate teams simply by setting forth the right performance challenge to the right set of people. When the performance ethic is weaker, however, top management needs to pay closer attention. In such cases, it probably ought to carefully select the potential teams it will monitor and help because, when all is said and done, unless top management's efforts result in one or more real teams, little else will matter.

The toughest challenge for potential teams that run things often comes in trying to identify specific team purposes, goals, and collective work-products. Too often, such teams confuse the broad mission of the total organization with the specific purpose of their "small group" at the top. This is easy to do because the purpose of the small group running the organization must be consistent with and central to the mission or purpose of the organization itself.

For a real team to form, there must be a team purpose that is distinctive and specific to the small group, and that requires its members to roll up their sleeves and work together to accomplish something beyond individual end-products. If all a group of managers does is discuss and decide on the basis of work delegated to others, it will lack the necessary work-product activity required of a real team. Moreover, if it looks only at the economic performance of the part of the organization it runs to assess its own effectiveness, the group will not have any *team* performance goals.

Top management can help such teams tremendously by working with them to think through what the group should do as a team, and how it should measure itself. This requires helping it find the right balance between individual work, delegated work, and team work-products, and the right potential skill mix and resource support. It is also important that top management pay continuing close attention to how well the team works these things out for itself over time.

In addition, top management can help the team by helping the executive in charge improve his or her team leader attitude and skills. As we suggested in Chapter 7, most leaders of teams, especially those that run things, must develop their team leader skills on the job because: 1) managing a working group differs from leading a team; and 2) each team challenge poses its own set of variations. Good managers, for example, expect—and are expected to—make most decisions and delegate most assignments. By contrast, good team leaders seek to develop a team approach to decision making and accountability. Thus, top leaders help a great deal by paying special attention and providing needed support to otherwise effective executives who are trying to make the transition.

When potential teams that run things do become real teams or high-performance teams, top management can contribute a great deal by carefully handling the team transitions and endings caused by membership and, especially, leadership changes. As we suggested in Chapter 8, a new member poses both a threat and an opportunity to a team. So top management can help simply by reminding the team to pay attention to how it integrates new members. A new leader, on the other hand, poses more than just a transition if he or she comes from outside the team itself. Thus, top management ought to favor current team members if possible. If someone new is picked, top leaders should work carefully with the team to avoid lost momentum and disappointment.

This last point about new leaders is too often overlooked, even by top management in companies with strong performance ethics. For example, Dean Morton's Medical Products Division described in Chapter 9 unnecessarily lost momentum when top management replaced Morton with Dick Alberting. Little visible attention was given to team preferences and, like people in many real teams, team members believed one of their number ought to have gotten the job. As a result, key people left. It took months for Alberting to regroup and develop his own team. The division continued to perform well, but everyone involved—Alberting, the team, the employees, the customers, and the shareholders—probably would have benefited from a smoother "baton pass."

## TEAMS THAT RECOMMEND THINGS

These teams include task forces, project groups, and audit, quality, or safety groups asked to study and solve particular problems. Unlike most teams that run, make, or do things, teams that recommend things typically have predetermined completion dates, although a few, like plant-level safety teams, might be ongoing. If top management asks such a group to address issues of performance as opposed to administration (e.g., organizing the annual sales conference), then almost by definition the group "matters." Accordingly, top managers can best manage the time and attention they need to devote to such teams by limiting how many they set up.

The two critical issues unique to teams that recommend things are getting off to a fast and constructive start, and dealing with the inevitable "handoff" required to get their recommendations implemented. The key to getting potential teams that recommend things off to the right start lies in the clarity of their charter and composition of their membership. In addition to wanting to know why and how their efforts are important, task forces need a clear definition about who management expects to participate and the time commitment required. Management can help by ensuring that the teams include people with the skills and influence necessary to crafting practical recommendations that will carry weight throughout the organization. Moreover, management can help the team get the necessary cooperation by opening doors and dealing with political obstacles.

One task force we learned about at Burlington Northern (not the Intermodal Team) illustrates the impact of management providing a clear charter and the right composition. The company asked fourteen people to take forty-five days to study and recommend the best organizational approach to marketing. The head of marketing appointed Steve Brigance to lead the effort. Steve had led a previous task force effort on labor strategy that suffered from an ill-defined charter and management commitment, and admitted to being less than thrilled with yet another task force opportunity.

He was determined not to repeat the labor task force mistakes. Consequently, he sent the head of marketing a four-page description of his concerns about the task force's mission. "While putting this in writing may seem overly formal and inappropriate," Brigance wrote, "I feel that this study has a very real potential to go awry unless we have a clearly defined process and charter agreed to in advance."

In particular, Brigance insisted that the task force have complete freedom to explore any organizational approaches it thought useful, including ones that might fundamentally challenge the assumptions of the head of marketing and other senior executives. Brigance also insisted on choosing a core team of himself plus only four of the fourteen task force members to do the real work of the project. He carefully picked people with the right mix of skills who knew the company well, had no axes to grind, and on whom he could depend for candor and hard work. Brigance's small group became a real team, and in forty-five days also delivered a set of "clean sheet" recommendations that compellingly challenged the existing approach to marketing. That's the good news.

Implementation, however, turned out to be another problem entirely. Neither Brigance's team nor higher-level management paid enough attention to involving the people who would have to make the new organizational arrangements work, either before or after the recommendations were made. In an all-too-typical pattern, the team made its recommendations, had a terrific discussion with top management, and then disbanded. Those in the marketing department most affected by the recommendations were neither asked to, nor did they, spend any time understanding the basis for the suggested changes. Not surprisingly, since the recommendations implied a number of risks for them, the marketing people, whether intentionally or otherwise, just waited top management out. Nothing much happened.

Even the most successful task forces can run into this handoff dilemma. To avoid it, the transfer of responsibility for recommendations to those who must implement them demands top management time and attention. Almost always, we have observed, the more top managers assume recommendations will "just happen," the less likely it is that they do. At its worst, as seen in the case of Brigance's team as well as the Brandywine task forces described in Chapter 9, the accepted recommendations are given to managers who have neither the understanding nor conviction to put them in place.

By contrast, the more involvement task force members have in actually implementing their own recommendations, the more likely they are to get implemented. Top management can exploit the performance opportunity inherent in task force recommendations by allowing the members to make them happen. However, to the extent that people outside the task force will carry the load of implementation, top management can boost the performance opportunity by ensuring that those people get involved as early as possible—well before the recommendations are finalized.

Such involvement takes many forms, including partcipating in interviews, helping with analyses, contributing and critiquing ideas, and conducting experiments and trials. At a minimum, anyone responsible for implementation should receive a briefing on the task force's purpose, approach, and objectives at the beginning of the effort as well as regular reviews of progress along the way.

The more they are involved, the more those who will be implementing benefit from the time to understand, buy into, and even shape the recommendations. The DH&S change teams, for example, intuitively understood this phenomenon and did not wait until their recommendations were complete before they actively involved hundreds of partners across the firm. Missing the handoff is almost always the Achilles heel for teams that recommend things.

## TEAMS THAT MAKE OR DO THINGS

These teams include people at or near the front lines who are responsible for doing the basic research, development, operations, marketing, sales, service, and other value-adding activities of the business. With some exceptions like new product development or process design teams, such teams tend to have no set completion dates.

In deciding which of these potential teams matter most to performance, we believe top management should concentrate on the performance challenge at what we call the company's "critical delivery points"—that is, places in the organization where the cost and value of the company's products and services are most directly determined. Such critical delivery points might include where accounts get managed, customer service performed, products designed, and productivity determined. If performance at the critical delivery points depends on combining multiple skills, perspectives, and judgments in real time, the team option makes sense. If, on the other hand, an arrangement based on individual roles and accountabilities is the best way to deliver the value customers require at the right cost, teams may be unnecessary and possibly disruptive.

Forces at work in the world today make it increasingly likely that teams will become the primary building block of performance in most companies. There will be more and more teams at the front lines whose performance challenge includes specific goals tied to customer service, total quality, and continuous improvement and innovation. *This does not mean, however, that teams are always necessary.* In many situations, the clear division of labor based on individual accountability will continue to make sense.

When an organization does require a significant number of teams at the critical delivery points, the sheer challenge of moving so many groups up the team performance curve will demand a carefully constructed and performance-focused set of management processes. Put bluntly, the problem for top management is how to build the necessary systems and process supports without falling into the trap of appearing to promote teams for their own sake.

This challenge is far more subtle and difficult than we thought at first. "Of course," most top managers would say, "we want performance. And, of course we would never build teams for the sake of teams." Yet, we have observed more than a few leaders who literally have set the number of teams as the primary goal. And we have seen even more who fall into that trap unintentionally.

The problem lies in how easily people in organizations convert managerial words into mandates. It is impossible, after all, for top management to speak about the important performance role of teams without talking about teams themselves. But so often, when they do discuss teams—even with explicit reference to performance—people down the line do not make the connection. And this unintended consequence is even more likely if management announces the team initiative without tying it to performance. All too often, and especially in companies with weak performance ethics, the organization "doesn't get it." Then, if management fails to pay persistent attention to the link between teams and performance, the organization becomes convinced that "this year we are doing 'teams.' " In the end, the team-based initiative loses most of its performance potential; it may even build cynicism.

This phenomenon is well illustrated by the story of a critical team initiative at a company we call "Liquid Tech." Like their counterparts in most organizations today, top management at Liquid Tech believes successful new product development depends on teams. It decided to build a "team culture" based on "performance, people, and process." It articulated a set of team values, formed a steering committee, and established other structural and process supports for teams. It published a guide on how to build teams that carefully defined the roles of team leaders and of executive champions for teams. It made it clear that participating in teams would positively benefit careers.

On the surface, Liquid Tech's management put together an impressive launch. But Liquid Tech does not enjoy a strong performance ethic. Notwithstanding the mention of "performance" along with "people" and "process" as part of the new team culture, the organization failed to make the all-important connection between each particular team and its specific performance challenge. Moreover, top management assumed that its impressive beginning would suffice. It provided no further guidance or evaluation other than the often-repeated admonition that teams would enrich new product development. Most critically, Liquid Tech's leaders paid no attention to whether *specific* teams were adhering to the team basics of number, skills, purpose, goals, approach, and accountability in tackling particular new product development challenges.

Predictably, the results were disappointing. In a typical comment, one employee pointed to a part of the organization that included scores of people and said, "If you take that 'team,' they may have a dozen or more different missions that, if you took them and ground them up, would basically spit out the old organization chart."

Liquid Tech's new team culture actually produced no new teams. The ones that already existed—and you can always find some in any organization—continued. The potential teams that had been struggling kept on struggling. Several promising product development opportunities that might have gained from a real team approach went on without it. In fact, using the terminology of this book, Liquid Tech's team initiative mostly produced a transitory gain in teamwork values, many pseudo-teams, and a fair amount of cynicism. Performance was virtually unaffected. Clearly not intending to initiate a regimen of teams for their own sake, Liquid Tech's top management had, in fact, done just that.

To avoid Liquid Tech's fate, top management needs to build structural and support systems that focus on the performance challenges, measurement, and skills necessary to broad-based team performance at the front lines. This may include organizing work around teams as the primary performance unit, and emphasizing just-in-time training. Such training might include team problem-solving, decision-making, interpersonal, and leadership skills. The choice depends on the performance needs of each team.

Top management can also help by instituting processes like "pay for knowledge" and "team performance" pay schemes, and by facilitating access to expertise beyond the team. More than anything else, however, top management must make clear and compelling performance demands on specific teams themselves, and then pay relentless attention to their progress with respect to both team basics *and* performance results.

# TEAMS AND THE HIGH-PERFORMANCE ORGANIZATION

We believe that focusing on both performance and the teams that deliver it will materially increase top management's prospects of leading their companies to become high-performance organizations. Again, we do *not* contend that teams are the only answer to this aspiration. They are, however, a very important piece of the puzzle—particularly because the dynamics that drive teams mirror the behaviors and values necessary to the high-performance organization and because teams are, simply stated, so practical.

More agreement exists today about the capabilities of high-performance organizations than about the specific organizational forms and management approaches that will support them. No one, including us, argues over the value of such company attributes as being "customer-driven," "informated," "focused on total quality" and having "empowered work forces" that "continuously improve and innovate." Behind these lie a set of six characteristics, only one of which—balanced performance results—is ever overlooked in discussions of where the best companies are headed. The six include:

1. **Balanced performance results.** At the outset of this book, we suggested the primary standard for the "new paradigm" organization ought to be performance itself. Companies that consistently outperform the competition over an extended period, say ten years, are high-performance organizations—regardless of how they get there. One can argue with the yardstick of a decade. Perhaps, for example, the only true high-performing organizations outperform competition in perpetuity. But we find it hard to question performance as the key criterion of a high-performance organization.

At one level, performance as a characteristic of the high-performance organization is obvious. But it often goes unstated—thereby leaving people assuming that the other characteristics of high-performance are ends rather than means to an end. One group of executives we know illustrates this point. When challenged to articulate the characteristics that would make their company qualify as a "high-performance organization," they ticked off every attribute on every list we know except one—none of them suggested a specific performance achievement.

Of equal importance is a balanced performance ethic that benefits the primary constituencies of any large business organization: customers, employees, and shareholders/owners. Proven high performers such as Levi Strauss, Procter & Gamble, Hewlett-Packard, and Goldman, Sachs are all well known for their balanced performance aspirations. They are relentless in delivering superior results to employees, customers, and shareholders. It is no accident that they attract the best people, serve enviable customer groups, and sustain the highest earnings. Equally relevant are the balanced performance goals of companies placing the highest emphasis on creating new paradigm, high-performance organizations for the future. Recognized organizational change leaders such as General Electric, Motorola, and American Express's IDS each are explicit about achieving performance results of multidimensions.

**2. Clear, challenging aspirations.** Whether it goes under the name of "vision," "mission," "strategic intent," or "directional intensity," the company's purpose must reflect clear and challenging aspirations that will benefit all of its key constituencies. Too many vision statements are just that: a written attempt by top management to meet the well-accepted "vision requirement." They may be read by all, and may even be immortalized in plaques on the wall, but they have no real emotional meaning to people down the line whose behaviors and values they are supposed to influence. The purpose, meaning, and performance implications of visions must communicate, to all who matter, that they will benefit both rationally and emotionally from the company's success.

Reaching for the stars is not just an idealistic notion. Past, present, and future high performers make "meanings" as well as money. Thus, for example, "being the best" is a common phrase in high-performing organizations, although it means different things in different places. At Hewlett-Packard it means earning unique customer loyalty, at Goldman, Sachs it means unparalleled clientele quality, at Knight-Ridder it means customer obsession, and at McKinsey it means client impact. Whatever the meaning that goes beyond the money, it makes people proud to be a part of a demanding and challenging total effort.

**3. Committed and focused leadership.** High-performance organizations follow leaders who themselves almost evangelically pursue performance. Through their time, attention, and other symbolic behavior, such leaders express a constant focus on where the company is headed and an unrelenting dedication to the communication, involvement, measurement, and experimentation required to get there. Truly committed leaders inspire confidence throughout the organization that the pursuit of performance is the single best path to economic and personal fulfillment.

Such leadership, of course, does not require teams at the top. But the power in such teams is undeniable because of how well the members keep each other committed and focused. Moreover, when an organization confronts what we described in Chapter 10 as major change, it is hard to imagine success without the committed and focused leadership provided by a real team at the top.

Perhaps it is a coincidence that enviable high performers like Goldman, Pepsico, Pall Corporation, and Motorola work hard to sustain team performance at the top. Perhaps not.

**4. An energized work force dedicated to productivity and learning.** The "learning," "adaptive," "self-directed," and "evergreen" characteristics of high performance organizations depend on a critical mass of people who are turned on to winning as well as to the change that winning requires. Performance in a constantly changing world demands change. And change, in turn, must be understood and tested before it can be mastered. Few companies can afford a work force caught in the trap of "it's not my job" or "not invented here" attitudes. Rather, the people of the organization must share an eagerness to ask questions, to experiment with new approaches, to learn from results, and to take responsibility for making changes happen.

No major company we know is pursuing an energized, productive work force without the conscious use of teams. We see this on the plant floors of industrial companies like Ford, Weirton Steel, and Sealed Air, in the high-technology labs and assembly rooms of Motorola, GE, and Martin Marietta, and in financial and professional services activities at Deloitte & Touche, IDS, and Goldman. Productivity and learning across the base of an organization means teams—plain and simple.

5. **Skill-based sources of competitive advantage.** Companies should always seek and make best use of intrinsically valuable assets like access to natural resources, control over powerful distribution channels, strong brand names, and patents and other government licenses. People generally agree, however, that most industries have entered an era in which sustainable competitive advantage will favor those who develop the core skills and core competencies that allow them to win a battle that now depends more on "movement than position." Indeed, innovation, customer-driven service, total quality, and continuous improvement are examples of the capabilities companies need for high performance.

Core skills invariably depend on team skills. To re-engineer work flows based on customer needs, for example, requires teams that integrate across functional boundaries. Whenever adding value depends on the real-time blending of multiple skills, experiences, and judgments, a team performance challenge exists. And teams provide an excellent (often unsurpassed) crucible for on-the-job skill development.

6. **Open communications and knowledge management.** A number of observers from academia, business, and the press believe that knowledge has become as scarce and important a factor of production as capital and labor. Few seriously doubt that information technology is critical to high performance. But that "technology" includes more than the hardware and software behind what some people call a new industrial revolution. It also includes the shared values and behavioral norms that foster open communications and knowledge management. For example, one commentator has suggested that in "information era organizations," there are no guards, only guides. In order to "informate" company performance, the

right information must get to the right people at the right time to affect performance. Moreover, those people must hold themselves accountable for their results. Otherwise, empowerment is dangerous.

We have seen how teams promote open communications and knowledge management. The Rapid Response Team at McKinsey (Chapter 5), of course, has knowledge management as an explicit part of its purpose. It literally helps consultants and their clients gain access to best practices from around the world. But, as we have noted several times, real teams *always* seek fresh facts and share information both within the team and with others beyond. Real teams communicate and learn whatever is necessary to get their job done; team "doors" are always open. Moreover, through the "extended team" influence, the communications and knowledge management of others work better.

Leading thinkers have come forth with a variety of intriguing images of what high-performance organizations with these characteristics and capabilities will actually look like. Peter Drucker pictures it as an "orchestra," Quinn Mills as "clusters," Robert Waterman as an "ad hocracy," and Ram Charan as "networked." Even one of us has a favorite entry, the "horizontal organization." Notwithstanding the range of concepts, however, these people seem to agree on three things. First, future organization designs will seek structures simpler and more flexible than the heavily layered command-and-control hierarchies that have dominated the twentieth century. Second, they strike a balance in favor of organizing work and behavior around processes instead of functions or tasks. And third, they all emphasize teams as the key performance unit of the company.

## CONCLUSION

The increased emphasis on teams that we observe and advocate enhances rather than replaces the value of other, more familiar aspects of organization direction and design. Top management will continue paying attention to where and how to compete (formulating strategy), changing individual roles and assignments (new job descriptions), realigning reporting relationships (reorganizing the boxes), and modifying management policies and processes (reworking the systems). Yet, we believe that top management is turning increasingly to teams for three compelling reasons.

*First, teams strengthen the performance capability of individuals, hierarchies, and management processes.* As we have illustrated throughout the book, team performance requires high-level contributions from every member of the team. Each must bring commitment, skill, and real work to bear on the team's purpose. Moreover, they must do so working together as well as working as individuals. Teams do not succeed without both mutual accountability *and* individual accountability. Accordingly, collective and individual achievement go hand in hand, making teams a primary vehicle for both extra performance and personal growth. Somewhat unexpectedly, perhaps, the people on the teams we learned about did not run into any career obstacles because of their team roles or participation. Quite the contrary, in fact. For example, several members of the ELITE Team, the Connectors Team, the Dallas Mafia, the Burlington Northern Intermodal Team, and the DH&S change teams moved on to higher management and broader responsibilities. We would be hard pressed to name any individuals who were disadvantaged by being members of real teams.

Teams also improve the performance impact of basic management processes such as planning, budgeting, and evaluating. For example, in the case of Fred Mott's *Tallahassee Democrat* management group, we saw a team-at-the-top approach to budgeting. By requiring each department's plan and budget to be prepared as a joint work product of the department head plus another member of the team, the *Democrat* benefits from better coordination and focus. The same effect arises when teams energize cross-functional work-flow processes such as new product development, logistics, and order generation through fulfillment. Motorola uses teams to manage and integrate its supply management process (Chapter 9), Kodak its black and white manufacturing process (Chapter 7), and the *Democrat* its advertising sales order through fulfillment process. In each case, teams are uniquely suited to apply the multiple skills and perspectives required by any truly cross-functional process on the ultimate performance objectives of the process itself.

Contrary to some popular opinion, teams do not imply the destruction of hierarchy. Indeed, quite the reverse. Teams and hierarchy make each other perform better because structure and hierarchy generate performance within well-defined boundaries that teams, in turn, productively bridge in order to deliver yet more and higher performance. For literally hundreds of years, hierarchies and structures have helped organizations create wealth through focusing, dividing up, and setting useful boundaries around jobs, tasks, and responsibilities. To be sure, the process view of organizations suggests that some of those boundaries will now shift and those hierarchies flatten. But hierarchy and structural boundaries will never disappear so long as each adds value to performance. And when that is so, a potential team opportunity exists at any place where hierarchy or boundaries inhibit the multiple skills and perspectives needed for optimal results. Thus, for example, new product innovation requires preserving functional excellence through structure while eradicating functional bias through teams. Similarly, frontline productivity requires preserving direction and guidance through hierarchy while drawing on energy and flexibility through self-managing teams.

*Second, teams are practical.* By that we mean most people can make teams work. Conversely, when confronted with calls for "orchestras," "networks," "clusters," and the like, many business leaders are hesitant, if not skeptical. However intellectually intrigued they are, tough-minded executives openly question if many of the newly proposed organizational concepts can help them deal with their company's immediate performance needs nearly as well as clear-cut, individual accountability. Some even see these images as nothing more than notional summaries of the underlying characteristics of high performance. As a result, they remain unsure about specifically how they are supposed to apply the new ideas. Teams pose no such how-to difficulties. Teams thrive on performance challenges; teams have leaders; teams demand discipline. Yes, there are important counterintuitive lessons about teams. But the vast majority of executives can rely on their common sense and current skills to make teams work.

*And, third, of course, teams get results.* As the stories in this book have repeatedly shown, teams advance each of the six characteristics of high-performance organizations, beginning with performance results. Real teams almost always perform better than any similarly situated set of individuals acting either separately or in a working group. Teams also help establish and communicate clear, performance-based aspirations. Perhaps no story illustrates this better than the DH&S teams that identified and then broadly inculcated an aspiration throughout their accounting firm to move from being "the auditor's auditor" to being "true business advisers." This new vision fueled a renaissance at DH&S which benefited the firm's clients, employees, and owners—the partners themselves.

We also saw committed leadership at work in the DH&S story as well as in the Burlington Northern intermodal unit. Certainly, companies will continue to gain from visionary individual leaders. But, as the Intermodal Team demonstrates so well, visionary leadership provided by a team at the top produces remarkable results. Almost inevitably, such leadership energizes others throughout the organization to take on the impressive extended team characteristics we observed in Intermodal as well as the Dallas Mafia (Chapter 4), which itself represents another example of vision-driven team leadership.

When this happens, of course, the team at the top helps generate the performance focus and enthusiasm so critical to building an energized work force focused on productivity and learning as well as skill-based sources of competitive advantage. Each of those characteristics also are advanced with the help of teams elsewhere in the organization, especially at the front lines. This was evident at many companies, including Motorola, Sealed Air, Knight-Ridder, Kodak, and General Electric.

In addition to the examples already mentioned, an excellent illustration of the power of teams to energize a work force and build key capabilities comes from GE's Ft. Edwards, New York, plant. Until about three years ago, Ft. Edwards was one of GE's more traditional plants—unionized, hierarchical, and relatively unprofitable. Today, the 400 workers operate in 27 teams all of which report directly to the plant manager. The teams vary in degree of achievement along our team performance curve. But all of them select their own leaders, set their own goals, and share their own working approach. In less than two years, the plant's productivity has turned up, costs are declining, and customers say they are being served much better. The enthusiasm and performance focus may strike you as odd in such a strong, traditional union shop. But no such concerns have prevented the rank-and-file workers from embracing an initiative they believe is good for them, good for customers, good for management, and good for GE. To us, this is a compelling illustration that most people instinctively want to perform better.

We cannot, of course, prove that teams are necessary to high performance, although we sincerely believe it. But we can articulate the logic behind why so many organization-of-the-future prognosticators continue to include teams in their visions. Real teams always thrive on performance. They cannot succeed without figuring out how to match their individual and collective strengths to the performance task at hand. Teams invariably are more powerful than individuals and more flexible than larger organizational units. Teams support the risk taking and experimentation so important to learning, change, and skill development. Finally, teams provide sources of motivation, reward, and personal development that can never be duplicated by companywide compensation and career planning schemes. In all these ways, then, we think it is fair to say that teams are a microcosm of the high-performance organization itself.

Top management can actively foster teams and team performance instead of simply waiting for exceptional teams to appear. Certainly, how and when top managers might best exploit team opportunities will differ from company to company. Moreover, top management must focus first and foremost on performance, not the number of teams. Still, we are convinced that every company faces a number of specific performance challenges for which teams are the most practical and powerful vehicle at top management's disposal. The critical role for senior managers, therefore, is to determine where teams matter, and then to pay careful attention to establishing the opportunities for such teams to perform. The best thing about teams is that they can make a difference now.

# Epilogue:
# A Call to Action

$I$N the end, the wisdom of teams is within the team itself. It is not in creating the high-performance organization, managing transformational change, enforcing corporate performance ethics, or inspiring new dimensions of leadership. It is in a small group of people so committed to something larger than themselves that they will not be denied.

Our final story is about such a group. At one time or another, each of us as well as our editors, publishers, researchers, and advisers has tried to eliminate this story for all kinds of logical reasons: it did not fit; it was not a business story; it was not typical; it did not make the right point at the right time. Like most high-performance teams, however, this one kept defying logic. Perhaps more than any other story we could relate, this team draws out the emotion and spirit that underlies our argument.

## THE KILLER BEES

In starting to write this book, we were determined to stay away from sports examples since they dominate the subject of teams and often present misleading analogies. But, in the end, we simply could not resist the Killer Bees, a boys' high school basketball team from Bridgehampton, New York. Bridgehampton is a small hamlet on the southern shore of Long Island populated, except during the summer, by hard-working people of relatively modest means.

Winter in Bridgehampton *is* high school boys' basketball. Nearly every permanent resident and even many summer seasonals from New York City religiously follow the Killer Bees—and for good reason. They are an incredible team. Since 1980, they have amassed a record of 164 wins and 32 losses, qualified for the state championship playoffs six times, won the championship twice, and finished in the final four two other times. Not bad for a school whose *total* enrollment has declined since 1985 from 67 to 41, and whose entire male student body numbers less than 20!

"I don't really know why we did so well," says John Niles, who coached the Bees until 1991. "None of the players was ever really a standout, but they always seem to play pretty well together. I think the community has a lot to do with it. They really back this team—and have for years. Fathers, brothers, and cousins have played on earlier teams, and mothers, sisters, and aunts cheer them on relentlessly."

Quite an understatement. Niles never had more than 7 players, never had a star who went on to the pros, and never had a very tall team. As a result, Niles and his boys had to develop different sets of skills and game plans every year. To win, the Bees had to be the ultimate in versatility, flexibility, and speed. Their game is "team basketball," and they are among the best at it anywhere.

As Niles hints, however, there is another strong explanation for the Bees' success: commitment. The Killer Bees have a richness and depth of purpose that eludes most teams. Their mission is more meaningful than just winning basketball games. They are committed to bringing honor and recognition to their community, to protecting and enhancing their legacy, and to one another. The Bees know what they are about and why.

Basketball makes Bridgehampton a tighter, closer community—and it makes those of us from other communities a bit envious. It creates lasting friendships among players, provides a social context and meaning to many families, and delivers honor and recognition to a small town that far exceeds what a few basketball victories could be expected to do elsewhere. This is the essence of meaningful purpose.

All of which, in turn, fuels the incredible work ethic and skill development that characterizes the team. Bridgehampton boys start back-lot basketball before they start school and they continue practicing 365 days a year up to, through, and beyond their school years. When someone fouls out, falls ill, graduates, or moves to another school, his teammates always fill in and carry on. Moreover, Niles was clearly not the only leader. On-the-spot leadership emerges and changes during each game, depending on the situation and the players on hand. When Niles retired in 1991 he was succeeded by Carl Johnson, a former Bee himself, of course.

The Bees always seem to rise to the occasion; they have been coming from behind to win against bigger, supposedly more talented opponents for more than twelve years. During 1989, for example, the state of New York threatened to close the school and merge it with another. Parents and friends fought the state regulators for months, but apparently to no avail. As the Bees prepared for one of their last games that season, the school appeared doomed.

That night, the Bees got off to a shaky start. Near the end of the game, they were behind, and it looked like they would lose when the news arrived that the state had relented and given the school one more year. Pandemonium broke out in the "Beehive," the gym they play in. The emotion and enthusiasm generated by the good news was overwhelming. The Bees rallied, won, and once again went on to the state playoffs—just another of dozens of come-from-behind victories in their rich history.

Like most high-performance teams, being a member of the Bees is its own reward. Niles insisted that scholastic performance come first; all his players graduated and most went on to college. Few Bees, however, have had the talent to play ball in college and none has gone on to star with the pros. There is certainly no financial gain in being part of the team. Instead, all the rewards come from membership in—and vivid memories of—a unique, inspiring, high-performance team.

And just in case you think it is all the coach, John Niles retired in 1991 along with three graduating senior players. Of course, this meant the loss of an incredible leader and mentor for the boys. At the very least, one would expect a couple of years of disappointment and rebuilding, maybe even the end of the high-performance Bees of the past decade. Those who follow the Bees, however, were not surprised to see them come out of the starting blocks the next season as though nothing had happened—still winning against larger, better opposition, still coming from behind to the delight of their fans, still bringing honor and recognition to their community. But we cannot describe the action or the community spirit half as well as Rick Murphy does in the *East Hampton Star,* describing a must-win game for the Bees against a tough Port Jefferson squad angling for a berth in the playoffs:

> It all added up to a Port Jefferson blowout, right? Wrong! . . . It was a blowout, okay, but it was the Bees who presided over the slaughter. . . . The Royals came out breathing fire. The Bees were content to sit back in a half-court zone, and the taller Port players found that strategy much to their liking. . . . The Bees closed to within 3 at half-time, but Port slowly built up an eight point advantage mid-way through the third stanza. . . . And then *it* happened: the press, fullcourt, in-your-face pressure that has been unnerving opponents for well over a decade was ordered by the (new) coach, Carl Johnson. So effective was the strategy that Bridgehampton had the game in the bag in a matter of minutes. LaMont Wyche, Terrell Turner, Robert Jones and Company turned the Beehive into a living hell for the visitors. . . . The Pierson mentor, Ken Hunter, summed it up best: "The Bees don't rebuild, they *reload*."

Maybe some day this will all end. Certainly we do not know another high-performance team of any kind that has lasted as long. But it will take a lot more than the loss of a coach to quell the spirit of this high-performance team. The *Star* sums it up well after a recent playoff victory:

> An equally large group of Bridgehampton fans, though giddy after the game, were not really surprised, despite the fact that their boys went into the fray as the underdogs, at least in the eyes of the Section Eleven seeding committee. After all, they are the Killer Bees. They expect to win, and they win. It is a tradition, and the record says it all. No other high school basketball team in the state has been as successful.

As with any sports team, of course, the Bees' story is not a perfect analogy for business. Still, they epitomize the characteristics of high performance seen in the Burlington Northern Intermodal Team, the Tallahassee ELITE Team, the Rapid Response Team, and the Dallas Mafia: extreme commitment to one another as well as to their team's purpose and performance, out of which blossoms an incredible ethic of work and fun, complementary and interchangeable skills, shared leadership, and dramatic results.

We would all like to play with the Bees.

## A CALL TO ACTION

We have listened carefully to all the logical reasons for not pursuing team options, many of which are rational and understandable if not compelling. Yet, while we respect this reluctance, we are not dissuaded from our basic contention: *most of the objections to pursuing the use of teams do not offset the advantages they offer.* The opportunity for increased performance is too great to let misunderstanding, inexperience, uncertainty, or false assumptions—or even past team failures—stand in the way. And the risks and actions necessary to team performance are well within the capability of most of us.

If deep down you are still not convinced that teams can make a significant difference in performance, despite the stories and illustrations in this book, we urge you to go see for yourself. Go watch the Killer Bees. Seek out the real teams that undoubtedly work within your own organization regardless of its culture and environment. Find them, watch them in action, check their results. Talk to them about what works, what doesn't, and why. Maybe you did not find the lessons you needed in this book, but you will find them by getting involved with the teams around you. When we started, we thought we knew all about teams too. But not until we actually went into the real team world did we learn to appreciate the potential they represent. We know of no better way to address a lack of conviction about teams than by seeing them in action.

For those who already believe in teams, we say, "Start making team performance happen!" Start with any group you are part of that has the potential to become a team. But do not challenge yourselves to be more teamlike. Instead, initiate open-ended discussions about the performance and purpose that can turn you into a team. Reexamine the goals of the group: are they clear, specific, measurable, and performance-focused? If not, figure out what to do about it. Ask yourselves if the goals require specific team work-products that will produce results. Don't worry about sensitivities and teamlike behaviors until you have wrestled with the basics of small number, skills, purpose, goals, approach, and accountability. Indeed, you may be surprised at how the suspected sensitivities disappear into a determination to find a way to get the results you all believe to be so important.

Give some attention to the skills and attitudes in the group, rather than styles or personalities. If some members have skill deficiencies, how can the group give them the focus, time, and support to help them develop skills *and* contribute to team performance? If any members just cannot deliver, find a way to work around them or have them replaced. Never be complacent about the skills of the group; it is far better to confront the issue head on, either within the team or with appropriate higher management, than to give up on your goals. Above all, do not simply try to make yourselves become a team; try instead to give yourselves the opportunity to deliver team performance. The results will surprise you.

If you are in a position to help teams you are not a part of, start with the pseudo-teams that plague all organizations. Do not let them fool themselves or others any more. Stop calling them teams, and do not let them pretend to be teams. Insist that they make the real choice between working group and team. Nothing is more discouraging than being on a pseudo-team. And nothing is more impressive than seeing the people on pseudo-teams as well as higher management face up to doing something about it.

Turn next to the potential teams that matter most to performance. Again, do not tell them to "become a team." Rather, demand performance from them. Encourage or insist that they work on a purpose that has real meaning to them, and on a set of performance goals to which they will hold themselves accountable. Make sure that their working approach builds on collective work-products that contribute to performance goals, and set up small wins all along the way. If necessary, "lock them in a room" until they can come out with an agreed on set of goals and measures. Look closely at their skills, and encourage them to do the same. Can they do what they are expected to do, or do you need to supplement the skill mix? Above all, be sure that something is done to fill critical skill gaps; no team can make it without the right skills. Send them to formal training, if needed, but first give them a chance to struggle together and even flounder and fight a bit. Most of all, do not get in the way when they start to get excited and even unrealistic about what they are trying to do. *Unbridled enthusiasm is the raw motivating power for teams.*

Finally, go to extra lengths to celebrate the victories of the teams in your organization. Reward them for their accomplishments as a team, and do not overlook the power of positive feedback. We all thrive on it. And when you are fortunate enough to spawn a high-performance team, get out of its way, and make sure the rest of the organization is aware of its unique accomplishments and attributes. And should you be fortunate enough to find yourself part of a high-performance team, then perform and enjoy!!

# Appendix

## TEAMS RESEARCHED
## FOR BOOK

| Organization | Team | Purpose | Results |
|---|---|---|---|
| Bridgehampton High School | Killer Bees | Build civic pride through winning basketball | More than 13 years of high standing, including two state championships and two final four finishes |
| BNR | Intermodal | Create new business amid deregulation | Became number one intermodal carrier within a year of formation |
| BNR | Marketing | Develop new organizational structure | Created new structure based on customer needs that overcame functional barriers |
| Citibank | War on problems | Improve customer service, responsiveness | Substantially improved customer satisfaction and service in eleven key areas |
| Conrail | Strategy | Deregulate the rail industry | Initiated deregulation passed by Congress, creating atmosphere for renewed financial health |
| Desert Storm | Log cell | Bring troops and tanks back from desert | Expeditious movement of hundreds of thousands of men and supplies back to U.S. in record time |
| DH&S | Multiple change teams | Develop new business strategy and leadership approach | Reversed 10-year trend in declining real profitability, went from last to first in new accounts won |
| Dun & Bradstreet | Clean slate | Reduce turnaround on report generation | Turnaround cut from 7 to 3 days |

| Dutchess Day School | Faculty/staff | Be better counselors to students | No substantial difference |
|---|---|---|---|
| Eli Lilly | Smart needle 1 | Bring new product to market | 1-year product rollout was fastest in Eli Lilly history for a medical product |
| Enron | Deal-to-Steel | Eliminate construction bottlenecks | **$10 million savings in 6 months, with systems in place for continued improvements** |
| Garden State Brickface | Irvington division | Become number one division | Became highest-revenue, most profitable division within 6 months |
| General Electric | Fort Edwards Salisbury | Multiple initiatives | Significant operating improvements in quality, flexibility, speed, with a 30% decrease in backlogs within first year |
| Girl Scouts | Innovation center | Recruit minority girls and volunteers | Greatly increased minority involvement in pilot area, creating structure, systems, and momentum to roll out similar efforts in other areas |
| Hewlett-Packard | Analytic products | Manage a business unit | Helped division become HP's highest-margin business |
| Hewlett-Packard | Medical products | Develop medical products business opportunity | Ran successful business for nearly a decade |

| Organization | Team | Purpose | Results |
|---|---|---|---|
| Knight-Ridder | ELITE | Eliminate errors in newspaper ads | Redesigned ad/production process, reducing error rate below 1% and cutting losses from errors |
| Knight-Ridder | *Democrat* leadership group | Run business side of newspaper | Became Knight-Ridder's top-performing paper for 3 years in a row |
| Kodak | Zebra (B&W leadership) | Run a business | Turned around failing business, inventory trimmed, and missed deliveries trimmed in half |
| McKinsey | Rapid Response | Develop knowledge-exchange network | Handled threefold increase in information requests from client teams, with more comprehensive and targeted assistance and faster response |
| Motorola | Connectors | Develop supply management system | Quality improved with 50% reduction in rejects and 70% reduction in late deliveries; new skills and systems instituted for continued improvement |
| Motorola | GEG leadership | Turn around major business unit | Between 1988 and 1990, profits moved from $25 million to $60 million, ROA jumped from 6.5% to 16.5% |

| NYC Partnership | Founding team | Help fix NYC's social/business problems | Greatly improved cooperation between public and private sector, with innovative programs for creating jobs and housing and reducing crime |
|---|---|---|---|
| Pall Corporation | Leadership | Build international business | From 1970–1980, had the highest return to shareholders among the Fortune 1000 |
| PBS-featured schools | Faculty and faculty/student teams | Educate disadvantaged kids | Dramatic rise in attendance, grades, test scores, and college admissions |
| Pfizer | E-beam | Build cutting-edge facility in record time | Built state-of-the-art facility under budget and ahead of schedule |
| Prudential | Leadership | Lead a multiple business unit company | Consistent performance improvement over 5 years |
| Sealed Air | Fort Worth foam | Best foam operation in the company | Record profit margins and changeover times |
| Sealed Air | Instasheeter | New product development | Designed and introduced new product in record time (13 months), instrumental in generating double-digit sales volume in key product area |

**APPENDIX (CONT.)**

| Organization | Team | Purpose | Results |
|---|---|---|---|
| Sealed Air | Rockingham | Manufacturing excellence | Waste cut in half for one product; downtime cut from 20% to 5% on another line; employee absenteeism down to 1.6% |
| Sealed Air | Totowa | Manufacturing excellence | Marginal improvements in productivity |
| Weyerhaeuser | Plywood | Recommend changes in business to improve performance | Persuaded management to keep and invest in business previously considered "dead" |
| Weyerhaeuser | Roundwood | Recommend changes in business to improve customer service | Delivery performance jumped from 85% to 95% with significant increases in quality and profitability |
| **DISGUISED EXAMPLES** | | | |
| Brandywine | Strategy | Improve corporate performance | No performance improvement |
| Company A | Leadership group | Manage business without team at top | No performance improvement |
| Company B | Leadership group | Work on team effectiveness | No performance improvement |
| Company C | Leadership group | Create team to turn around business | Too early to know |

| Com Tech Cellular | Leadership | Manage national business | No substantial difference |
|---|---|---|---|
| Cosmo Products | Leadership | Run troubled business | Performance continued to stagnate |
| Dallas Mafia | Leadership team | Upgrade business quality, profitability | Changed mission and strategy, resulting in improved skills, morale, and profitability; completely reversed the mix of business in less than 3 years |
| Lake Geneva Multinational | Leadership | Executive evaluation and development | Improved quality of leadership through better definition and measurement of goals and performance; increased pool of executives by 25%, with significantly higher performance levels |
| Liquid Tech | Multiple | Product development | Similar to performance without "teams" |
| Scintil & Cleve | Not used | Strategy and succession planning | Disappointing |
| Metronome | Disk Drive | New product development | Not yet known |
| Metronome | Fiber optics | New product development | Not yet known |
| Metronome | On-time delivery | Reduce missed deliveries | Missed deliveries cut from 10% to under 4% |
| Slader Field | Executive Group | Executive-level reorganization | No mutual accountability |

# Selected Readings

## Books

Beer, Michael, Russell Eisenstat, and Bert Spector. *The Critical Path to Corporate Renewal*. Boston: Harvard Business School Press, 1990.

Clifford, Donald K., Jr., and Richard E. Cavanagh. *The Winning Performance*. New York: Bantam Books, 1985.

Goodman, Paul A., and Associates. *Designing Effective Work Groups*. San Francisco: Jossey-Bass, 1986.

Hackman, J. Richard, ed. *Groups That Work (And Those That Don't)*. San Francisco: Jossey-Bass, 1990.

Hillkirk, John, and Gary Jacobson. *Grit, Guts and Genius*. Boston: Houghton Mifflin, 1990.

Hirschhorn, Larry. *Managing in the New Team Environment*. Reading, MA: Addison-Wesley, 1991.

Kidder, Tracy. *The Soul of a New Machine*. Boston: Atlantic-Little, Brown, 1981.

Kotter, John, and James Heskett. *Corporate Culture and Performance*. New York: Free Press, 1992.

Larson, Carl E., and Frank M. LaFasto. *Teamwork: What Must Go Right/ What Can Go Wrong*. Newbury Park, CA: Sage Publications, 1989.

Mills, D. Quinn. *Rebirth of the Corporation*. New York: John Wiley, 1991.

Pascale, Richard Tanner. *Managing on the Edge*. New York: Simon & Schuster, 1990.

Peters, Tom. *Thriving on Chaos*. New York: Alfred A. Knopf, 1987.

Peters, Thomas J., and Robert H. Waterman, Jr. *In Search of Excellence.* New York: Harper & Row, 1982.

Rummler, Geary, and Alan Brache. *Improving Performance.* San Francisco: Jossey-Bass, 1990.

Schaffer, Robert H. *The Breakthrough Strategy.* Cambridge, MA: Ballinger, 1988.

Senge, Peter M. *The Fifth Discipline.* New York: Doubleday Currency, 1990.

Smith, Douglas K., and Robert C. Alexander. *Fumbling the Future.* New York: William Morrow, 1988.

Smith, Preston G., and Donald G. Reinert. *Developing Products in Half the Time.* New York: Van Nostrand Reinhold, 1991.

Stewart, Alex. *Team Entrepreneurship.* Newbury Park, CA: Sage Publications, 1989.

Waterman, Robert. *Managing the Adhocracy.* Knoxville, TN: Whittle, 1990.

Weisbord, Marvin R. *Productive Workplaces.* San Francisco: Jossey-Bass, 1989.

## Periodical Articles

Bassin, Mark EdB. "Teamwork at General Foods: New & Improved." *Personnel Journal* (May 1988), pp. 62ff.

Chandler, Clay, and Paul Ingrassia. "Just as U.S. Firms Try Japanese Management, Honda Is Centralizing." *The Wall Street Journal,* April 11, 1991.

Dubnicki, Carol. "Building High-Performance Management Teams." *Healthcare Forum Journal* (May–June 1991), pp. 19–24.

Dumaine, Brian. "The Bureaucracy Busters." *Fortune,* June 17, 1991, pp. 36–38ff.

Hardeker, Maurice, and Bryan K. Ward. "Getting Things Done." *Harvard Business Review* (November–December 1987), pp. 112–119.

Hoerr, John. "Work Teams Can Rev Up Paper Pushers Too." *Business Week,* November 28, 1988, pp. 64ff.

———. "The Payoff from Teamwork." *Business Week,* July 10, 1989, pp. 56–62.

Hoover, John, and Michael A. Pollack. "Management Discovers the Human Side of Automation." *Business Week,* September 29, 1986, pp. 70–75.

House, Charles H. "The Return Map: Tracking Product Teams." *Harvard Business Review* (January–February 1991), pp. 92–100.

Jacobson, Gary. "A Teamwork Ultimatum Puts Kimberly Clark's Mill Back on the Map." *Management Review* (July 1989), pp. 28–31.

Katz, Ralph. "High Performing Research Teams." *Wharton Magazine* (Spring 1982), pp. 29–34.

Kotkin, Joel. "The 'Smart Team' at Compaq Computer." *Inc.* magazine (February 1986), pp. 48–55.

McCowan, Peter, and Cynthia McCowan. "Teaching Teamwork." *Management Today* (September 1989), pp. 107–111.

Nulty, Peter. "The Soul of an Old Machine." *Fortune,* May 21, 1990, pp. 67ff.

Ostroff, Frank, and Doug Smith, "The Horizontal Organization." *The McKinsey Quarterly,* no. 1 (1992), pp. 148–168.

Pantages, Angeline. "The New Order at Johnson Wax." *Datamation,* March 15, 1990, pp. 103–106.

"Pat Biedar Stumbles onto the Right Path," *Industry Week,* April 15, 1991, pp. 66–70.

Reich, Robert. "Entrepreneurship Reconsidered: The Team as Hero." *Harvard Business Review* (May–June 1987), pp. 77–83.

"Team Tactics Can Cut Product Development Costs." *Journal of Business Strategy* (September/October 1988), pp. 22–25.

# Index

**W**

Waterman, Robert, 50, 254
Weinberg, John, 216
Weirton Steel, 253
Welch, Jack, 17, 197
Weyerhaeuser, 49
Whitehead, John, 136, 142, 143, 216
Winters, Robert, 212, 215–216, 241
Working group. *See also ComTech Cellular*
    appropriate situations for, 92, 213–216, 235, 237
    definition, 91
    and individual accountability, 89, 213, 222
    need for clear purpose, 89

    senior working group, 213–215
    vs. potential team, 96–98
    vs. pseudo-team, 167
    vs. team, 85, 88–90, 131, 166, 214, 233
World-class manufacturing, 121, 206–208, 210
Wormwood, Dale, 206

**X**

Xerox, 22
    invention of personal computer, 50, 196

**Z**

Zero defect rate, 53, 69